NARRATIVE MACHINES

MODERN MYTH, REVOLUTION, AND PROPAGANDA

ISSUE 0

MYTHOS
-MEDIA

CREATING AND EXPLORING THE NARRATIVES WE LIVE BY

www.MYTHOSMEDIA.net

First B&W edition

Mythos Media, 2017

Illustrations: a selection from an intentionally derivative art series is explored theoretically within the text itself, using a mix of collage, bricolage and palimpsest repainting. The forthcoming color edition will include the full series.

PRINTED IN THE UNITED STATES OF AMERICA

Special Thanks:

To the many contributors of ModernMythology.net between 2007 – 2017, against and amongsts whose voices this assemblage came to be, especially Mr. VI, who contributed many seed ideas for the first section. This assemblage is dedicated to anyone who can find a means of recognizing that theory is a performance, and get on with the show...

NiHiLiST
NEWS

view seminal fine
al age, it's refreshing
at—oil on stretched
:ists have done for
Rock was chosen t

vintage Art Deco
e's watched the
ne art dealer in
ries nationally), Me
gallery a few steps
and renovating a t
uglas, Mell plans
ell also added a lar
r-expanding collec
Pantera (see "Icons

ace, with new
tly. At the heart
late strip of sha
ogether different
nning, Greg Esse
of it has been acti

d desirable, inevitab
ling the arts district,
nial issue of retainin
is coming to a head
s are beginning to
to an area. Just look
amage there. Hopef
)C, the arts district
artists who helped b
ings to Come," p. 12

nt and interview three
:ient tradition to a
of her life experience
arks, and organizing
g, hip and energetic
n with the *Arizona*
s. Dan Hull is part of th
vntown. His Yarnball
Gnome Publishing, an
curated experience (s

"Reality itself is material for artistic construction, and they there-fore naturally demand the same absolute right to dispose of this real material as in the use of materials to realize their artistic intent in a painting, sculpture, or poem. Since the world itself is regarded as material, the demand underlying the modern concep-tion of art for power over the materials implicitly contains the demand for power over the world. This power does not recognize any limitations and cannot be challenged by any other, non artis-tic authority, since humanity and all human thought, science, traditions, institutions, and so on are declared to be subcon-sciously (or to put it differently, materially), determined and therefore subject to restructuring according to a unitary artistic plan." —Groys

TABLE OF CONTENTS

PROPAGANDA

Note: The subject of this project was begun with a chapter in Disinfo's 2005 *Generaton Hex*. Further pieces first appeared online in Rebel News, Alterati, Reality Sandwich, or in anthologies such as the *Immanence of Myth* and *Apocalyptic Imaginary*. They have been substantially re-written, edited, and appear for the first time here as one piece.

00: THE FUTURE IS THE PAST

Explosion falls upon deaf ears
While we're swimming in a sea of sham
Living in the shadow of vanity
A complex fashion for a simple man
And there is no hell
And there is no shame
And there is no hell
Like an old hell

—"The Motel," Bowie

We live in an age which most of all resents itself, a painful awakening to a present that is at odds with our most cherished wishes and hopes, a future which never arrives until it is too late. It is always in the process of arriving, of accelerating. We feel alternately, paradoxically, that we must be saved from progress, or from tradition. "Save us from the future," cries one protester, while the other shouts just as loudly, "save us from the past!"

Who writes the greatest fictions and who pen the greatest truths? Even superheros have to be placed within the hyperreal to become believable again. We can only take irony seriously, and must heap scorn on the serious, and risk the heresy of laughter always at someone's expense. It is most of all to myths of the retro-future that we all seem to look. The only questions we can ask are aesthetic: which parts of the past do we include in this Frankenstein's monster, and which do we omit? Which fits the personal brand of ourselves, of our imaginary, glorified Movements? We have never been quite so alone, in terms of the fragmenting and atomization of communities. And yet never have we been so surrounded by a diversity of myths, in which we can dream ourselves and our world. So it is that the coming retro-future is an invention most of all of editors and artists. Worst of all, few of them know it, and yet it would seem terrible artists make great dictators.

Meanwhile, it is becoming the scientists and anthropologists that preach the End, should we continue upon the course on which we find ourselves. The End of History as a static utopia has been revoked. Or perhaps, it has been revealed for what it truly is: an eschatology. But it is also likely that Fukuyama has been consistently misread. The End of History is either a gravestone, or a high point from which we must recede. Every major geopolitical event of this decade seems to point in this direction.

The present is, in some sense, *always* an End of History, a point of departure where a future without end along the lines of thought of our present conditions seems possible. The spirit of the postmodern age is seen precisely in this anxious clawing forward and backward at the same time. Maybe it is a "new" modernity, inasmuch as anything is truly new. At this very moment we too are subject to this "new" force of mythic history and culture, and are under their sway as if they flowed from reality itself, Hegel's *zeitgeist*, but we can't see it from the inside. We need our myths to situate us, to frame the boundaries and horizons. It is to the artists to help us see the contours of that narrative, to help us see ourselves. This link of mirror and myth makes the social role of the artist finally clear.

Our dreams of revolution and apocalypse too are weapons that have been used against us. We would all like to start again, an opportunity for a cosmic "do over." Our uncertainty about the spirit of the age raises a significant problem. Are we still living in the shadow of World War? Is post-modernism really a path to the End of History or has it proved itself, as many have determined, a cul-de-sac? Are we still trudging through a psycho-historical framework that was shaped by the mutual annihilation of modernity in the fires in Dresden, the death camps, or the leveling of Hiroshima? How did it get to be 4AM and where is our pants?

We can only begin here, wherever "here" happens to be, using the materials that are available to us, provided by our misremembered past, and whomever's graves we can plunder. Psychology is always rooted in history, but what it reacts to is rarely clear to the conscious mind except in retrospect.

This assemblage also presents a certain departure from what is now a sort of orthodoxy in cultural theory, while at the same time following in its footsteps. The spectacle distracts us from ourselves, and that is the only apparent value of art in the age of propaganda. (And don't let the self-parody postmodernism has turned to lead us astray: we still live in the modern, the prefix "post" only signifying a fun-house mirror of so-called "schizophrenic times.")

Games, movies, books, have no need to interrogate us about who we are, though they may challenge or vilify our fears and desires. Only so far as it is done primarily in service to the market. Movies can be ranked in quality based on ticket sales or votes at the ballot box, and so we have universally come to determine "the good" by consensus. They commodify and entertain, allowing us to build identities as one might shop in a virtualized shopping mall. We are an assortment of Simpson's quotes and repackaged ideologies.

"Whatever I say is good, is good" is the mantra of the masses. The popular is always great, by this standard. Metrics of this sort have allowed corporate interests to turn the world into Reality TV, an ongoing performance that we must undergo to demonstrate that we are valuable enough to have the privilege of human rights.

The problem is always in the fact that everything is remade in our minds, but it isn't remade from scratch. We will come to see how little we have managed to escape the clutches of the past. Its story calls to us still.

Yet this is ever as it was, no ontological sea change has actually occurred, beyond an accelerative cultural leap of the sort that followed the printing press. Baudrillard recognized that "Everywhere socialization is measured by the exposure to media messages. Whoever is unexposed to the media is des-ocialized or virtually asocial." The question, then, is what follows. In his estimation, a collapse. "Where we think that information produces meaning, the opposite occurs."

But maybe it isn't quite so univocal. This isn't a Marxist attack on capital, nor a Frankfurt school style tirade about consumption. There is no use in a class battle over which symbols and forms of media are high and which low, which messages are vulgar and which refined. In this sense, we are engaging in a sort of theoretic burlesque. This work is for people who are engaged in understanding and creating culture, but it isn't purely for academics. We will appropriate instead from whatever suits our purpose, without any consideration for the rigidity of academia or the myths of common sense or plain speech. Pretension is our friend, so long as we can use it to get up on that stage and start the show. So long as it remains playful. We may take our ideas seriously, but should never do the same ourselves. Laughter is the final form of freedom.

We may wonder what purpose a text such as this can possibly serve. For the philosophers Deleuze and Guattari, a book is an assemblage: "Comparative rates of flow on these lines produce phenomena of relative slowness and viscosity, or, on the contrary, of acceleration and rupture. All this, lines and measurable speeds, constitutes an assemblage. A book is an assemblage of this kind, and as such is unattributable. It is a multiplicity..." much like a Self or a Society, visions and voices gathered together to speak as if we are One. It is edited, curated, but without any appeal to the authority of authorship, as it is composed from a multiplicity of sources, which is fitting for any work which embraces pluralism, and the ethic and aesthetic implicit within assemblage as a concept. This concept must remain immanent rather than transcendent because it is the codification of experience and intuition, ideas ground from our collective bones and flesh, contrasting *mythos* with *logos*, a unified attack against the supposed authority of a singular demiurge, a transcendental reason that defies fracture. Whereas the *logos* is the word of God, the divine *fiat* that structures and moves our universe, so the *mythos* is an indefinite set of articles, tales told for the telling itself, with no hard and fast authority, no assertable Ultimate Truth, no attributable origin grounded in cold solidity.

And yet, despite all that, this winds up in many ways a critique of the postmodern flight from truth, to whom such methods are quite familiar. Brian Eno once said, "The question, 'What does it mean?' really asks, 'What does it symbolise?' Well, my notion is that art does something, not that it means something. Its meaning is what it does." The systems thinking heuristic "the purpose of a system is what it does" (POSIWID) says much the same.

Nothing is original, in the sense that it has never before appeared in some guise. But it is nevertheless unique, for it has appeared nowhere else, at no other time, in this configuration. The re-purposing of image and idea is the theoretic art form of the present moment—it is re-contextualized for new use. To what future use any of these present puzzle pieces will be put, of course, we can only now guess.

The explicit purpose of theory is not necessarily to act, though theory is always a covert action, in another sense. Our words are without fixed, absolute meaning, but they always *do* something. Poetry, it might be said, is the art of misunderstanding. Nothing in this text will seem by any traditional measure poetic, but its aims remains more poetic than scientific, more *mythos* than *logos*, merely performed at another level of remove, the critique of a modern *meta-mythos*.

It is our pretension that we might get out the filleting knife and lay bare the mechanisms through which we understand ourselves. That can hardly be done within a few hundred pages. But directions can be suggested, those one might explore after it is done.

At best, this is a launching pad, a manifesto toward a movement of artists and theorists who recognize that both art and theory are acts within the world. At worst, it is degenerate philosophy, proudly made by degenerates, for degenerates.

Only this much is certain: we are narrative machines. We combine, reconfigure, and regurgitate material that is never in an essential sense our own. We are *never* one. We are many disparate bodies, never fully unified, except for through our myths. The only question is whether we embrace or resist our isolation, and dance with our masks on, or hide in the darkness.

As Antonin Artaud said in *The Theater and Its Double*, "All writing is filth." Help us give birth to an abomination.

—The Editorial We.

MODERN MYTH

"You, ordinary fetishists, believe you are free but, in reality, you are acted on by forces you are not conscious of. Look at them, look, you blind idiot..." —Latour.

NARRATIVEMACHINES

WWW.MODERNMYTHOLOGY.NET

SEX IS THE ABATTOIR OF BEAUTY
BEAUTY IS THE VOYEUR OF UTTER DESTRUCTION

I. MYTHS ARE STRANGE ATTRACTORS

> Leave aside the assumption—itself very questionable—that a rational life must be one without myths. Rational or not, life without myth is like life without art or sex—insipid and inhuman. —
> The Silence of Animals, Gray.

The absolutely central role of myth in our lives shouldn't need explanation or qualification. And yet it does, now more than ever. It will quickly become apparent why this is so.

It's not even entirely clear what we mean by "myth," unless we want to merely play at semantics. Myths would seem not only stories, for aren't some stories myths while others are not? Maybe. However, the stories we tell ourselves and one another can become myths. All we can say for certain at the get-go is that myths collectivize our sense of self. It's not good enough that you know a story, what's important is that we both do, and can orient ourselves in relationship to our interpretation of it. There is no static, codified interpretation of any text, and the authority to hierarchize or prioritize an interpretation is the centralizing principle of tradition.

Outside the arcane framework of semioticians like Roland Barthes—who approaches the subject in his book *Mythologies* as one might prepare specimens in a museum—it is surprisingly hard to make a clean distinction between "story," "narrative," and "myth." Maybe stories are simply myths that have not gained mythic resonance. That's a frequently employed, but entirely vague way to say they are stories which haven't yet sprouted from the seed of some collective belief. But fundamentally, myths, stories and narratives are made of the same stuff. Stories we tell ourselves, stories we tell one another, stories we tell about what those stories mean, on and on.

"Mythos" means "by mouth." It is that which is spread, a fabric woven of memes. A "story" implies a series of events. A "narrative" feels somehow at once less and more grandiose, and might encompass either. These distinctions break down further in the hands of narrative theorists and semioticians, by level of mediation.[1]

So, stories—once they've become culturally embedded or repeated—are generalized into myths, and those myths serve as a kind of connective tissue for human societies. There may be some sense in considering myth a story that has been repeated, and solidified with that collective repetition and remembrance, which at one and the same time permutes with each retelling, in each mind.

---

[1] Those connotations are descriptive rather than prescriptive, with distinct meanings in formal or subtle ways, but functionally there is venn-diagram overlap and a high amount of ambiguity outside academic contexts, even if that is philosophically problematic. Throughout Narrative Machines, we will attempt to stick to using "myth" to refer more to the communal aspect of narratives, "mythos" to their communicability, "story" to refer to the personal dimension, and "narrative" as the overarching structure. But the closer one looks the more they blur into one another, so this may prove an empty promise.

Renowed scientist and professional crank Richard Dawkins defined "meme" as a self-reproducing and propagating information structure analogous to a gene in biology. Various theorists have adapted the concept of memes to other domains, mythemes, narremes, and so on.

In light of amplified reproducibility online—a more fertile culture for them to grow in—this subject has also expanded from social and pop science to political and even military import. A tutorial on "Military Memetics" presented at the 2011 Social Media for Defense Summit defines a meme as, "information which propagates, has impact, and persists," going on to elaborate that it could include "words, ideas, symbols, icons, logos, tunes, poems, catch-phrases, fashion, technological processes (e.g., making arrowheads or gumbo), fables, religion, graffiti, images, novels, movies, narratives, culture (functional or dysfunctional; national, tribal, or organizational)."

Analysis of myth is, by virtue of this, inherently a discussion of memetics, though the inverse may not always be the case. As much as we may want to reduce memes to silly photos shared on Facebook, these are just the tip of a very large iceberg, and as this narrative research is better wedded to information and systems theory analysis, we can be sure there will be more to come. As one example of many, the Defense Advanced Projects Research Agency (DARPA) has supported a series of memetics-related projects with multidisciplinary teams from industry and academia.[2]

A meme suffices, at the very least, as a metaphor for any idea that has the potential to be turned into a social act. As with most metaphors, there are ways in which it is accurate, and ways that it is not. More importantly, what are the repercussions of the idea within memetics of the overlapping relationship of genes and culture? In other words, do myths play a role in our evolution, as a part of our mirrored relationship with one another?

We would like to provide a quotation from *A Thousand Years of Nonlinear History* on this subject, and then give commentary more aligned with our specific line of inquiry.

> Darwin's basic insight was that animal and plant species are the cumulative result of a process of descent and modification. Later on, however, scientists came to realize that any variable replicator (not just genetic replicators) coupled to any sorting device (not just ecological selection pressures) would generate a capacity for evolution.

---

[2] Epidemiology of Ideas (2006) Military Memetics (2006-2009) Social Media in Strategic Communications (SMISC) (2011-in progress) Narrative Networks (N2) (2011-in progress)

The "best" in terms of survival depends in large measure on the conditions of the environment and all the possibilities that can be defined within that space. What we hold as virtuous may not be well suited, but the aesthetic appeal of virtue, to the extent that aesthetics increases adaptation in an environment, is one of the many ways we can re-determine value in a utilitarian sense. The attraction or repulsion we feel when encountering a certain facial structure, or from a pattern of symbols constructed—we might say—right out of the genetic intelligence of an individual, helps provide one of the key sorting mechanisms in literal and figurative mating rituals. Sorting is taking place when we are attracted to one book and not another, or one song and not another. When we find a common movie or favorite show with someone, there is a bond there. Think about the sorting and matching occurring when we recognize we've both seen the same movie, how we compare mutual reactions to the story, and how it might affect far more than mere entertainment.[3] Shared referents are social currency. This is not, at the same time, a top-down sort of brainwashing, nor is it entirely fixed and embedded in indelible biology; it is instead the pre-existing conditions that structure all societies.

Sexual attraction recapitulates an inherent biological imperative to produce offspring; yet humans have in various ways circumvented or sublimated that drive, and so the "children" that can be born from the co-mingling of our ideas needn't be physical or literal. Power structures are navigated and codified through externalizations of "sex" commodity value, often implicitly, and often in a sense which has no direct connection to sexual reproduction or intercourse. Artists are inherently mythically promiscuous. Nevertheless, the ideas that are most compelling to us, the art that attracts and changes us, seems to operate on the same principles that determine a mating selection process. This is part of the central role aesthetics plays in our lives—in politics, in identity, in religion, in economies...

Thus, we can use a genetic metaphor in regard to our myths. Read that again. Selection processes, sorting mechanisms, and other systemic relationships apply to the ways myths replicate, spread, feed, and die. And these myths have an effect on our own breeding, as well as the basic relationships we form with one another and the environment around us. They are a part of these feedback mechanisms.

> Richard Dawkins independently realized that patterns of animal behavior (such as bird-songs or the use of tools by apes) could indeed replicate themselves if they spread across a population (and across generations) by imitation. (ibid)

---

[3] Economy as sex, representing social and material realities (compare the market behavior / psychology of the art world, to commodities, to blind speculation). There are always bound to be "realists" that think the model is the reality and behavior is driven by that image. This really puts a fine point on the infuriating and confounding issue of beauty as commodity, which contrary to popular opinion is not the product of capitalism, any more than beauty as innate preference in some way began with global trade. Capitalism merely emphasizes the fungibility of such commodities.

This has clear repercussions in the study of the diffusion of language and culture. No matter how many layers of regress are added here, it is the relationship formed by a myth that gives it a defining motive. Here we see the undercurrent of all forms of human representation, a collective shadow that looms over societies, which we've taken to refer to simply as "myth." This opens up the door for new approaches to mythic study which go far beyond what can be accomplished in a single introductory volume, but we are hopeful that more work will continue in this direction in the future. Not that the basis for this perspective is new to those familiar with the history of psychoanalytic thought. In 1901 Freud wrote the following in the *Psychopathology of Everyday Life,*

> A large part of the mythological view of the world, which extends a long way into the most modern religions, is nothing but psychology projected into the external world. The obscure recognition ... of psychical factors and relations in the unconscious is mirrored—it is difficult to express it in other terms, and here the analogy with paranoia must come to our aid—in the construction of a supernatural reality, which is destined to be changed back once more by science into the psychology of the unconscious. One could venture to explain in this way the myths of paradise and the fall of man, of God, of good and evil, of immortality, and so on, and to transform metaphysics into metapsychology.

And today we echo this sentiment, though it should be directed toward operative psychology in the world, rather than solely the mythologies of Psychology, the discipline.

The relationships myth allows for can be forged in many directions, both from the inside out (sense- and identity-making, defining who "we" are), from the outside in (placing ourselves in relation to one another, conceptualizing the structure and nature of the outside world, and our relationship to it), and they are also self perpetuating and, to an extent, self structuring or replicating (myths as heuristic, pedagogical, or mimetic device).[*]

Myths define who we are, defines where we are in time, what role we serve, and what the nature of that role should be. They ask "what if," little realizing that fantasies are informed by the same impulses as the rest of the psyche, ideas which feed back directly into the material world—the myths of nations, of gods and kings, have had a direct effect on human history, as the genetic and ecological future is shaped by such phantasms, whether an institution erected after the fact, or as inspirational motive.

---

[*] For example, a traditional motif for myth as pedagogy appears in folklore such as Frau Perschta, Krampus, or Saint Nick, winter tales original told to teach children discipline. When this is attempted by the state, for instance as is explored in the BBC article "Moscow fairytale comics to help migrants 'behave'", it feels forced and overtly propagandic, to modern sensibilities. Further, as indoctrination, it is unlikely to be successful for outsiders who don't already feel a connection to those myths of common origin. However, most advertising and similar messaging serves many similar roles, in a way that feels natural to those already inculcated by the implicit logic of Western capitalism.

All our relationships with ourselves and with one another are composed of stories. Identity, especially, is grounded in myth. All that is represented, all that we form an opinion on, as we form an opinion on it, is in that process entering the realm of myth.

In *I Contain Multitudes*, a book by Ed Yong, the ecological structure of both microbiomes and ecosystems are laid out, and it is further observed that they behave according to similar self-determined rules. That is, the context of an ecosystem are dependent on every other component element of that system, and vice versa, and the same is true of the microbiome of our body and the billions of organisms that live within us, or we might more accurately say, which are a part of us. We are "always a we, never a me."

The same point holds for myths. An analogy can be drawn between the relationship of the two (microbiomes and mythologies) in a manner of scale, emulating the Gnostic motto, "as above so below." The observations drawn in the world of biogeography might be applied to the behavior of narrative as a part of an ecosystem. Further, as the Internet further acts as a representation of social networks, analysis can be assisted through elaborate real time modeling and analysis of the global narrative machine. We will deal with this in only the most general sense—we will explore many of the philosophical problems that are liable to be overlooked within any such purely analytic approach.

Myths are a primary selector for social motility, even if not a motive,[5] as it's not as if we read and enact our lives like a play. We are tugged and pulled by them, as they are simultaneously created by us and creating us, existing at all the junctures where our worlds overlap with one another. Myths arise as relationships, points of intersection. They present within a context, and it is in that context in which they must be understood. These relations are complex, and involve an open ambiguity about their power dynamics. The relationship between ritual object or work of art and individual audience member, the relationship between audience members, all occur within the framework provided by our myths themselves, especially the almost inaudible but ever-present whispers of the past.[6]

Finally, myths are strange attractors, the set of values toward which a system tends to evolve.

> A body plan defines a space of possibilities (the space of all possible vertebrate designs, for example) ... The formal study of these possibility spaces is more advanced in physics and chemistry, where they are referred to as 'phase spaces.'

---

[5] Though do we recognize our motives for the first time when they are reflected back to us in our myths? This is the primary function of psychoanalytic critique.

[6] This assemblage looks exclusively at those in-between spaces, the connective tissue that holds us together. It is not an exegesis of any one particular mythology.

Their structure is given by topological invariants called 'attractors', as well as by the dimensions of the space, dimensions that represent the 'degrees of freedom', or relevant ways of changing, of concrete physical or chemical dynamical systems. ...

In the biological and social sciences, on the other hand, we do not yet have the appropriate formal tools to investigate the structure of their much more complex possibility spaces. —A New Philosophy of Society, Delanda

This means that the tools of literary, psychological, and social analysis may all be set loose on our myths, with a recognition that this is considerably more than a purely academic issue. Beyond that, assuredly neurological and mathematical-linguistic models will continue to have a place, using multi-discipline approaches. It is an open discussion that could benefit as much from exploration of cognitive psychology as it can from the analysis of literary symbol or the direct experience of a shamanic ritual. This is not a science, but that doesn't make our aims any less legitimate. And science can even provide us with some of our most useful metaphors.

What we learn in this domain may never be certain—many of the difficulties that lie between us and such a comprehensive systems theory approach to myth will be sketched out in the pages to follow—but it is nevertheless vital to do so. Not only in the hope of understanding ourselves, but more troublingly, because these semantic and sentiment systems are already at work in our social-technological ecosystems, our media, our political systems, our markets, all as a part of the ever-evolving web of language darting around the globe and bouncing off our satellites.

It is our objective to reassert the role of *mythos* in a nominalist pan-psychic materialism, which is to say that by denying universal reifications—in the sense that souls or political parties, gods or spirits or even minds refer to an essence which itself exists in the world—we can still affirm the existence of common narratives. Like the poststructuralists, we only need to drop an appeal to universality, objectivity, or even centralized coherence. If we are honest, this is already the state of affairs in the world, and it is not one from which there is any acceptable return.

We hope this re-appraisal of myth leads us to new ideas and questions which none of us would have formulated on our own. It is a group endeavor and benefits the most from the interaction of minds in the commons. What it becomes is in all of our hands.

NARRATIVE**MACHINES**

HOW TO
DISAPPEAR
DISAPPEAR
DISAPPEAR
DISAPPEAR
DISAPPEAR
DISAPPEAR

COMPLETELY
AND NEVER BE FOUND

THERE IS NO EDG

THE WORLD IS BOUNDLESS AND FORBIDS US FROM FLEEING

II. MYTH IS DEAD; LONG LIVE MYTH

THE ABSENCE OF THE SACRED

We are unbridled pattern recognizers and profligate theorizers. Often, our theories are good enough to get us through the day, or at least to an age when we can procreate. But our genius for creative storytelling, combined with our inability to detect our own ignorance, can sometimes lead to situations that are embarrassing, unfortunate, or downright dangerous—especially in a technologically advanced, complex democratic society that occasionally invests mistaken popular beliefs with immense destructive power (See: crisis, financial; war, Iraq). As the humorist Josh Billings once put it, "It ain't what you don't know that gets you into trouble. It's what you know for sure that just ain't so." (Ironically, one thing many people "know" about this quote is that it was first uttered by Mark Twain or Will Rogers —which just ain't so.) —Confident Idiots

We can hardly know ourselves without myth. Myths convey meaning, or rather, are a meaning that we participate in creating.

All of our retained history is recalled as narrative. The value that myth provides is demonstrated in the fact that we have history at all, and not only in the historic record of stone figurines and arrangements of cave bear bones. The history of civilization is, at one and the same time, myth. It is not a singular, universal and static truth that myths represent, but instead an ever shifting mirage of order, coherence and meaning, shared stories that in aggregate comprise a culture.

History, even if we allow it to be in its broadest sense a single kind of activity, is nonetheless a highly diverse one. Plagues, invasions, emigrations; the foundation, workings and development of constitutional arrangements and political systems; wars, external and civil, revolutions, changes in religion and culture, gradual or abrupt, the formation of various kinds of collective identity—confessional, national, ideological—providential history in the sense of the dealings of God with man: all these and much else are properly regarded as history. Some histories are virtually pure narrative; others are virtually pure, almost atemporal, analysis, being essentially structural or cultural surveys. —A History of Histories, Burrow

Our history is reflected in these narratives that we construct of ourselves and one another. This history forms a patchwork, a collective memory only partially remembered. The art and religions of antiquity sprung into existence together, and were a way for us to relate to one another as populations grew beyond small wandering tribes. The earliest artistic artifacts are religious, or is it the other way around? It is hard to say.

Myth and art—nearly inseparable terms until the Modernist wrecking ball tried (and failed) to smash them asunder—provide a distorted mirror for us to regard ourselves in. We see ourselves in a new light, the best artists showing us existential truths through the distortion or even complete abandonment of empirical necessity.

In the best case, myths can provide a kind of collective psychological nourishment, and cultures who are devoid of the ability to distinguish myth from literal fact suffer for it. Such a thing could hardly be called a culture at all. In *The Work of Art*, Walter Benjamin writes, "The uniqueness of the work of art is identical to its embeddedness in the context of tradition." This also seems to work conversely, so that art objects provided a means of encoding symbols in the various ways we've already alluded to.

He continues, "An ancient statue of Venus, for instance, existed within the traditional context for the Greeks (who made it an object of worship) that was different from the context in which it existed for medieval clerics (who viewed it as a sinister idol). But what was equally evident to both was its uniqueness—that is, its aura." He defines this 'aura' in various nebulous ways throughout the course of his essay, it is "A strange tissue of space and time," it is something that vanishes when an object can be reproduced endlessly, when it ceases to be another other than the image of itself.

This aura is none other than a particular instance of what can more broadly be called the sacred. If you bear with us a moment in the premise that the sacred can be something vital to our nature, then an absence of it, or more accurately, an absence of the ability to recognize it, let alone find it, would present a pressing cultural and existential crisis. A glance at the Newstastrophe of 2016-17 in the U.S., the global resurgence of retro-futurist Traditionalism, etc. makes it clear that we are in just such a position, even though no solid connection between the two has yet been drawn.

An obvious conclusion of modernity is that we have no unifying myth, as Georges Bataille proposes: we live in an overarching myth which is an absence of myth. America seems a fast-paced, materialistically oriented, cultural melting pot, in which it seems that any need for centralizing mythology would quickly boil away.

To anyone who winces at the thought of a story being just fiction, the relegation of myth to the status of untruth should appear unfortunate. The modern definition, "a commonly accepted but untrue belief," is not at all what we mean by "myth" here. However, the myth as the false or the true tacitly defines a predominant conception of our times; it serves as the dividing line between the archaic past and the modern. Even amongst the ranks of those who are generally most sympathetic to the psychological value of myth, there has been increasing question of if myth has any place in our lives. For instance, Michael Vannoy Adams presented this material at the "Psyche and Imagination" conference of the International Association for Jungian Studies,

Recently, one Jungian, Wolfgang Giegerich, has argued that, at this stage in the history of consciousness, myth no longer has any psychological function... Ancient mythological figures, he contends, "do not suffice." They are insufficient because, he says, "even though they may display certain formal similarities" to the modern situation, "they are incommensurable" with it. ... Giegerich, however, maintains that the modern psychological situation is utterly without precedent, without parallel. It is so radically different—or, as he says, so logically different—from the ancient mythological situation that any similarity is merely formal and thus insignificant. Giegerich says that the modern situation has "fundamentally broken with myth as such, that is, with the entire level of consciousness on which truly mythic experience was feasible."

Yet, the most obvious conclusion is often not the most poignant one. We clearly *do* have myths, though they frequently exist in mediums not surrounded by the aura of the sacred. Media narratives have become increasingly paranoid—and to some extent rightly so—about how myths are being used as a weapon, perhaps missing the irony that it is the media which serves as the delivery mechanism for memetic warfare.[7] In the wake of God's death, we have only the clustering of personal and clan identities and then an overarching framework—Nature, or the State, or celebrity—really whatever collective pantheon meets the need of a given time and place. As a society, we hardly know what *isn't* a myth, as modern myths are so pervasive that they are nearly invisible. Those that are considered archaic, that is, they have ceased to function in the manner that they were meant to, become more apparent to us. We call these relics "myth," but they are not. They are their empty husks, no longer sacred, myths that have died. But the impulse that once gave them life is still there. Perhaps they are more like the cast off shells of a growing crustacean.

Neil Stephenson's novel *Anathem* deals with the modern crisis of the sacred. The following passage is especially relevant,

> So I looked with fascination at those people in their mobes, and tried to fathom what it would be like. Thousands of years ago, the work that people did had been broken down into jobs that were the same each day, in organizations where people were interchangeable parts. All of the story had been bled out of their lives. That was how it had to be; it was how you got a productive economy. But it would be easy to see a will at work behind this: not exactly an evil will, but a selfish will. The people who'd made the system thus were jealous, not of money and not of power but of story. If their employees came home at day's end with interesting stories to tell, it meant that something had gone wrong: a blackout, a strike, a spree killing.

---

[7] And online "we are the media," which is to say we serve as amplifiers for various interests. Memes don't spread if there aren't selves to incubate in.

The Powers That Be would not suffer other to be in stories of their own unless they were fake stories that had been made up to motivate them.

We cannot as a race lose our myths—certainly not before such a point that we have no beliefs or culture whatsoever.[8] We also cannot so easily separate myths from the sacred, nor can we extricate ourselves from the biases of a specific culture, least of all the ones we are immersed in.

Myths often seek to make us feel more connected to sacred origins. Artistic movements such as the Surrealists were fixated on this goal, and this was a fixture in the work of the great popularizers of myth, Carl Jung and Joseph Campbell. There was in this a general desire to rediscover, reconnect with some primal, sacred source. Consider this quote from Bataille's essay "The Surrealist Religion,"

> Everything Breton has put forward—whether it concerns the quest for the sacred, the concern with myths, or rediscovering rituals similar to those of primitives—represents the exploration of the possibility we again discover, possibility in another sense; this time it is simply a question of exploring all that can be explored by man, it is a question of reconstituting all that was fundamental to man before human nature had been enslaved by the necessity for technical work.

It is easy to make this distinction, and feel a need to somehow return to a state of sacredness, real or imagined, which seems to have been stripped from or lives, from our very psychological beings, by the realities of global industrialization. But what does that mean, exactly?

For our purposes at the moment it should be enough to highlight that the sacred represents not a single idea, but rather an entire category of ideation, which allows for the separation of the world into ontological categories. It is a constituting element in the formation of worldview, serving a psychological need if not a material reality, which perceives the world manifest to our senses as itself symbolic of an invisible world. Mircea Eliade explores this subject in *The Sacred & The Profane,*

> By manifesting the sacred, any object becomes something else, yet it continues to be itself. A sacred stone remains a stone; apparently (or, more precisely, from the profane point of view), nothing distinguished it from all other stones. But for those to whom a stone reveals itself as sacred, its immediate reality is transmuted

---

[8] "Dōgen is not concerned with "sacred mountains", or pilgrimages, or spirit allies, or wilderness as some special quality. His mountains and streams are the processes of this earth, all of existence, process, essence, action, absence; they roll being and non-being together. They are what we are, we are what they are. For those who would see directly into essential nature, the idea of the sacred is a delusion and an obstruction: it diverts us from seeing what is before our eyes: plain thusness. Roots, stems, and branches are all equally scratchy. No hierarchy, no equality. No occult and exoteric, no gifted kids and slow achievers. No wild and tame, no bound or free, no natural and artificial. Each totally its own frail self. Even though connected all which ways; even because connected all which ways. This, thusness, is the nature of the nature of nature. The wild in wild." —"Practice of the Wild", Snyder

into a supernatural reality. This conception of the sacred seems to demand the transcendent, the invention of the supernatural.

It stands to reason that everything is natural; even if an event or entity is unexplainable, it still remains natural. Forgive the tautology: nature is what is. The distinction between "natural" and "supernatural" is only relevant, only meaningful, in the context of the profane when contrasted with the sacred. Needless to say, inventing the supernatural, a new category of being to house the sacred, creates its own slew of problems that must be dealt with, such as superstition, religious literalism, or even the metaphysical reifications of Gnostic spiritualism.

In Eliade's conception, and it is a point well taken, a sacred object is so because it is a symbol, a link, with the archetype standing "behind" the physical, profane object. A sacred canoe is not just a canoe, it is "canoe," or it is a canoe within the context of a specific myth pertaining to canoes, or the sacred river, etc. It has meaning precisely because of its resemblance to the myth, rather than the other way around. This is the sense in which fetishes are meant to link practitioners with some spirit world,[9] and it is the core idea of occultism: that there is, an implicate order at work in Bohm's sense,[10] even within the apparent chaos of the manifest world. This too underlines both the theoretic and historic groundedness of science in occultism.

The sacred and profane show themselves not only in the perception of *things* but also in the perception of *time*. For instance during a sacred festival —a concept that we have mostly lost touch with in purely profane holidays —one enters into the time before time, recapitulating the birth of the world, or some other mythological event which occurs outside of profane time. The phrase "time before time" is an odd approximation, a metaphor created from within the field of time. Sacred time and sacred objects do not truly stand outside, behind, or before their profane counterparts; they are distinguished as occupying two separate ontological categories simultaneously, and there may even be some kind of exchange or interplay between the two, as sacred festivals and rituals demonstrate. Yet also the sacred always maintains a sense of the undefinable. The second it can be clothed in words and grows comfortable in them, it is has become orthodox and profane.

---

[9] "Religion originates in the Oedipal murder and devouring of the primeval father by the horde of his rival sons; their repression of the memory of the deed; their unconscious remorse and consequent worship of the father in the guise of the totem animal; and the guilty through veiled recollection of the murder itself through its periodic re-enactment of the totem feast." —Freud's Moses, Yerushalmi

[10] "In the enfolded [or implicate] order, space and time are no longer the dominant factors determining the relationships of dependence or independence of different elements. Rather, an entirely different sort of basic connection of elements is possible, from which our ordinary notions of space and time, along with those of separately existent material particles, are abstracted as forms derived from the deeper order. These ordinary notions in fact appear in what is called the "explicate" or "unfolded"order, which is a special and distinguished form contained within the general totality of all the implicate orders" —Wholeness and Implicate Order, Bohm.

The constructed supernatural realm loops back into the otherwise inaccessible elements of our own being, as a piece of psychological sleight-of-hand that allows us to conditionally stake a claim in the ever-shifting chaos that is nature itself, un-sculpted by human sensation, consideration, organization and expectation. Collective fictions give us our sense of meaning and purpose. The condition we must accept when engaging with myth is that we pretend the shadows on the wall, the image on the screen, or the entities in our dreams represent some type of reality.

> The realm we call the sacred cannot be left to sociologists, even if ... the use of this word has become questionable if we do not frame with reference to sociology. ... Science always abstracts the object it studies from the totality of the world. ... It might in turn be pointed out that the sacred can just as easily be envisaged on its own. ... But a question remains: suppose that the sacred, far from being like the other objects of science, subject to separation, is defined as the exact opposite of abstract objects (things, tools, and clearly definable elements), precisely as the concrete totality itself is resistant to it. (ibid)

Finally, the sacred can define myths of place. We might consider the post-holocaust resurgence of the idea of Israel, or the *axis mundi* itself. Psychogeography plays a chief role in defining a *volk*, and sacred geography often seeks to define a center to construct a universe around. Carl Jung followed this very idea in the ways he envisioned his models of the Self, and we can apply a similar critique to all such metaphysical ideas. Again from Eliade, "When Scandinavian colonists took possession of Iceland (land-nama) and cleared it, they regarded the enterprise neither as an original undertaking nor as human and profane work. For them, their labor was only repetition of a primordial act, the transformation of chaos into cosmos by the divine act of creation." The land itself must first be claimed by myth before it can be of any use. Every element of our environment is open to mythic interpretation, further, it must be consumed and reformed, reclaimed, through a mythology so as to be rendered a part of the human sphere of concern that we imagine to exist separate from nature. This appears a fundamental principle of culture. Like a living being, a culture must feed, or it will die.

There is no universal agreement about what is sacred, and what profane. Our histories could never encapsulate the range of diversity in the stories and selves of the past, although they speak through us in various ways. If new myths are born, re-tethered to something sacred, they must come from that sense of being overwhelmed, of outright possession as if to unavoidable gravity, they must be anything but contrived, planned, and developed with the intention of delivering the sacred to us. (She does not come to us on a platter. More likely, the platter will have your beating heart on it.) This provides an innate tension between the sacred and propaganda.

The sacred is homologous to love—consuming, destroying, and transfiguring old structures. Neither are mechanically reproducible.

We can visualize the transmission of myths, and their constituent memetic parts, and say each new myth has a ripple effect on every other, rendering an interference pattern in its wake. Some may consider those results positive or negative, and those determinations depend on the biases of the interpreter. For every action, it is likely that some will benefit, and others suffer.

And the mass psychological factors that inculcate and drive mass religion do not vanish when we kill our Gods. No matter how we destroy our idols, they arise anew.

So, if myth is something long dead, a corpse exhumed with philosophical disinterest, then please consider this work an attempt at necromancy. But if myth is considered something dangerous; full of falsities, dead ends and mazes luring the unwary into a fugue of superstition, then consider it a whispered pass-phrase into another world: the world beyond the wallpaper. A world that recognizes the real is in the effect rendered, rather than in the thing symbolized. Conflicting fictions drive Holy wars. How is a history born of spilled blood unreal? How is it meaningless, even if all the Gods are just shadows cast on the wall by finger-puppets?

Myth is not dead, nor is it false; it is living, and misunderstood. And the sacred presents a deep existential necessity, and an equally serious existential threat.

THE IMMANENCE OF MYTH AND TYRANNY OF THE LITERAL

It is only through active, ceaseless interpretation that we might catch a reflected glimpse of the human subject at the heart of literature. It is by only by acknowledging artifice that one can move beyond artifice. Reading is a creative act. Unlike almost everything we are encouraged to consider entertainment, it is an active pursuit. Without this process of interpretation we cannot know ourselves. —"The Tyranny of the Literal," Autralian Book Review

As a youth, who can remember staring at the television in befuddlement as documentaries would attempt to discover the supposed "historic truth" of a myth? Did giants actually walk the Earth before the time of King Arthur's court? How did Noah manage to get every species of animal aboard a single ship?

These are the wrong questions to ask, and for the wrong reasons. Myths speak to our need of stories and images, both grand and mundane, for us to relate ourselves to. They aren't meant to replace the method of science, any more than *mythos* should occlude *logos*.

This is of course only what need they fulfill, but not what use they serve within human society—what they *do*. In the public mind, "myth" has become the opposite of fact, something that is generally accepted but untrue; so we might say "it is a myth that reading by flashlight ruins your eyesight." The popular Discovery Channel show Myth Busters uses this definition, attempting to disprove myths with something vaguely resembling science. The myths of antiquity are looked upon as quaint stories, despite the fact that they shaped history, how it is interpreted, even how it happened. This secular, occidental conception (which is the root of modern myth) says the myths of the past were erroneous explanations about the nature of reality— fanciful stories, which, though colorful and interesting curiosities, surely bear no particular use to our lives.

In this, we misunderstand how myths function. As has been expounded ad nauseum by an expansive list of scholars and authors, including Mircea Eliade, Carl Jung, Joseph Campbell, Karly Kerenyi, etc. etc., many myths do not principally intend to explain the world in an analytic sense. And even if they once did intend to serve as an instrument of science, we can put that intention aside, and find that myth is a reflection on us more than it is a reflection on the world without us in it. Spiritual metaphors are useful inasmuch as they describe mental states, but the considerations of Model Dependent Realism should be applied here as much as in the sciences. This view, presented by Hawkings and Mlodinow in their 2010 book *The Grand Design*, states that *models are to be judged by their confluence with observations*, but that *can't be retroactively used to demonstrate the absolute reality of the model.*

> Like the overlapping maps in a Mercator projection, where the ranges of different versions overlap, they predict the same phenomena. But just as there is no flat map that is a good representation of the earth's entire surface, there is no single theory that is a good representation of observations in all situations — The Grand Design, Hawking and Mlodinow

We place ourselves within a world as defined by myths. This world may or may not correspond to the facts, which is maybe how "myth" came to mean simply false. Myths are quite often psychologically true, when you understand what it is they're saying. Of course the world wasn't made in seven days, of course Odin wasn't suspended from a tree, ... This misunderstanding bites both ways, as literalism dominates religious and even literary as well as secular thinking.[11]

> To say that a thing is imaginary is not to dispose of it in the realm of mind, for the imagination, or the image making faculty, is a very important part of our mental functioning. An image formed by the imagination is a reality from the point of view of psychology; it is quite true that it has no physical existence, but are we going to limit reality to that which is material? We shall be far out of our reckoning if we do, for mental images are potent things, and although they do not actually exist on the physical plane, they influence it far more than most people suspect. — Spiritualism and Occultism, Fortune

The difference between the supernatural and natural is, as we've already explored, nothing more than a different narrative context, encoded within myth. So too with all the categorical distinctions that we think of as ontological, save one: the only true ontology, which is only relatable through representational models. This is the quandary we forever find ourselves in, to which we may contemplate the famous passage from Chuang Tzu, perhaps outside its original context,

> Zhuangzi and Huizi were strolling along the bridge over the Hao River. Zhuangzi said, "The minnows swim about so freely, following the openings wherever they take them. Such is the happiness of fish."

> Huizi said, "You are not a fish, so whence do you know the happiness of fish?"

> Zhuangzi said, "You are not I, so whence do you know I don't know the happiness of fish?"

---

[11] This blind-spot can present a tactical advantage to those who would use it, so it bears consideration.

Huizi said, "I am not you, to be sure, so I don't know what it is to be you. But by the same token, since you are certainly not a fish, my point about your inability to know the happiness of fish stands intact."

Zhuangzi said, "Let's go back to the starting point. You said, 'Whence do you know the happiness of fish?' Since your question was premised on your knowing that I know it, I must have known it from here, up above the Hao River."

The myth of annulment provides a sense of time-keeping. We begin and end modernity with the death of myth, generally accepting that mythology once served a central role in human life, up until the time when science and industry somehow stole away or otherwise replaced our need for "childish things". This is the central thesis of Bataille's *The Absence of Myth*. The belief in this absence itself serves as a framing myth which allows us to establish a place within history for ourselves. Modernity, so defined, is the point at which myths ceased to hold sway. At the dawn of reason, man stepped out of the imaginal world of myth, and entered the real. Yet it was precisely at this point that the true anxiety of the relationship between real and imaginal began to take hold. Spiritual mysteries are manifest in the same way anything else is, as an emergent property of systems operating in the real world, which is to say they are immanent.[12]

The chimerical aspect of this topic lies in its immanence; myth is organic, as organic as the bodies it springs from, irrespective of whether they are living or dead. Myth is often the closest we come to immortality, as creators, and the closest we come to speaking with the dead, for the living—whether a lifelong quest, the death masks of immortal ancestors lining the walls, or the momentary act of impossibility that propels us beyond normal status, from mere mortal into hero, into spirit, perhaps even to divinity. The forces that move and motivate us are not structures to be weighed in the balance of validity, and judged either viable or wanting. They are, as Deleuze and Guattari would have it, "lines of flight," though they can destratify as well as stratify social orders. They are pathways, transportation machines. Meaning is not paramount; the content should not merely be rated in terms of signal vs. noise.[13]

---

[12] There is room for distinction between sign and representation, beyond the tendency to see a schema of thing represented and its meaning. We need to get past this dialectic of certain inner meaning contained within a thing (sign) and its objective existence (representation) to recognize both as a part of the same field of experience. This flattening is laid out in Baudrillard's Simulacra and Simulation. We feel a need to distinguish between the inert existence of matter (rocks, etc) and living organisms, and tend to take offense when they are conflated, since organisms can have meaning, we are told, whereas objects are at best put toward to some use, despite the fact that rocks may have given rise to life, and exist as a sort of proto-life, much as all matter is, to one extent or another, proto-life.

[13] We should also consider the entirety of Deleuze's final essay, Immanence, A Life, "...we shouldn't enclose life in the single moment when individual life confronts universal death. A life is everywhere, in all the moments that a given living subject goes through and that are measured by

One does not ask what the tales of Herakles or Odysseus *mean*, unless the intent is to use myth as a mirror of the personal psyche. Meaning is an exuded by-product, like a snake's shed skin. Myth is not purposed, nor a thing (in and of itself) purely of sign and symbol.[14] It may be treated symbolically—the lance and the cup may symbolize the generative organs of either gender, but they do not *mean* such things.

Any encoding in mythical terms fail the test of transmission, when relevancy is dependent on meaning. Myth is essentially meaningless. If utility and purposefulness are the grand arbiter of validity then myth is an irrelevancy—it has no end goal in itself. It remains at odds with industry and capitalism even as its organs are used to create brands and fascist regimes.

So be it, we say. Far better when myth is discarded from consideration by those who would use it to justify and perpetuate their agendas, far better that it is viewed as backward and irrelevant. For us, in embracing a form of metaphysical nihilism in common with Nietzsche[15]—as a stage towards greater awareness rather than a bleak end provided by the singular—myth is co-equal with all collective human activity. It is as intimate as breathing, as internalized as metabolism.

The reason myths exist after thousands of years is not that they contain information which must be preserved. Rather, it is because they shift and mutate. Any attempt to fix it in place, to say for instance "this is the final word on what Moby Dick means" robs myth of its creativity and turns its ossified corpse into dogma. There are no truly final words, at least until all the lights go out and humankind is no more. The myths themselves roll forever downhill, accumulating new cultural fragments, personal nuances, dying and reborn every time someone new chooses to sing along.

If representation and meaning are so important—if politicians, philosophers, priests and other authorities insist that a given myth has a specified, singular meaning—it is for one purpose alone. That purpose is the appropriation of the limitless power of myth for their own ends. Fascism and myth can go hand-in-hand, and this certainly has soured it for some, (such as Horkheimer and Adorno), but this is like blaming the tool for the use it was

---

given lived objects: an immanent life carrying with it the events or singularities that are merely actualized in subjects and objects. This indefinite life does not itself have moments, close as they may be one to another, but only between-times, between-moments; it doesn't just come about or come after but offers the immensity of an empty time where one sees the event yet to come and already happened, in the absolute of an immediate consciousness."

[14] Here we may distinguish between symbol that is chosen, a superficial veneer, and sign which chooses us. Though they may be hard to distinguish at the moment of their appearance, in retrospect, it is generally clear.

[15] "The project of nihilism is to unmask all systems of reason as systems of persuasion, and to show that logic—the very basis of metaphysical thought—is in fact a kind of rhetoric. All thought that pretends to discover truth is but an expression of the will to power ... of those making the truth-claims over those being addressed by them; in particular, the disinterested, scientific, rational search for the objective, neutral truth of a proposition is an illusion produced by metaphysical thought for its own benefit." —The End of Modernity, Vattimo

put to. Myth is a powerful tool of fascism because, when the spark strikes tinder, at the right time, with the right people, it can burn the world to ash. It is not itself fascistic.

But we say, "Myth is essentially meaningless." Myth *manufactures* meaning, but that element of its nature cannot be singularly codified. From its meaninglessness, meaning arises, as plants arise from soil. Without Tiamat or Ymir, there are no worlds. It is said that from the Tao came the ten thousand things, and so it is with myth—the ground of being is vast and heaving, with myriad lines of flight surging upward.

Nature is madness. It has processes, but no myths to tell. We are the ones who bear our stories on our backs. We carry them everywhere, even when we write it out there, upon the canvas of that silent, dark world. This is primal chaos, wild and unpredictable, dangerous to life but never inimical to it, merely indifferent to man's attempts to structure experience. Multiplicity appears to derive from totality, from a singularity, but perhaps these two are inseparable. Hierarchy and teleology both result from this idea of "the one to many." So the one returns to the many, but this still deludes us, following from and contributing to a teleological worldview, that we might return again to the one, to the primal unity of heaven, at the heart of an atom bomb.

We cannot resist the temptation of building schemas, pictures from random dots, constellations from random stars. And in that tendency, we can first glimpse the true paradox of the mythological impulse: the unending process of turning chaos into apparent order, and yet the root of that impulse seems to arise *from* chaos.

Creativity derives from this multiplicity of conflicting ideas and symbols; the butchery of the singular, of chaos, of nature. Eliade observes, "Life is not possible without an opening towards the transcendent; in other words, humans cannot live in chaos." Myth tells us this, over and over in innumerable cultures, giving us a myth of the transcendent in the process. Consider this quotation, from Joseph Campbell's *Masks of God,*

> Mythological, theological, metaphysical analogies, in other words, do not point indirectly to an only partially understood 'metaphysical' term (God, Brahman, Atman, the Self, the Absolute, for instance), but directly to a relationship between two terms, the one empirical, the other metaphysical; the latter being absolutely and forever and from every conceivable human standpoint, unknowable: unconditioned as it is by Time, Space, Causality, the categories of logic – and to such a degree that even to speak of it is to represent, and so to misrepresent it, which cannot be represented…

> It is evident that Kant's metaphysical Ding-an-ich (being in itself), therefore, is equivalent to the Brahman of the Upanishads, the void of the Buddhists, and the 'Nameless' of the Tao the Ching.

If symbols are a means of reaching into the unknowable, that unknowable is transcendent of our immediate experience. Yet, at the same time, *it is the transcendental necessity in spirituality that most threatens to cut us off from the immediacy of the sacred, and the immanence of myth.* This conflict between the chaotic order of nature and the ordering chaos of man begins, interestingly enough, in what we have rightly or wrongly referred to as the "cradle of civilization." Consider the slaughter of Tiamat in the Babylonian epic of the Enuma Elish—with its ranks upon ranks of deities and monsters in which humanity springs from the blood of a fallen singular chaos, dissected and enslaved by the very gods themselves. Or perhaps the colder, but similarly brutal murder of the primal giant Ymir in Norse myth, wherein the mountains are the bones of that giant, the seas and oceans his blood, the dome of his skull the sky and his brains the scudding clouds. In such an opening we see the guts of our world revealed—Kali pleasures herself on the cold, hard lingam of Shiva the corpse. Sex and death, murder and theft, crime and punishment, the entire potential of human experience is encoded in such myths. The darkest realities of existence can be dealt with mythologically, allowing us an intermediary for dealing with our demons.

> Since "world" is a cosmos, any attack from without threatens to turn it into chaos. And as "world" was founded by imitating the paradigmatic work of the gods, the cosmogony, so the enemies who attack it are assimilated to be enemies of the Gods, the demons, and especially to the archdemon, the primordial dragon conquered by the gods at the beginning of the time. ... This is the reason the Pharaoh was assimilated to the God Re, conqueror of the dragon Apophis, while his enemies were assimilated to the mythical dragon. Darius regarded himself as a new Thraetaona, the mythical Iranian hero who was said to have slain a three-headed dragon. In Judaic tradition the pagan kings were represented in the likeness of a dragon... —The Sacred and The Profane, Eliade

The list of associations between the singular, primordial chaos and the symbol of the dragon goes on and on, including Tiamat herself. This process of slaying and reconsecrating runs through our process of individuation, a child crying in a new, dry world, separating from that umbilicus; claiming and defining.[16]

---

[16] A concise outline of the Enuma Elish is expanded on pg. 24 of Puhvel's *Comparative Mythology*, which includes the primordial pantheon before the time of the established order, "In the beginning there are a male/female pair; Apsu and Tiamat, or freshwater and saltwater deities respectively. Their bodies commingle and engender a host of deities, notably Ea, the god of wisdom and magic. When this new generation becomes unruly and troublesome for the old pair, Apsu wants to destroy it, but Ea is quicker and more decisive and slays Apsu first, leaving Tiamat widowed. Apsu remains an inert entity from then on, the mythical sweetwater ocean beneath the earth that is the abode of Ea, where he sires Marduk. ... In a great struggle he (Marduk) slays Tiamat, wipes out the monsters ... Marduk and Ea then bisect Tiamat's body to form heaven and earth, and Marduk's rule is consolidated forevermore." This pattern is not unlike what we see in Greek myth, with Kronos and the other titans the precede the Olympic pantheon.

This pattern distinguishes a variety of cultural traditions that lead, inevitably, from polytheism to monotheism, as it underlies many of the myths of the near East,

> In [Psalms] 74:12-17 we have an account of how Yahweh, in a contest with the waters, smote the many-headed Leviathan, and then proceeded to create day and nigh, the heavenly bodies, and the order of the seasons. We have already seen that in the Akkadian Epic of Creation Marduk's slaying of the chaos-dragon Tiamat is followed by his ordering of the universe, and by the building of Esagila. It is also accepted by the majority of scholars that in the Hebrew word tehom used to denote the abyss of waters in Gen 1:2 there is a reference to the chaos-dragon Tiamat ... But in the passage from Ps. 74 the name of the water-dragon, Leviathan, is the same as the Ugaritic Lotan, the dragon slain by Baal.

This is not indicative of all creation myths. The Enuma Elish espouses an original or primordial chaos that pre-existed any structuring principles, but there are others which are based on an underlying order, established by neo-Platonic strands of thought that believe there is an implicate order concealed within manifest chaos, such as Qabbalistic and Christian theology. Sky-God mythologies also often follow immediately after the rendering of the world from chaos to order, must then deal with the transition from the order of the gods to the order of man.[17] Scientific cosmology itself seems divided on this matter, since it methodologically derives from the necessity of repetition and testability, and yet cosmological theories like the big bang, or cyclical views that include a big bang and big crunch, bring into question the framework creation myths have employed since the earliest dawn of recorded mythic thought, even if the application of meaning goes beyond the strict scope of scientific inquiry.

More than calling into question the actual historic origins of the universe, this raises a more immediate cognitive one: what is the significance of "order," and "chaos" in this context, how do we distinguish one from the other? This question is reduced quite simply by the realization that we are pattern recognition machines, the "master who makes the grass green," to refer to a famous Zen koan. The organizational principles, the schemas which we attribute to reality may in some sense originate in the neural architecture with which we *create* apparent order from chaos.

In simplest terms, though there may appear to be an inherent order in the progression 1,2,3,... and no coherent order in another assortment of numbers, that "order" is a representation of our structural expectations. All number theory includes invisible logical underpinnings. 1, 2, 3... represent-

---

[17] "A shadowy first god is succeeded by one whose name means heaven. "Heaven" is deposed and castrated by his son, who in his turn feels threatened by his unborn or newborn offspring and tries cannabilism as prophylactic. But nothing avails; he is overthrown by his son, who becomes the ruling storm-god. The deposed father creates a monstrous enemy as his last-ditch champion, but the storm-god and his cohorts eliminate this threat and consolidate their rule." (ibid)

ing, among other things, an expectation of chronological and linear progression.[18] Cosmology is recapitulated within us all.

Ordering of the world is aesthetic. Our predispositions, be they biological, cultural, personal, or some fusion of all of the above, are revealed in the patterns we see. To us, they will appear self-evident. As Robert Anton Wilson put it, "what the thinker thinks, the prover proves." Even if there is no fundamental value in the idea of order or chaos without a structuring principle whatsoever, primacy can be placed on the idea of chaos for this very reason. Thus, we find immanence in myths that recognize a primal chaos underlying the structures and laws even of nature and the gods, more than those that do not.[19] And it is literally the Order of the Gods which structured our societies, at least up until fairly recently.

On the other hand, primordial chaos is not merely random, or formless, or ever-changing, though it can represent all of these things. It is the world unclaimed, unshaped by human consciousness. Thus, it is undifferentiated life, the terrifying abomination which the orderly, monotheistic traditions try to yoke. The void, primordial nature, is often portrayed as the mother goddess, in the guise of her darker aspect. Myth says she must be "slain", or tamed by man. But her inevitable return is the basis of apocalyptic philosophy, for nature can never be truly put down.

Nowhere is this as clear as in the Hindu image of Kali Ma, "Black Time," representing the creative and destructive womb of the universe. This is also symbolized as the "womb and the tomb" often referred to by Joseph Campbell, among others. This space has been recreated throughout the ages in an initiatory sense in caves, or other explorations into darkness. Thus initiation is a "second birth," and while the womb represented by the cave, by darkness, by sensory deprivation is easily linked with birth and death, it is also life itself. Life outside the walls erected by human hands and minds.[20]

Can we look behind a repeated image, and see the root impulse at work? In a profane world, can we recognize the immanence of myth in our lives at this moment without returning to myths of transcendence, of salvation, apocalypse, or revolution?

---

[18] There is also the technical definition which pertains merely to the measure of entropy in a system. Our discussion here pertains to what chaos and order symbolize, rather than what they measure.

[19] Immanent *mythos*, at its core, implies a poly- rather than mono- ontological frame, that is, without any final, unassailable, authoritative center. The very concept of being is in this light somewhat suspect. This poly-ontology applies equally to imagined spirits, as well as our imagined selves.

[20] This womb exists before birth, and after death; it is in its own source formless and timeless, as to the identity, there is no "before" birth, "after" death. It is the eternity that undercuts our illusions of time and space (or so we imagine). In a basic sense this is a Saturnine image, Saturn personified both as an old man and young child, as the lord of the Underworld; however the female inflection shifts the emphasis to birth, sex, and death. There has been a general historic trend in myth to move from mother-chaos to an orderly, patriarchal order. Perhaps, it seems that many of us now hear the siren song of Kali Ma strongly once again.

Myth is immanent. This is the final sense of sacredness. But the existential plight of secularism is revealed in the desire to flee the sacred, to escape myth entirely in the architecture of modernism, in its 'externalities of action' and its annihilation of the spirit. We yearn to gallop into a utopian future devoid of a need for ornament, gods or spirits. Belief only grounded in certainty, an architecture of benign, practical reason. No more myths or superstitions. No bangs. No surprises.

Instead, we got the horror of two world wars.

> ...in the heart of the cemetery, there is a sudden lightening of tone, and you find you are strolling through what might be a Modern suburb of Tunis or Tel Aviv. The lines of family tombs resemble cheerful vacation bungalows, airy structures of white walls and glass that might have been designed by Le Corbusier or Richard Neutra. One could holiday for a long time in these pleasant villas, and a few of us probably will. So, there is one place where modernism triumphs.
>
> As in the cases of the pyramids and the Taj Mahal, the Siegfried line and the Atlantic wall, death always calls on the very best architects. —"A Handful of Dust," JG Ballard

NARRATIVE**MACHINES**

THIS MEMES ARTWAR

III. THE GEOPOLITICS OF MEMEWAR

MINDSCAPES

What is French? This question cannot be answered by sounding out empty shells: Charles Martel, Joan of Arc, etc. On the subject of identity, the best distinction is the one Paul Ricoeur makes between idem and ipse identity. The permanence of the collective entity throughout constant changes (ipse identity,) cannot be reduced to something with the status of an event or of repetition (idem identity.) On the contrary, the former is linked to a complete hermeneutics of the self, to the whole work narration. This is the very condition of self-appropriation inasmuch as narration gives rise to a "place," a space-time which configures a meaning. "It is the identity of the recounted history which makes the identity of the individual," Ricoeur claims. To defend one's identity is not to be satisfied with a little ritual vulgate. It is to understand identity as something preserved in the play of differentiations and to attempt to recreate conditions in which it is possible to produce such a story. —Alain de Benoist

We are never too far from the trappings of mythology in our daily lives. They are the substance of movies, books, our mutually created narratives on the Internet, even on television. They permeate our ideas about ourselves, our relation to the world, and our relationships with others. They may be insightful or vapid. Fungibility can even have an inverse relationship with quality. The very drive for people to make complete fools of themselves on Reality TV also attempts to fulfill a mythic need. To be famous is to be mythologized. What many of us find so repellent about these trends in pop culture is how utter reproducibility has leveled the "aura" of the sacred. Myth is not absent.

The ancient truth expressed by Heraclitus, that those who are awake have a world in common while each sleeper has a world of his own, has been invalidated by film—and less by depicting the dream world itself than by creating figures of collective dream, such as the globe encircling Mickey Mouse. —The Work of Art, Benjamin

Yet there seems to be something different about how we experience stories from those who lived in a world before iPhones, or computers, or televisions or typewriters, even though these are all merely more reproducible forms of their predecessors, and the analogy of campfire storytelling and Internet communication is occasionally drawn.

There is a liminality to our modern myths, much as we can say a movie is real, and yet also understand that there is a sense that this is not so. They don't seem to strike their audiences as deeply as ancient rituals must have gripped their adherents. Even the fanaticism of fandom doesn't invalidate this claim.

Human sacrifice, which Benjamin saw as the final form of traditional ritual, certainly takes a certain amount of commitment to narrative, one would think. Modern myths are seductive precisely because they pretend not to be myths, they are *just* stories, or movies. It would seem peculiar to sacrifice a newborn child to Harry Potter, no matter how big a fan you are.

> Thus not only communication but the social functions in a closed circuit, a *lure*—to which the force of myth is attached. Belief, faith in information attach themselves to this tautological proof that the system gives of itself by doubling the signs of unlocatable reality.

> But one can believe that this belief is as ambiguous as that which was attached to myths in ancient societies. One both believes and doesn't. One does not ask oneself, "I know very well, but still." ... Myth exists, but one must guard against thinking that people believe in it: this is the trap of critical thinking that can only be exercised if it presupposes the naivete and stupidity of the masses.
> —Simulacra and Simulation, Baudrillard

The lights come up in the theater and the illusion is dispelled, we lose attention entirely mid-stream and surf to another channel or web-page, to take another fragment into the bricolage of our wandering consciousness. We tell ourselves those half-imagined worlds we binge-watch on Netflix have no real effect, no reality.

> Do not be lulled into believing, that just because the deadening American city of dreadful night is so utterly devoid of mystery, so thoroughly flat-footed, sterile and infantile, so burdened with the illusory gloss of baseball-hot dogs-apple-pie-and-Chevrolet, that it exists outside the psycho-sexual domain. The eternal pagan psychodrama is escalated under these modern conditions precisely because sorcery is not what '20th Century man' can accept as real. —King Kill 3, James Shelby Downard

There are many examples of modern myths embodied in media. Rather than saying that *The Lord of the Rings* is a modern myth, though clearly it is, it is more accurate to say that media contains and is at the same time built upon layer upon layer of myth, any of which implicitly requires context to be rendered coherent and accessible.

We can look at this somewhat poetically, as Tolkien was want to do, "When we can take green from grass, blue from heaven and red from blood, we have already an enchanter's power—upon one plane; and the desire to wield that power in the world external to the mind awakes....In such "fantasy", as it called, new form is made; Faerie begins; Man becomes a sub-creator." Or we can consider its implications within newsrooms, boardrooms and war rooms. In all cases, this power of the word and fascination of the will is what centuries of occultists were aiming at perfecting, without necessarily recognizing it themselves. Faust requires no deal with the devil, he's got video cameras.

> The representation of human beings by means of an apparatus has made possible a highly productive use of the human being's self-alienation. The nature of this can be grasped through the fact that the film actor's estrangement in the face of the apparatus, as Pirandello describes this experience, is basically of the same kind as the estrangement felt before one's appearance [Erscheinung] in a mirror—a favorite theme of the Romantics. But now the image [Bild] has become detachable from the person mirrored, and is transportable. —The Work of Art, Benjamin

In a capitalist society, myths too take on a capitalist bent. They serve its ends—consumed as if they are products, this does not mean that they do not leave their mark. All of this hearkens back to the absence of the sacred.

The formative or even subliminal effect of the media we're steeped in is hard to say, but certainly the multi-billion dollar industries of marketing and advertising would be useless if it was not far-reaching. For instance, there are a variety of common myths which allow access to the viewership of a news broadcast with a particular political agenda. The broadcast further establishes its narratives, but it works upon existing expectations and pre-conceptions. We believe what we are already primed to believe, and experience resistance otherwise. So, you don't find many polyamorous bisexuals watching Fox News in rapt attention. This is another example of myth acting both as amplification and sorting device, as part of our evolutionary selection processes.

We are untethered from any common shared myth, so that the task of simply creating a new mono-myth that possess the collective imagination is generally less fruitful than the artist may hope, as Bataille himself discovered in his rather ill-conceived idea of re-instituting human sacrifice. We may find in this deep desire for collective unity—whether in the Gardnerian pagan revival or nationalism.[21] This is key to understanding both the common arising of nationalistic or fascistic tendencies within occultism or religion, and contrasting the fact that they can arise as a purely atheistic phenomenon—indeed that is often one of their defining characteristics, to replace All-father with Fatherland. Nationalism subscribes more to an aesthetic of primal kitsch, a desire to find that root of common unity in a form of patriotism,[22] while fascism engenders a more occult aesthetic, even when its reality is entirely banal.

---

[21] A methodological but not moral equivalence

[22] Yukio Mishima's "Patriotism" is worthy of consideration in this light. The analysis given in John Nathan's biography in particular highlights the aesthetic metaphysics of Mishima's artistic and then literal commitment of body to a kind of literary perfection, even in the failure of his final "performance."

Further, this may only serve to distinguish between the character of American and European nationalism, irreverence for centralized truth in the blind worship of the cult of celebrity, and the egregious power of the spectacle. Time will tell.[23]

THE MAP IS THE IDEA OF THE MAP

The anxiety that underlies the wholesale exchange of the profane for the sacred can produce a nostalgic throwback to the "old time religion." The yearning for sacred origins has long been a political tool of those who would wield it. The aura of a fondly remembered yesterday drives such cultural movements as we see demonstrated in the movie "Jesus Camp," and this trend is evident in many revivalist, traditionalist, evangelical, and reactionary groups across the world, not just Christianity. It has a basis of an American *mythos* that sprang up about the paranoid 1950s, repainting it as a golden age of idyllic family values, "when men were men and women knew their place," which reach from that time, and before, right up to the present. They were mostly fictional even in their time. Now, they are hyperreal. The Trump campaign's call to Make America Great Again, strikingly similar to a defunct slogan of Reagan's from the 80s, is in either event an appeal to an alternate history that never was. Authoritarianism is not an appeal to truth, it is an appeal to power, and fundamentally, the power that imaginal myth can have *upon* the real.

This defensive reaction, to look backwards in times of chaos, cannot be restricted to one ideology. It is one of the forms of modern mythology that we most frequently encounter. According to Samuel P. Huntington in his (in)famous book *The Clash of Civilizations and the Remaking of World Order*, the coming world conflicts will be driven along ideological and cultural fault lines, even if underlying motivational factors in some cases include more material concerns, such as territory or overburdened resources, the interests of individual actors, or even blind organizational output.[24]

Perception of conflict driven by these factors itself can be a veil, as we see further afield in Russia's apparent insistence on following the mythology of Mackinder's Geopolitics,

---

[23] There is some blurring bound to occur between "nationalism" and "fascism," especially outside academic use, and the latter has been so colored by Godwin's Law that Fascism has gained a sort of fascination precisely because of its inscrutability. Our reference to it is in the sense of its etymology, "strength through unity," as well as the proto-religious/occult power of the myths that emanate from this imagined source. To the extent that both evoke a yearning for a common origin, a doctrinal and even ontological center, they are similar, though there are considerable differences that have already been well established in the extensive literature now available on fascism.

[24] Ideology is generally a distillation of power relations rather than the other way around, so we shouldn't seek to distinguish our myths and ideology from the real dynamics that they arise in.

Russia's push into Georgia in 2008, into Ukraine in 2014, and its recent campaign in Syria, as well as its efforts to consolidate a sphere of influence in the inner Eurasian heartland of the former USSR called the Eurasian Union, all are eerily foretold in geopolitical theory. Mackinder held that geography, not economics, is the fundamental determinant of world power and Russia, simply by virtue of its physical location, inherits a primary global role. Under President Vladimir Putin, the slightly kooky tenets of Mackinder's theory have made inroads into the establishment, mostly because of one man, Alexander Dugin, a right wing intellectual and bohemian who emerged from the Perestroika era in the 1980s as one of Russia's chief nationalists. —"The Unlikely Origins of Russia's Manifest Destiny," Foreign Policy

If we accept the conjecture that Mackinder's Geopolitics is central to current Russian foreign policy, and this is no certain proposition, then we must also accept that a purely mythological story about the world is informing what happens in the real world.[25] The map is, literally, the idea of the map. We must also come to terms with the fact that Dugin's interpretation of this ideology explicitly uses the methods of postmodernism to attempt to strike at the West, or as he calls it, "Atlanticism."[26] Perhaps what is most interesting about Duginism is not that it actually directly describes Russian foreign policy, but rather that it invents a myth out of cobbled together parts—a very postmodern gesture—and thereby attempts to retroactively take credit for actions that happen to fall in line.

Though everything else about Dugin's critique is regressive, a fun-house mirror inversion of theories developed mostly by the Left for decades, he is right about one thing: Liberalism, or specifically the moderate Rightwing neo-Liberalism and Benthamite utilitarianism that has increasingly taken its place, fractures innate community—constructing it instead through reducible and reproducible acts, and individual identity is then lent us purely through our external function and esteemed value.

Not even rebellion is safe from this process, but in light of current events, we need to dig deeper into the political repercussions of a 4th estate based on principles being co-opted by the far Right. Dugin's prevarications are

---

[25] "Drawing on the extensive twentieth-century literature on geopolitics—and especially on the interwar German school of Karl Haushofer—Dugin posits a primordial, dualistic conflict between "Atlanticism" (seafaring states and civilizations, such as the United States and Britain) and "Eurasianism" (landbased states and civilizations, such as Eurasia-Russia). As Wayne Allensworth noted, once one penetrates below the surface of Dugin's seemingly rational and scholarly language in *Foundations of Geopolitics*, one realizes that 'Dugin's geopolitics are mystical and occult in nature, the shape of world civilizations and the clashing vectors of historical development being portrayed as shaped by unseen spiritual forces beyond man's comprehension.'"—Aleksandr Dugin's Foundations of Geopolitics, Dunlop.

[26] "Ideologically the problem is liberalism as the unique and only ideology imposed on the Europe and the rest of humanity by anglosaxon world. The liberalism affirms only individual identity and prohibits any kind of collective or organic identity."—Aleksandr Dugin, "What's Wrong With Europe?"

precisely in line with how myth and ideology collude to instruct, or rather *construct*, geopolitics, and we can also see in this a glimmer of our methodological objectives. Through the imposition of a mythology, we thereby shape the world in its image. We mustn't confuse the one for the other, merely because the methodology may have similar foundations. Consider,

> Also striking are attempts to identify the continuity of 'unreason' in fascism and poststructuralism. In an effort to combat the 'philosophical anarchism' of modern social theory, intellectual historians such as Wolin (2004) suggest obliquely that because both fascists and poststructuralists question the premises of occidental rationalism and American cultural leadership, there is an equivalence between the right-wing assault on democracy in fascist and neoconservative ideology and the poststructuralist critique of the democratic basis of western culture. Not only do arguments of this kind ignore the obvious substantive distinction between radical right-wing and radical left-wing criticisms of liberalism in an attempt to implicate the 'soft totalitarianism' of the left as an amoral betrayal of Enlightenment universalism, but are oblivious to the real and present danger implicit in neoconservative, neofascist and right-wing fundamentalist attacks on emancipatory politics." —Fascism and Political Theory, Woodley

Postmodernism as "skepticism toward all meta-narratizes" (Lyotard) claims to expose the flaw in both centered and de-centered worldviews. But what does an absolute skepticism toward all frames of reference do but create an unending regress of deconstruction in the hands of academics, while the powerful institutions in society use those same techniques to create a corporatist state that appears in-assailable to traditional methods of cultural subversion? We mustn't forget that the methods of post-modernism are available for appropriation to any end, as we can see in their use not only by the neo-liberal or centrist corporate power structures but also the authoritarian Right, and in some cases this use is quite explicit, as we see in Alexsandr Dugin's inversions, subversions, his *theoretic propaganda*.

The great debate of history is fundamentally literary. While intended to level the playing field and put power under critique, this approach can have unintended effects. All tools can be a weapon. Decentering can also be an implement of the state—one world, apprehended by pure logic. This is how one Gnostic-Transhumanist narrative of the future runs: if we can just find the optimal equations and frameworks, the world will run itself. One of many possible "ends of history," its true meaning is "the end of progress." We will have Arrived.

Yet, there is a growing anxiety about how this sort of appropriation is having real effects on our ability to agree on the basic facts. We are, increasingly, not even operating in analogous maps. No longer "Left" and "Right," it is "Universe A" and "Universe B".

The Singularity has yet to appear, and the darkness of the past beckons. Latour's "Why Has Critique Run out of Steam? From Matters of Fact to Matters of Concern" engages with this concern directly,

> In which case the danger would no longer be coming from an excessive confidence in ideological arguments posturing as matters of fact—as we have learned to combat so efficiently in the past—but from an excessive distrust of good matters of fact disguised as bad ideological biases! While we spent years trying to detect the real prejudices hidden behind the appearance of objective statements, do we now have to reveal the real objective and incontrovertible facts hidden behind the illusion of prejudices? And yet entire Ph.D. programs are still running to make sure that good American kids are learning the hard way that facts are made up, that there is no such thing as natural, unmediated, unbiased access to truth, that we are always prisoners of language, that we always speak from a particular standpoint, and so on, while dangerous extremists are using the very same argument of social construction to destroy hard-won evidence that could save our lives. Was I wrong to participate in the invention of this field known as science studies? Is it enough to say that we did not really mean what we said? Why does it burn my tongue to say that global warming is a fact whether you like it or not? Why can't I simply say that the argument is closed for good?

We are instructed how to read the world through our "texts," and in this sense, we are indebted to the postmodernists, though as we've seen this can be taken too far. Myth is neither pure fantasy nor a true material force. For as central as narratives are to human life, gravity is not merely a matter of interpretation. According to DeLanda, only by looking toward a method implied by emergent non-linear systems can we even hope to find a way out of this maze.

> One of the ideas that I attack in my book is precisely the primacy of "interpretations" and of "conceptual frameworks." Ideas and beliefs are important, and do play a role in history, but academics of different brands have reduced all material and energetic processes, and all human practices that are not linguistic or interpretative (think of manual skills, of "know-how") to a "framework." The twentieth century has been obsessed with positioning everything. Every culture, given that it has its own framework of beliefs, has become its own "world" and relativism (both moral and epistemological) now prevails.

> But once you break away from this outmoded view, once you accept all the nonlinguistic practices that really make up society (not to mention the nonhuman elements that also shape it, such as viruses, bacteria, weeds, or nonorganic energy and material flows like wind and ocean currents) then language itself becomes just another material that flows through a much expanded picture. Language, in my view, is best thought of as a catalyst, a trigger

for energetic processes (think of the words "begin the battle" triggering an enormous and destructive process). —Roy Christopher interviews DeLanda

Observant readers might recognize that there is a philosophical quandary here: do we prioritize the myth, or the mind, or the body? Where is the line between *mythopoesis* and *logos*, does that "frame" of myth even have an end? The nested holarchy of models, (models all the way down), seems to be a theme with this line of inquiry, but how does one make a model with nothing "real" to base it on? As Nietzsche recognized, philosophy, whether epistemological or ethical, often amount to juggling this hierarchy of values, and that is nothing more than the power struggle which has always defined human societies.

Even resource-driven conflicts are likely to be conceptualized in ideological terms, especially to the people who make up the backbone of any military. The US as a "global peacekeeper saving the world from itself" is such a myth as well, piggybacking on the overarching myth of American exceptionalism. This sort of myth is in no way exceptional. We paint in-groups and out-groups in mythic terms. We might see an echo of this in such disparate times as the crusades of the middle ages. After Richard the Lion-Hearted captured Acre in 1191, he ordered 3,000 captives—many of them women and children—taken outside the city and slaughtered. Some were disemboweled in a search for swallowed gems. (Spoiler: they didn't have gems in their bowels.) Rather than being a classic example of the removed brutalities of the past, this is not so different from the rhetoric that is used to embed fear of the immigrant Others of today.

The drive behind fanaticism, and fascism—which is an affliction not unlike fanaticism—is psychological, not material. William Reich explored this in *The Mass Psychology of Fascism*. And this, taken from a chapter appropriately and perhaps ironically named "Ideology as a Material Force,"

> Those who followed ... the revolutionary Left's application of Marxism between 1917 and 1933 had to notice that it was restricted to the sphere of objective economic processes and government policies, but that it neither kept a close eye on nor comprehended the development and contradictions of the so-called 'subjective factor' of history, i.e., the ideology of the masses.

The fascism of the state is the fascist within. This alchemy produces poisonous splinter factions, fundamentalist groups that cause many of the pathological habits our cultures otherwise exhibit, in concentrated form. Though always a sort of mass movement, it is contained in miniature within each individual psyche, since after all, *the center of the circle around which all turns is only a product of the collective imagination.* The extremists at the front lines of ideological conflicts hear the echoes of myths originating thousands of years ago, catalyzing the existential fear, hate, or desire latent in a culture, and more pointedly, within the individuals that comprise that culture. Fascism is, in a striking sense, an art movement gone horribly wrong.

The literalization of a mythical aesthetic can be the first step of this process. Here Lacan's observation that the unconscious is structured like a language is key.[27] This has bearing on myth as mass dream, most crucially at the times revolution strikes, or at the point of any state change.[28]

Politics or even religious ideology shouldn't form the only lens to gaze at myth in modern culture. Military memetics is itself congruent with notions of the epidemiology of ideas, and the level of scrutiny in this direction has already been considerable.

> Using the analogy that ideologies possess the same theoretical characteristics as a disease (particularly as complex adaptive systems), then a similar method and routine should be applied to combating them. Memes can and should be used like medicine to inoculate the enemy and generate popular support. —"Memetics: A Growth Industry In US Military Operations"

According to a memo spread in 2006 written by former Secretary of Defense Donald Rumsfeld, the "long war" against terrorism is a war of ideas,

> "Today the centers of gravity of the conflict in Iraq and the global war on terror are not on the battlefield overseas. Rather, the center of gravity of this war are the centers of public opinion in the U.S. and in the capitals of free nations. The gateways to those centers are the international media hubs and the capitals of the world. Zawahiri has said that 50 percent of the current struggle is taking place in the arena of public information. That may be an understatement. Osama bin Laden, Zawahari, Zarqawi had media committees that consistently outpace our ability to respond."

The propagandic methods of ISIS follow precisely from this observation.[29] There are considerable risks contained in the future synthesis of mythology and psychometrics—the measure of personality through scientific means, as we've seen in a nascent form in the rise of Trump and other populist long shots, who leaned quite heavily it seems on Cambridge Analytica, and other data firms who have become quite adept at interpreting and manipulating mass narratives. This news story follows what was 'fictionalized' before the fact, in House of Cards' 4th season, where the Underwoods rely on advanced psychological models to structure and simplify their narratives, and ultimately, to win an election.

---

[27] "You see that by still preserving this 'like' [comme], I am staying within the bounds of what I put forward when I say that the unconscious is structured like a language. I say like so as not to say—and I come back to this all the time—that the unconscious is structured by a language. The unconscious is structured like the assemblages in question in set theory, which are like letters."

[28] Analysis of mass narratives, with the aid of technology, can bear fruit in this direction, though as we will see, it is not an endeavor without its difficulties and dangers.

[29] Though it is a notable irony that they also follow a historical path that Rumsfeld shares some personal responsibility in paving.

The age of polling as the leading edge in political analysis may be through. (Or perhaps, our attraction to such narratives drives their own propagation in an economy sculpted by the ad value of a click.)

> Trump's conspicuous contradictions and his oft-criticized habit of staking out multiple positions on a single issue result in a gigantic number of resulting messaging options that creates a huge advantage for a firm like Cambridge Analytica: for every voter, a different message. Mathematician Cathy O'Neil had already observed in August that "Trump is like a machine learning algorithm" that adjusts to public reactions. ... The granularity of this message tailoring digs all the way down to tiny target groups, Nix explained to Das Magazin. "We can target specific towns or apartment buildings. Even individual people." —Das Magazin, translated to English by Antidote zine

Suddenly our "fanciful stories" are anything but coffeeshop talk, and we're paying a little more attention. Myth is on the lips, minds, and knifepoints of those in the midst of active revolution, as well as those working in the media.

> Memes influence ideas, ideas influence and form beliefs. Beliefs generate and influence political positions combined with feelings and emotions, eventually producing actions, which inform and influence behavior. Using this logic progression, any attack upon an ideology must consider an assault on a central or transcendent 'idea' or group of ideas as means of achieving success. Memes as ideas are then 'in play' as tools (or means) to attack ideologies.
> —"Memetics: A Growth Industry In US Military Operations"

Group narratives are always being re-purposed, whether we speak of the selective use of scripture by religious fundamentalists, or the more bizarre relationship between National Socialism and occultism, which underlined the rise of the Third Reich despite Hitler's professed abhorrence for the occult. Fringe elements are at most times culturally inert, but have the potential to overcome the whole of a culture during crisis points, as the Nazis did after World War I. Some of the recent concern over the rise of the loose conglomeration of alt-Right, paleoconservative, and various openly white nationalist groups has been along these lines, though the shape it will take is unclear.

However, myth as a whole cannot be considered at fault for such misuse. Religion is not to blame for witch burning or terrorist bombings. Nor can the instinct behind myth be "killed," in any event. We can replace people's myths, but we cannot take them away. It can be a healing, as well as destructive, force.

MYTHEMES AND MIMESIS

"For there is always going on within us a process of formulation
and interpretation whose subject matter is our own selves."—
Mimesis

This much is certain: misappropriation is one of the many powerful propagandic tools available to anyone with a mind to find a new use for an old
idea. Symbols have no one single specific meaning, no one specific purpose,
but they can have many guises and uses. They're like a coat-rack for personal and collective identity. Memes like Pepe The Frog demonstrate this
perfectly clearly. The cartoon was put to use by racists much as the
Swastika was re-purposed by the Nazis, but that does not make cartoon
frogs or Swastikas inherently racist. Symbols aren't just ripe for appropriation, they are a means for it. Yet, at one and the same time, symbols refer to
something, and the meaning of the whole can be changed as we collectively
wrestle over what the significance of that reference actually is.

So we might see culture as the fundamental struggle between unconscious complexes, all vying over the meaning of the signs that we toss back
and forth. Who is really in control of their symbols? Certainly, it is we who
are under their thrall. Myth supersedes us. For instance, the self is a narrative, by which we narrate to ourselves our memories and relationships with
one another, and ourselves. We live in relation to the narrative, as much as
any real world that dwells beyond. There is reason to believe that each time
we call a memory to mind, we edit it slightly. We draw over it, lightly in
watercolors or etched in broad ink strokes.

If at this point we have any lingering doubt about the centrality of myth
in our extended, communal, and personal lives, one need only to witness
how, without changing our behavior, someone can change you from hero to
villain, friend to foe or back again. Imagine if everyone who knows you suddenly had their memories of you erased. Your wife, your friends, perhaps
your children. What would have changed? Whatever you are independent of
their stories would be the same. And yet, you would find yourself a stranger
in your own home, in a sense, a stranger in your own skin. You would be
forced to rebuild yourself anew.

This is precisely why breakups can be so excruciating. Perhaps your part-
ners memory of you isn't erased, but it has been overwritten. Ten years of
shared memories, a collectively built identity, and now you are simply "the
crazy ex." Our relationships and identities are stories. The dimensions of
this process are endless, and try as we might to extricate ourselves, it is our
investment in one particular narrative over another that defines the ethical
sphere. This may be a choice, or it is habitual, but it is always an added
layer, not something drawn from an *axis mundi* such as transcendental reason.

Who's pulling your strings? Now that's a really good question. One of the things Jung said, was: "People don't have ideas, ideas have people." Think about that for three months. It should make you afraid for the whole time. Because as soon as you get that, you think "Uh oh." Let's say you're an ideologue of some sort: socialist, fascist, environmentalist, something that has 'ist' on the end. You think those are your ideas. They're not. You're their tool. And that's fine, if you want to be a tool of those ideas, go right ahead. But you don't know where those ideas are leading, and they could well be leading somewhere you do not want to go.
—Dr Jordan B Peterson, Professor of Psychology

To his initial question, we can only pose a further question of our own: Does an organ exists to serve a purpose, or did it arise coincidentally out of specific contexts, only later to develop to available uses as the context changed? We are the same, organs adapted over time in relation to the demands of a changing world—without intrinsic purpose, but not without use.

Myth is the battlefront of the future, as well as the past. It determines who we are to one another, who we are to ourselves. The culture war is innately occult: he who controls the Word (*logos*) controls the world.[30]

While current US military practices may view ideologies as diseases, they do not acknowledge the emergent properties of memes as the disease vector...to amplify this disparity, there is a nexus at the crossroads of sociology, anthropology, cognitive science, and behavioral game theory that can help us to intentionally persuade (inoculate) large audiences (or hosts) through subtle or overt contact. —"Memetics: A Growth Industry In US Military Operations"

The social realm is always dictated by forms of performance. But despite how this may seem, it is not a role we choose. This has always been the failing of systems such as Peter Carroll's early approach to Chaos Magick in *Liber Null*, or Robert Anton Wilson's "reality tunnel manipulation," that we can simply jump from one internal narrative or belief to the next, like flipping a switch. This presupposes not only complete psychological agency but control of the narratives we have already been cast in by fickle fate. As Jung wrote in *Psyche & Symbol*, "...just as our free will clashes with necessity in the outside world, so also it finds its limits outside the field of consciousness in the subjective inner world, where it comes into contact with the facts of the self." We cannot merely remove how others perceive us and replace it with another, as if identity were a simple mask, with a single True Self lurking beneath it.

---

[30] These forces act through us like lightning rods, via culture. If there is some kind of higher order hive mind, that's a part of the cultural matrix as well. Our cultural consciousness, the "hive mind" is a crucial and yet ignored component of the total human being.

Generations of accumulated myth and history don't vanish simply by changing our beliefs, as most non-white Americans will probably attest to. We're cast a role in a play that was running long before we showed up. However, we can *participate* in the rewriting of the code that informs our constructs, and this is the only way we can sensibly speak about "doing magick": as artists, engaging ourselves and one another in a semiotic negotiation—or interrogation—with necessity. It is an uphill, nearly insurmountable battle. The pay is terrible, and there's little glory in the victories. But what else are we going to do with ourselves?

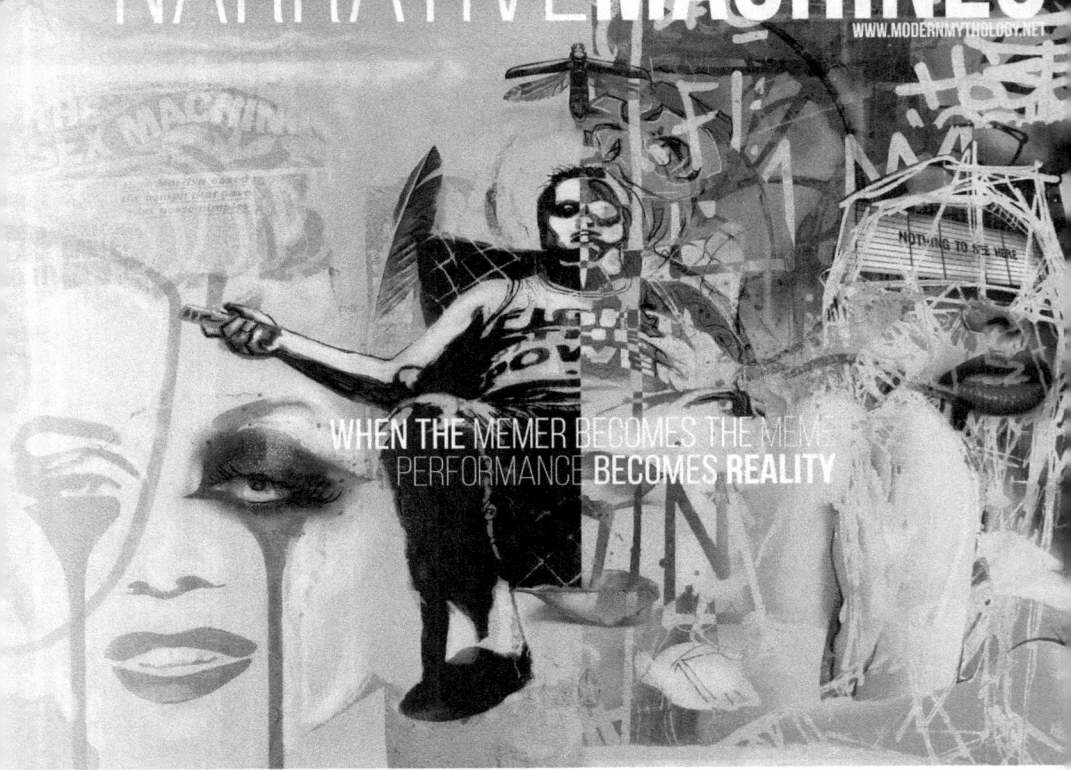

NARRATIVE MACHINES

WWW.MODERNMYTHOLOGY.NET

WHEN THE MEMER BECOMES THE MEME
PERFORMANCE BECOMES REALITY

IV. PATCHWORK SELVES

PALIMPSESTS ALL THE WAY DOWN

A palimpsest is a manuscript page from a scroll or book from which the text has been scraped off and which can be used again. The word "palimpsest" comes through Latin from Greek παλιν + ψαω = (palin "again" + psao "I scrape"), and meant "scraped (clean and used) again.

W e're always changing our stories, re-prioritizing or even wholly inventing our memories. We re-write our past, and we do it so constantly that it is unimaginable that our histories are anything other than a series of overlapping stories. Some stick around to become a myth—shared and permuted by eight or eight million—and others vanish. Consider this except from a New Scientist article, "Storytelling 2.0: When new narratives meet old brains":

> "We are our narratives" has become a popular slogan. "We" refers to our selves, in the full-blooded person-constituting sense. "Narratives" refers to the stories we tell about our selves and our exploits in settings as trivial as cocktail parties and as serious as intimate discussions with loved ones. We express some in speech. Others we tell silently to ourselves, in that constant little inner voice. The full collection of one's internal and external narratives generates the self we are intimately acquainted with. Our narrative selves continually unfold.

> State-of-the-art neuro-imaging and cognitive neuropsychology both uphold the idea that we create our "selves" through narrative. Based on a half-century's research on "split-brain" patients, neuroscientist Michael Gazzaniga argues that the human brain's left hemisphere is specialised for intelligent behaviour and hypothesis formation. It also possesses the unique capacity to interpret—that is, narrate—behaviours and emotional states initiated by either hemisphere. Not surprisingly, the left hemisphere is also the language hemisphere, with specialised cortical regions for producing, interpreting and understanding speech. It is also the hemisphere that produces narratives.

This is the process through which we come to interpret anything: we make a story to understand it, and understand ourselves through our own involvement in these stories. Yet how, then, do we distinguish between the story and the real world? Everything is "outside," stratifications of exteriority; there is no "true" self, no certain center *anywhere*. Even language itself presents this puzzle, as Wittgenstein's private language argument demonstrates:

> If I say of myself that it is only from my own case that I know what the word 'pain' means — must I not say the same of other people too? And how can I generalize the one case so irresponsibly? Now someone tells me that he knows what pain is only from his own case! — Suppose everyone had a box with something in it: we call it a 'beetle'. No one can look into anyone else's box, and everyone says he knows what a beetle is only by looking at his beetle. — Here it would be quite possible for everyone to have something different in his box. One might even imagine such a thing constantly changing. — But suppose the word 'beetle' had a use in these people's language? — If so it would not be used as the name of a thing. The thing in the box has no place in the language-game at all; not even as a something; for the box might even be empty.

Our language is not a referent to innate essential meaning, but to an approximation of shared experience, and the same can be said of our myths. Even natural processes can only be understood when they're brought into relation through some sort of meta-narrative. We sneer and scoff at this postmodern catch 22 of self-awareness, but are only right to so far as postmodernism and poststructuralism turned to excess, thinking narrative runs the real, rather than our collective bargaining over meaning, use, and identity.

> I don't believe there is such a thing as postmodernism. It's exhausted. We truly need a complete new thing, and [Deleuze and Guattari's] A Thousand Plateaus is the direction. Those guys are fifty or sixty years ahead of everyone else. You read it at first and you think you're reading poetry: "Metals are the consciousness of the planet." Get out of here, what the fuck is that? Then you read about metallic catalysts, how in a way they are like probing heads that unconsciously accelerate certain reactions and decelerate certain others. They allow the exploration of an abstract chemical space by probing and groping in the dark. And you realize those two are right. —"Destratified", DeLanda

We can agree or disagree about whether a given narrative is good or bad, accurate or not, but this discussion is in a sense adding a layer, not cutting down to the indelible truth. This is why the palimpsest is such a poignant metaphor. Our received myths are Talmudic, which is to say, they contain commentaries upon commentaries upon commentaries. Sacred texts attempt to serve as a stand in for a true essence or origin point around which this constellation of commentary is arranged. To do so we must sidestep their fictional nature.

We can never hope to clear away the intermediary of interpretation, and view the world directly as it is. When we interpret we define, and everything we touch is turned, in some regard, into fiction. We can only become initiates by learning the tricks we play on ourselves, and developing a kind of heightened sense of curious skepticism.

We have to be willing to accept uncertainty and incomplete knowledge, and always be ready to update our beliefs as new evidence comes in… Our best approach to describing the universe is not a single, unified story but an interconnected series of models appropriate at different levels. Each model has a domain in which it is applicable, and the ideas that appear as essential parts of each story have every right to be thought of as "real." Our task is to assemble an interlocking set of descriptions, based on some fundamental ideas, that fit together to form a stable planet of belief. —The Big Picture, Carrol

Even when the veneer of our ideology is shiny and new, if you scratch that surface, you will find layers tracing back into our distant, collective past. Certainly, the worldview of the fundamentalist is grounded in such an archaic origins. The re-occurrence of the patterns behind myth, its so-called deep structure, may seem to arise from a mutuality of human experience. Most of us are born with five fingers on each hand, and even that obvious observation can have significance,

"We move on to the magic numbers your authors are so fond of. You are one and not two, your cock and my cunt is one, and we have one nose and one heart; so you see how many important things come in ones. But we have two eyes, two ears, two nostrils, my breasts, your balls, legs, arms, buttocks. Three is the most magical of all, because our body doesn't know that number; we don't have three of anything, and it should be a very mysterious number that we attribute to God, wherever we live. But if you think about it, I have one cunt and you have one cock, shut up and don't joke, and if we put these two together, a new thing is made, and we become three. So you don't have to be a university professor or use a computer to discover that all cultures on earth have ternary structures, trinities." —Foucault's Pendulum, Eco

Inherited myths define our way of being in the world, and when the results they yield are abhorrent, we either cling to them to the bitter last, or mutate, opening ourselves up to other forces in the cultures we expose ourselves to. Instinctive reactions can be passed on, even bearing in mind the polarization that seems to happen from one generation to the next. These often unspoken dictates are the children of archaic beliefs that are incongruous with the universe as we currently know it. A modern veneer is painted over top, but to any history buff, the headlines bring few true surprises.

Myth accumulates like layers of sediment, a process that operates exactly like geological stratification, including the sorting mechanisms that inhibit or excite the flow of particles, such as mountains and rivers, which block and aid in cultural diffusion. In myth-space, barriers and accelerators are not only physically geographic, nor merely temporal-historic.

It is never a simple, linear progress; each layer is composed of a selection of some myths, and yet not others. For example, the initial American government was founded on Masonic ideals, themselves predicated on myths that can be traced back to Rome and Greece, and so on, leapfrogging through time, and each time reinterpreted, repurposed.

Repurposing of at-hand symbols, signs, and ideas can create some interesting juxtapositions. Consider the Roman fasces, a "bundle of sticks" which symbolized power through unity. It appears in many seals and symbols across many cultures, and certainly factors into American iconography. Even the bundle of arrows clutched by the bald Eagle is a form of fasces. Yet the fasces is also the root of the word "fascism," and not only incidentally. This didn't mar the meaning of the symbol enough to keep it from continued use in countries that at least claim to be anti-fascist, perhaps because it was already so embedded in their iconography. This seems probable, based on the history of other symbols, such as the swastika, which has been tainted in the West ever since the Nazis co-opted it. Similarly, though Americans attribute the origins of Democracy with ancient Greece, much of the iconography of the young American government was more accurately Roman.

> On top of such symbols as the fasces that still adorn the chamber of the United States House of Representatives on Capitol Hill, Rome handed down a lore of patriotic anecdotes. ... The Founding Fathers were so steeped in Roman lore that the great seal of the United States bears three legends from Virgil: "NovusOrdo Seclorum" (Eclogues 4.5: Magnus ab integro saeclorum nascitur ordo 'The great succession of ages is born anew'); "Annuit Coeptis" (Aeneid 9.625:Jupiter omnipotens, audacibus annue coeptis 'Almighty Jupiter, beam on bold beginnings!'); "E Pluribus Unum" (Moretum 103: color est e pluribus unus[When you mix a salad,] there is one color out of many'). Perhaps unwittingly but certainly appositely, Jefferson picked the image of the melting pot from a Vergilian salad bowl.

This merely serves as illustration of a general observation. Even etymological diffusion carries with it a sense of the mythic as well. For instance, "Kaiser" and "Tzar" being derived from "Caesar." Nothing that is recalled occurred in a social vacuum. Cultural heritage remains a palimpsest; the beliefs held in the past continue to affect the world we live in today, regardless of if we see them, or presently believe in them. Over time they create a mesh-work that contributes inevitably to new variations in coming generations—the Qabbalistic permutation of the divine name, 72 characters endlessly shuffled, DNA speaking in its alphabet of 4 letters, many analogies present themselves. These cultural underpinnings may co-exist harmoniously, or they may lead to acts of war or genocide, depending on the combination of influences and circumstance.

History does not repeat, as the common saying goes, but rather it is a series of ongoing narratives which do not die at the beginning or end of generations. We all exist in the middle, carrying on the ghosts of past lives and ideas we may only dimly recall, and vanishing without ever seeing the end of the play. Editorial decisions are made, but they exist within the same narrative continuum. There are no true fresh starts, no *tabula rasa*, in the social world. Civilization is a process of accumulation, of accretion, though much is always lost.

We see this process in miniature even in the construction of an assemblage such as this one. A first draft is written in the course of ongoing research. More time passes, and ideas are expanded, cut, rebuilt, and those previous decisions become a sort of deep structure for the final result, even in passages that have been cut. If the original draft had been lost, and it had to be rewritten from scratch, the text that would result would be entirely different, because it would be constrained by a different deep structure. The necessities of publishing make all writing in a sense precocious, literally "pre-cooked," not yet actually done. The rewriting could, theoretically, continue forever.

This is a useful metaphor for the cyclical repetition and difference of history. There seems to be a sense that it is a kind of merry go round. But in actuality, everything that is happening now is happening for the first and only time. That's also not to say there isn't an endless recapitulation. This is the premise behind Colin Woodard's book *American Nations*, that the foundational culture of a region is instrumental in its shape generations later, even if that land changed hands and centers of power many times since. The core document that is being edited, essentially, is the same. Just as a wave can continue to move through the ocean even as the individual water molecules are left behind, so too, certain tendencies of consciousness may persist, independent of phantasms such as essentialist identity. Many so-called spiritual ideas can be seen in a new light, without requiring any deference to metaphysics: the *mythos* that we carry, mutate and propagate in the course of our lives does not die with our physical body; though it is clearly meaningless noise without re-interpretation, the endless game of telephone that is history. A literal soul is in no way required, in fact, it would seem to muddy the water.[31]

---

[31] There's a broader point to make about materialism vs. metaphysics, that both are only a framework defined with any priority ahead of time. The mind precedes matter, or matter precedes the mind. Materialism remains an idea of itself. When we drill down into the question "what is matter?" we can quickly see the problem. Scale seems to define its behavioral context almost entirely, and what "it" amounts to is defined by physics of frequency or particles. This observation itself becomes troublesome since it's so often a route to jump from poorly understood versions of Einstein or Heisenberg's theoretic models to spiritualism, even though that should not at all be the kind of conclusions we draw, for instance, of "matter and energy being one." To convert the state of matter to energy you get a nuclear blast, so those who talk about how we are "Beings of Light" should settle down. The periphery of our myths may be boundless, but we're still nothing but meat. Spirit amounts to a metaphor, as does the body, in another sense, and little else more need be said of it.

State change is the dividing line, where we say an entity ceases to be one thing and becomes another, and so it will present a metaphor for us to return to and build upon. In certain configurations of "matter," we get "mind," just like water is solid at some temperatures and gas in others. These amount merely to the configuration of their constituent parts, and the interior and exterior relationships of those parts. This is one of the ways we can say the Self or any concept of God is a construct. Nor does Self refer to any single essential unity: we are palimpsests, ghosts of the past, echoes of the future, pulled by forces we falsely attribute to ourselves. Nature is nameless.

> Your body is not a word,
> it does not lie or
> speak truth either.
>
> It is only
> here or not here.
> — Margaret Atwood, Power Politics

POST-MORTEM OF THE POST-MODERN

Some consideration needs to be given to the philosophical debates that serve as intellectual history for our implicit mythologies of self and world. The concerns that lead to post-modernism—which was really a revolt against authority, universality and of the priority of materialism—can be seen in their infancy in the debate of ideas, artistic, philosophical, psychological and otherwise, that formed in the context of *fin de siecle* Vienna. This is examined thoroughly in Janik and Toulmin's *Wittgenstein's Vienna*, using the lens of both place and time to draw out peculiarities of thought that might otherwise remain opaque. For our purposes, we begin here with the nominalism of Mauthner, who in many ways stated the case to which Wittgenstein was reacting to. The central philosophical issue that gripped Vienna in this period was the relationship between ethics and aesthetics, which is rightly a question about the significance of representation. Mauthner concluded that phenomena require no proof on their own ground—after all, analytic logic rests upon tautology—but when we seek verification, repetition or explanation, then myth comes into play, whether or not the model it presents creates a satisfactory representation of that phenomenon or not, as,

> ...the idea that there exists such a thing as logic, in the sense of something universal and immanent in all languages, is another illegitimate reification. Belief in such a thing, even though it appears to comprise a body of knowledge, is superstition. "Everything about thinking is psychological," Mauthner insists; "only the pattern [Schema] of our thinking is logical." However, the pattern of a man's thinking—and of his speaking—is determined by, and reciprocally determines, the culture in which he lives, as both develop simultaneously; it is not something pre-existing which can be derived from "immutable laws of thought." — Wittgenstein's Vienna, Janik and Toulmin

This is a big idea, and deserves adequate consideration. Within Mauthner's nominalism, the method of philosophy and modern mythology become virtually indistinguishable except for in this regard, where the former uses rigor and the latter additionally embraces the truth of the single instance, the irreducible, the ephemeral, rather than that which has been generalized by a rational process.[32]

---

[32] In a sense Wittgenstein's Tractatus was a reaction to Mauthner's nominalism, in addition to the mathematical modeling of Hertz and the Machian philosophy of science, but it was ultimately unsuccessful in all the ways he seemed to hope, much as it was successful in feeding another sort of mythology, that of logical positivism.

The belief that life is an arc of narrative logic is a damaging fallacy, and yet, narrative is the result of anything we try to make sense of. Meaning is an act of narrative will, it is the expectation of logic within it that is dubious. Though there are different sorts of "logic," and it is within this that we can —should—question our faith in syllogisms, as well as the forms of logic always at work within our narratives, from the everyday to the spiritual.

In deference to the introduction to Will Durant's dated but still incisive *Story of Philosophy*, we must recognize that philosophy is for our times an analytic art of synthesis, a means of tempering wild but far-seeing intuition with scruple and rigor. It never attains the analytic insight of physics, or the purity of mathematics, and nor should it. To that strictly analytic approach to philosophy, the casual assertions of Scientists like Stephen Hawkings that "philosophy is dead," are quite right. Although we have no intention of parroting Mauthner's philosophical project entirely, his approach to these issues is illustrative of the gesture through which we are seeking to free *mythos* from Plato's ghost. Our aim is something quite else.

> What disturbed Mauthner, above all, was the tendency ordinary people have to attribute reality to abstract and general terms. The natural tendency to reify abstractions he regarded as the origin not just of speculative confusion, but also of practical injustice and evil in the world. In science, these include such misleading notions as force, laws of nature, matter, atoms and energy; in philosophy, substance, objects and the absolute; among religious ideas, God, the devil and natural law; in political and social affairs, obsession with notions like the Race, the Culture, and the Language, and with their purity and profanation. ...

> There is no such thing as language, but only individual human beings who use language. For Mauthner, then, language is an activity, not some sort of entity. ... A culture's language is part of its operating equipment—*specifically, it is the communal memory.* ...

This reveals the troubled relationship between *logos* and *mythos*. There is much connective tissue that cannot so easily be pared away despite the natural desire to draw strict boundaries between the two, and correlate it with the divide between reality and fiction. Nothing is ever so simple.[33]

> The distinction between personal myth and all other forms of myth remains a misleading one.

> Precisely because the cosmos can be understood and interpreted only through the human spirit (ed: so far as we are concerned) hence through subjectivity, what would seem to be the purely subjective content of mythology has at the same time a cosmic significance. ...

---

[33] We have worked hard to avoid this desire in the first section, drawing the contours out slowly through the implications of already existing Continental thought. This assemblage is a collection of such implications.

[Myth] is objective insofar as it is recognized as one of the determining factors by which consciousness frees itself from passive captivity in sensory impressions and creates a world of its own in accordance with spiritual [or psychological] principle. If we formulate the question in this sense, the "unreality" of the mythic world can no longer be said to argue against its significance and truth. The mythical world is and remains a world of mere representations–but in its content, its mere material, the world of knowledge is nothing else. *We arrive at the scientific concept of nature not by apprehending its absolute archetype, the transcendent object behind our representations, but by discovering in them and through them the rule determining their order and sequence.* The representation gains objective character for us when we divest it of its accidents and demonstrate in it a universal, objectively necessary law. Likewise, in connection with myth, we can only raise the question of objectivity in the sense of inquiring whether it discloses an immanent rule, a characteristic "necessity." —Philosophy of Symbolic Forms Vol 2, Cassirer

Some equivocation is required on this point, because of the inefficiencies of language. As Janik and Toulmin observe, "...Precisely because it is essentially metaphorical, language is well adapted to poetry, but ill adapted to science and philosophy." Poetry and myth derive their power from the unknown, the unspeakable, and even from misunderstanding itself; projection as a mechanism for a kind of gnosis. Any linguistic reification is a gesture toward some descriptive quality, a sense in which X shares the apparent qualities of Y. Such metaphors are conditional. They are not free-standing objects with fixed edges.

Further, literature, philosophy, and indeed all the humanities are compartmentalized from a materialist approach to science. "After all, what are any of these words except abstractions?" We forget that materialism is in this sense nothing more than the *idea* of materialism. But nominalism can avail us here. One of the central tenets of materialism going back into antiquity has been skepticism toward metaphysical absolutes, especially those which are thought to survive beyond the being they are attributed to.

We can distinguish between reductive materialism, which seeks to reduce everything to atoms, discrete individual irreducible "real" parts or concepts, and a sort of model-dependent, systems-theory realism that is properly more nominalist than materialist, based on function within the context of the system. What's even more poignant is how DeLanda's philosophy, which seems more of the latter sort, rests somehow within our very idea of immanent mythology, and yet at the same time, that kind of materialism—which removes us as actors, almost completely abrogating our narratives and ideologies—would seem to be completely contrary to any philosophy that centralizes myth.[34]

---

[34] The path presented in the following assemblage will show how the mental semiotics or symbolics of myth-theory (such as in Barthes or Levi-Strauss) and the material of DeLanda's "nonlinear history" are not such irreconcilable opposites. We will see that they are indeed mutually

The immanence of the past distilled into the present is the closest we come to eternity; one wonders what else there might be to transcend? Once the self is understood as a construct—formed by the interior and exterior relations of narratives, much as the physical processes that determine systemic relations in the material world, operating in terms of models that follow their own sets of mechanics—the linchpin is firmly in place.

---

complementary. While immanent myth might seem the pinnacle of the post-modern project, the reification of narrative in all elements of life, it is not the case. There are many ways that even an analytic realism can be appropriated to the purposes of immanent mythology. This appropriation is almost certainly not what DeLanda had in mind, but his framework serves our uses all the same.

MYTH IS OUR MIRROR

> The split in him caused by his contact with her would be recon-
> ciled by his actually having returned to her. From a religious
> point of view, one could say it is as if God used this girl to capture
> him, and yet the girl herself is not an actuality but is like the
> laced-winged fly with which a hook is baited. —Repetition,
> Kierkegaard

When we look out into the world, we sense its otherness, and are drawn
to expand beyond the already established self-territory. The myth of Manifest Destiny was merely retooled atop the natural impulses of a toddler,
exploring and thereby owning its world. We experience self in the other, in
all our points of real and imaginal intersection; of those areas where there is
none, we simply cannot know. We yearn for the real, but can never touch it
without transfiguring it into narrative. Much like that mythologized "meeting of the eyes" in the Troubadour tradition, or the white stag in the forest,
a nymph, a siren. We are lured forward toward the image, though whether
that winding path leads we do not know. As we chase, the boundary of our
self expands. Mirroring is a key component of self formation, and this is
amplified most of all by love and the things that destroy it.

The self is a story, but it is not itself generally a myth. However, we do
use the narrative structure we learn from popular myths to understand our
place in the world. We need a series of inciting incidents to enter into our
life, as the hero is tossed into the adventure unwittingly in the process of
giving pursuit to this fleeting ideal. So we see in many myths, where one is
lured upon a path of outer exploration or conquest, but the real journey is
one of self-discovery and definition. And yet, what is the self in any of that?
It too is merely a mirror, reflecting what is presented to it, and what preceded it.

The lure for union on the other side is the fiction that sets us all upon
that path that becomes our lives. This is at once the call to action of heroism
or romance, which is a classic mythic construction of the Western world, as
Campbell explored, putting "libido over credo." This shares the same motive
force under stories about conquest and discovery, and after all none of us are
confused when we learn that the Iliad is a tale at once about love and war.
Western myths of love may have developed out of a certain rebellious,
Romantic ideal, but that myth is driven by something far more primal, as all
successful myths are.

To love is to become transfixed by the mirage of your best selves. It is
also often the rocks you are broken upon. When this myth takes you—as it
oftentimes does, completely by surprise—you can know it most of all
because of how it is at once so familiar and yet so other, so overwhelming
and yet so completely intangible. Of course, sex and love both are linked to

death, *la petit mort,* most of all in that they both move towards a unification. However brief that moment may be, it forms a singularity in itself if the involved parties are transformed in one way or another by way of the inter-action. All the components of our previous life can be re-mythologized in a near instant, so that we feel we have fallen through the rabbit hole, into a new world, through the eyes of another.

We speak of "chemistry" in sex and love. This may be more apt than many of us realize. The initial terms are reformed in a new shape. A+B=C, or C=A+B. Sexual beings think of this as death though it's doubtful if those that reproduce asexually by mitosis would see *thanatos* within *eros* and vice versa, if they thought of themselves at all.

This gets at the discontinuity between beings, which Bataille uses as part of the framework for *Erotism,* wherein he supports the general thesis that eroticism, a truly human act, is the "assenting of life up to the point of death."

> Reproduction implies the existence of discontinuous beings. Beings that reproduce themselves are distinct from one another, and those reproduced are themselves distinct from one another, just as they are distinct from their parents. ... This gulf exists, for instance, between you, listening to me, and me, speaking to you. We are attempting to communicate but no communication between us can abolish our fundamental difference. ... It is my intention to suggest that for us, discontinuous beings that we are, death means continuity of being. Reproduction leads to the discontinuity of beings, but brings into play their continuity; that is to say, it is intimately linked with death.

By saying that myth is a mirror, we are getting at the thread of continu-ity and discontinuity that underlies perception, sex and death. We feel a pull, almost like gravity, which tugs at us from the other side of the looking glass. It needn't be a person, an activity, a mythic image, or even a dream of ourselves as a perfected whole rather than an incomplete fragment; it might appear as any of these, or most anything else. We seek control by naming the spirits we glimpse on the other side, yet aren't we also an other, a "they", when we see ourselves in the mirror? The nature of this doubling is always in some sense ambiguous. Where do you end and your lover begin? How do we know ourselves if we are not reflected in the stories of another?

> Love begins with the awareness of the curve of a back, the length of an eyebrow, the beginning of a smile. "It happens!" The pres-ence of another being mobilizes your attention, your senses. That feeling grows, becomes a desire to repeat the experience. It becomes an itinerary. A voyage. The imagination takes over that reality and starts building fantasies, dreams, projects ... It creates its own necessity, and in some people encompasses the whole of life. It becomes that voice in the night that tells you "I love you," and that knocks your whole being off balance. Ultimately, it reaches the zones where you question the whole universe; it

domesticates thinking, it ends as an addiction. And then, in the tragic cases, it falls into an abyss, where there are cries of pain, where the lovers lose sense of all dimensions, of all reality. These are times when a poet can say that love changes the direction of time. This state of being in love is an uneasy state: it is unstable, permeable to all winds, almost irrational. It easily creates a sense of terror, becomes obsessive. That's when heartbeats accelerate, and one puts out the lights, lies down with another body, and sinks into a kind of desperate bliss. How can one bear such an intensity? Love becomes a river of "re that replaces blood in the arteries. It leaves one breathless. One wants to stay still, not moving, having forgotten the hour. Even the sense of one's body disappears. The body disappears from memory. There's an immobility due to the total mobilization of the senses functioning henceforth in an altered state. Desire itself is eventually overcome. Strangely enough, this state approximates the experience of death. Who can endure for a long time such an internal upheaval? The lovers themselves end up fearing their happiness and feel ready to destroy it. And society itself suspects such love and represses it with all its might. It considers it to be a potential subversive revolution. Love always acts like an earthquake. It strongly affects not only lovers but also those who watch it happen. —"Etel Adnan: on Love and the Cost We Are Not Willing to Pay Today", Adnan

This transfixing image catches hold of us, driving us to frightful and even dangerous extremes in an attempt to break through, to immanentize, to revolutionize, to behold the divine vision, in any of these cases, to realize that metaphysic here on Earth. And we cannot break through to this ideal, to "unlock the Gates of Heaven," for we are discontinuous, but in pursuit we asymptotically "approach the limit," up to the point of death, which is to say, union with that image. We say it is asymptotic because our lives don't actually move in absolutes—no one is completely reformed, no revolutions truly remake the world without utterly destroying it—but our fortunes are written in our pursuit of such symbolic images.

Without this fascination, there would be no exceptional artists or thinkers, there would be no one willing to put their lives on the line, or do much of anything except what is simple and practical. And there would also be no cult leaders, no Jihadists and Crusaders willing to trade blood for myth. We are living, and myth too is living; a part of us, a mirror. It is like the moon in relation to the sun—without the sun, the moon would cast no light, but in the presence of the sun, it appears to have a light of its own.

A self turned into a myth-mirror is possessed, half-mad at the least. At the same time some might say they have been touched by God. So it is that shamanism, art and magic all root in the same soil.[35]

---

[35] In Ronald Hutton's *Shamans*, a varied counterpoint to Eliade's more staid *Shamanism*, this is spelled out in no uncertain terms, "The final characteristic shared by all the practitioners whom scholars have placed in the category of Siberian shaman is that they were all performing artists. If

In a month-long series of talks titled "Living Your personal Myth" at Esalen Institute, Joseph Campbell said "Mythology begins where madness starts, where a person is seized or gripped by some fascination for which he will sacrifice his life, his security, his personal relationships, his prestige, and his self-realization... it's not always easy or possible to know by what it is that you are seized."

This penetrates all human cultures, whether we're speaking of the overtly mystical immanence of Sufi or Qawwali music, or the other worldly forms of disseminating and enforcing a narrative that define traditional religious or secular institutions. The outward journey is always ever inward. We can never escape the mirror. After all, the only difference between sacred and profane, and maybe even mind and body, is orientation toward an aesthetic. It's all *magic*.

> Aesthetic cannot be fixed, immutable. It has to change as the occasion demands because in our understanding, art is made by man for man, and, therefore, according to the needs of man, his qualities of excellence. What he looks for in art will also change... We are not simply receivers of aesthetics ... we are makers of aesthetics. —Conversations With James Baldwin, Achebe

---

shamanism was part craft and partly a spiritual vocation, it was also an aspect of theater, and often a spectacularly effective one."

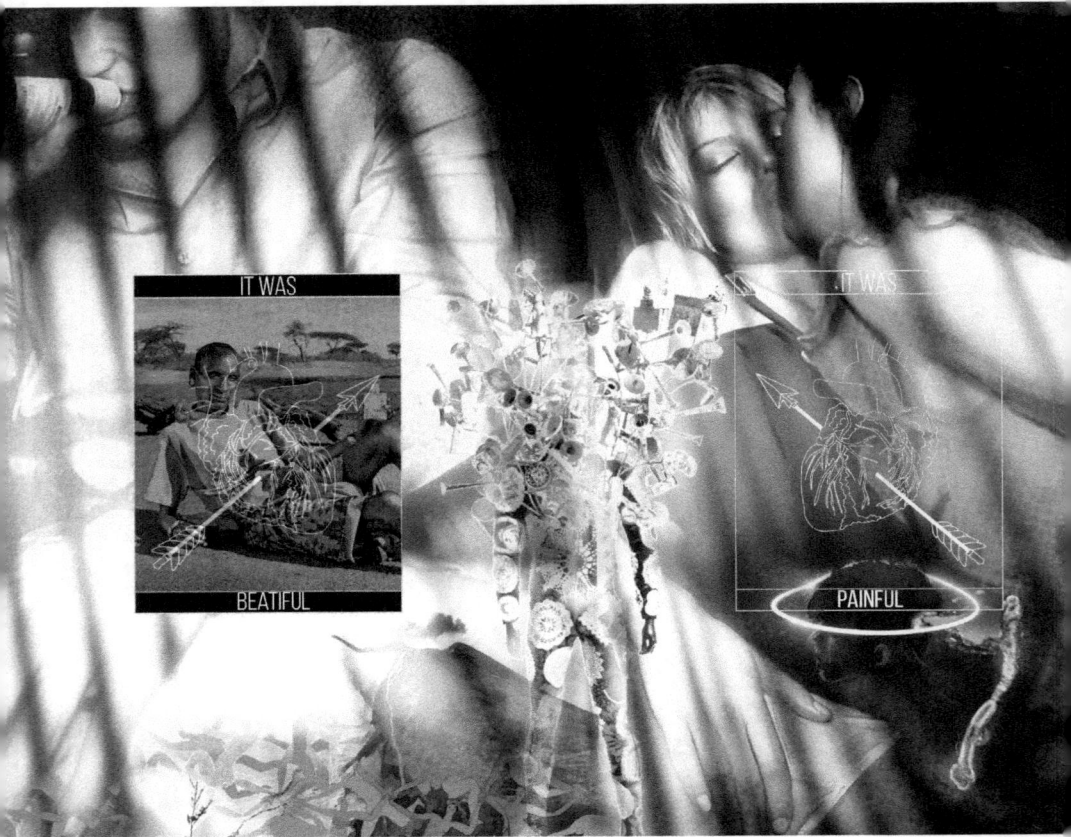

V. WITH WHOSE VOICE DO WE SPEAK?

"Human beings live in their myths. They only endure their realities." —Robert Anton Wilson

Dreams, memories, the sacred—they are all alike in that they are beyond our grasp. Once we are even marginally separated from what we can touch, the object is sanctified; it acquires the beauty of the unattainable, the quality of the miraculous. Everything, really, has this quality of sacredness, but we can desecrate it at a touch. How strange man is! His touch defiles and yet he contains the source of miracles. —Yukio Mishima

L ife is a dream you won't remember upon awakening, and myth is that dream, retold, those pieces that are forgotten seeming to reoccur in the subconscious of future generations. This retold dream is the realm of myth, and concurrently, its representatives take the form of art, music, and literature. Myth borrows from the realm of the unconscious, much as the unconscious is said to draw from the ancestral halls of death, and in some ways they share a similar dual nature as both real and unreal.

However, myth cannot be simply reduced to dream images. Dreams on their own do not define, transform, or destroy cultures. The source in us that seems to speak in dreams speaks also in our myths, if not in the same way. They are after all always conditional, still only real "in a sense." You might have been raised in a culture that worships fire as a benevolent force. It'll still burn you if you sit in it long enough. And yet nothing could be more real than the dreams that shape our lives, or the stories we use to give our names a meaning.

Our life passes in a procession of moments, all remembered fictionally after that bubble in time. There is a mysterious process of growth which follows its own laws and takes place behind the biographical *peripeteias* of life, and goes from childhood to old age. Viewed in mythological context, the greater human being, the *anthropos*, is likened to a tree. The trees of life and trees of knowledge are, in this symbolic sense, the same.

Living or dying, awake or asleep, we forget, and then we remember ourselves. Hold on too tight, and be trapped forever. Let go, and disappear as if you never were. The only way to remain is to carry another's story inside us a while, for in compassionate hands our own stories are not quite so heavy. It is the word's inner meaning that is resurrected time and again in flesh. Ideas are not just ideas, when they take hold of us.

Everything that has had a major effect on your life was started by sheer happenstance. We can embrace it, accept it, or run, but not change the substance of our story. Destiny was never a choice. Even our bodies are just a rental. But who writes this story, then? Who truly controls the narrative?

Put another way, myths are fiction, but they can enter the real through us, to the extent that we are transformed, and remake the world in their image. Stories about the world intuitively inform our judgments and actions in the world. And it is wise to ask what drives us to lend one particular myth our voice, and to not hear another...?

It's easy enough to say our lives have all been a sort of dream, but that's a trite way to treat life. Yet it's no less true. The part of us that doesn't feed the rivers and oceans is myth, poetic as it may be for our teeth and bones to one day pave a river-bed.

REVOLUTION

"Nothing on the face of this earth—and I do mean nothing—is half so dangerous as a children's story that happens to be real, and you and I are wandering blindfolded through a myth devised by a maniac."—Master Li Kao

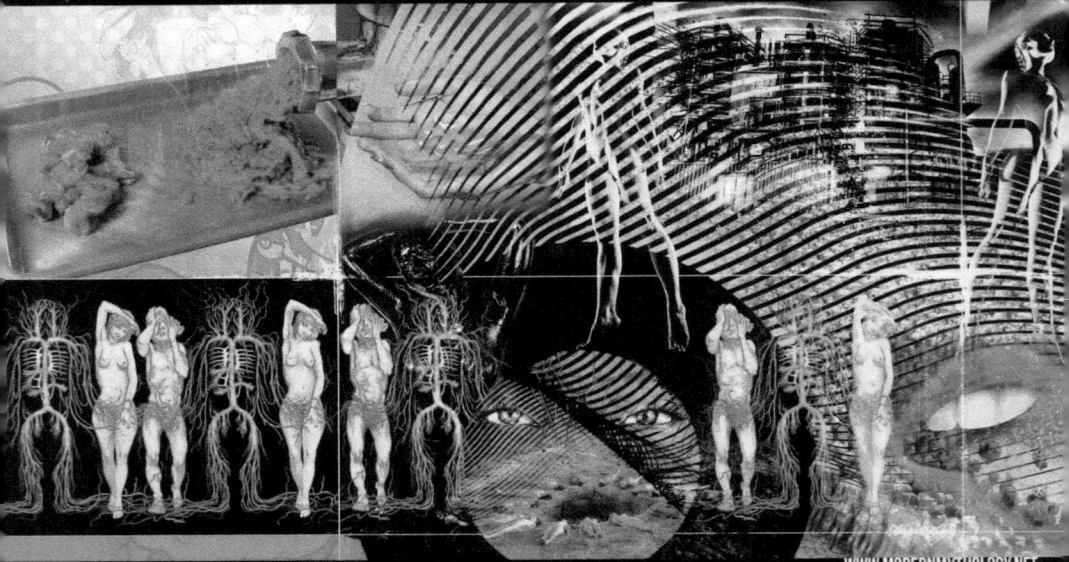

NARRATIVE**MACHINES**

WWW.MODERNMYTHOLOGY.NET

THE FUTURE IS HERE.
EVERYTHING HAS TO BE **DESTROYED.**

I. REMEMBERED AND REMEMBERED AGAIN

TEAR DOWN THE WALL

"If you want a vision of the future, imagine a boot stamping on a human face ...forever." —1984, Orwell

Many still remember when the Wall fell. November 9, 1989. If you were alive, you remember. A newscaster on the television, his image warped and tattered by static around the edges, was talking about the end of nuclear threat. It was a revolution of culture, some said. Then President Reagan appeared, and took credit for the fall of Communism.

Revolutions leave an indelible stamp on those lived through them. But how did a falling wall end the Cold War, let alone stanch the tide of violent revolution? This is the kind of rhetoric we are fed. We're given the pieces to this puzzle, but never told what image they're supposed to make.

If it wasn't already painfully obvious in 1986, it certainly is now. No one should have thought that violent uprising was a thing of the past. The legacy of globalization has generally been more revolutions, not fewer. It's as if, with every generation, we forget the lessons learned by those that came before. This "nightmare of history," to refer to Joyce's famous quote, calls to mind several essential questions. Are revolutionaries incapable of hearing the ghosts of the past? Is this forgetting itself the nature of revolutions? Finally, how can we keep others from using our own hopes and ideas against us? These questions are hard to answer, and any analysis is likely to sound irrelevant to those that have lived through the horror of violent conflict.

Still, we must wrestle with this legacy if we are to have any hope of freeing ourselves from it. The cycle of loss and vengeance itself is a crucible for revolutionary ideology—the longing for the innate eschatology, for salvation and apocalypse, for a metaphysical order to finally reveal itself as a *certain* reality.

WHAT GOES AROUND

"All stories begin before they start and never, ever finish." —The Crane Wife, Ness

The squall seemed to kick up in the 1600s. From our 21st century vantage point, we can see many simultaneous and interwoven causes. As lines of trade grew, corporate egregores[36]—groups that behave as if they are entities with a singular self-interest—began to crystallize. As cause and effect, we saw the destabilization of religious hegemony, as people started looking through telescopes and microscopes, expanding colonial empires that forced cultures into frequent, if often uncomfortable, contact. All these contradicting histories, in aggregate, seemed to carry the evanescent and as-of-yet unfulfilled promise of the myth of human rights. Whatever the cause, the old structures of authority were losing their hold, and the de-centering or even collapse of the old order was an inevitable result.

The scientific and industrial revolutions moved in accord with the coming waves of social unrest, and helped give us the lie of endless progress. Like any wave, in the troughs, it seemed it might taper off, never to return. Nations were all reformed by revolution over this 300 year period, clustering most around the *fin de siecle* periods. First in Britain (Glorious Revolution 1688), then America (1763–83), France (1789–99), China (Taiping 1850–64, Xinhau 1911, October 1917, Nationalist 1923–28, etc.) and Russia (1917) those ripples started at home but spread to the furthest reaches of colonial empires and crumbling imperialist states. In 1914, a new hell on Earth was unleashed—world war—which has cast a long shadow from that date to the present. But it too was significant most of all in its place in this ongoing history of revolution.

In *The Anatomy of Revolution*, Crane Brinton notes that, of these, only America thusfar has avoided totalitarianism in the wake of idyllic uprising and ideological struggle, though whether it ever lived up to the promise of its own revolutionary mythology is dubious at best. All these conflicts were alike in one way: it was the idealism of a new collective future for the masses, not blind obedience to the monarchic godhead that served as initial fuel and tinder. And that same fire still burns.

---

[36] "Egregoric entities, whether gods or demons or dictators at the center of a cult of personality, are powerful entities, even as they are imaginary—wholly created by and consisting of thoughts, speech, and behaviors. The human mind is a powerful entity, and becomes more powerful in coordination with others. To say that an "imaginary" entity, existing only in human minds, has agency, is not much stranger than suggesting that humans themselves, inscrutable piles of preferences that we are, have agency." —"Weaponized Sacredness," Ribbonfarm

GLORIOUS REVOLUTIONS

The promise of revolution rarely lives up to the reality. Britain's Glorious Revolution, also known as the Bloodless Revolution, installed parliament and led to the formation of the Bill of Rights. (Though it was not, in fact, entirely bloodless.) But Bonaparte, Stalin, Mao, even Hitler ascended to power by way of revolution, big or small.

When you step back, it's hard not to see the pattern. Though the word "revolution" originally referred to planetary bodies, it is frequently noted that it's a recurring cycle. One power is deposed, and replaced with another. Over and over again, forever.

And this storm has never truly ceased, though it has its troughs and poles, its accelerations and decelerations. As Vladimir Lenin said, "There are decades where nothing happens; and there are weeks where decades happen." The bleak certainty of struggle-without-end has hardly stalled the yearning for a glorious revolution to sweep in and wash away our problems. There have even been social uprisings that seemed to deliver on their longer term hopes, like the Velvet Revolution or arguably the Prague Spring. But for how long?

The question, from the liberal point of view, is if progress toward humans rights goals is actually being made, and for whom, or are we merely spinning in place?

Angus Deaton's book *The Great Escape* attempts to tackle this issue, showing some of the hidden complexities behind this question, and ultimately moving beyond platitudes or doom-saying. Statistics seem to back up the claim that we are progressing.

But, upon closer scrutiny, there are any number of problems with the argument that the world's getting better all the time. Numbers lie, to the extent we think they represent inarguable realities. We can falsely interpret them, or misunderstand what they are actually telling us. How far afield should we be looking? There are countless issues with trying to quantify human rights goals. Even the concept of progress itself is enmeshed in the conflicted history of the Enlightenment, a history which includes the invention of penicillin and the Bomb, liberation and colonization. Humans are nothing if not morally ambiguous when taken all in all.

The social legacy of revolutionary progress is murky as well. For example, in Egypt in 2011, Mubarak was ousted to much celebration, and replaced by The Muslim Brotherhood's Mohamed Morsi. Morsi has since been deposed and sentenced to death. Elements of Mubarak's regime are back in power, and Tahrir square protest leaders sit in jail. It is hard to predict Egypt's political future, but it serves as ample demonstration of a grim narrative arc.

Yet the hope for progress continues, as reported in Foreign Policy's "Egypt's Quiet Revolution," though how that stacks up against the other factors in the region remains to be seen. What this report under emphasizes is the brutal crackdown that continues as well. The "Quiet Revolution" conflicts with the considerable risk faced by those that are perceived to threaten establishment values, and the price already paid by those that have already had their lives ended or irrevocably altered by revolutionary violence. Even hope is a two edged sword. The dream of revolution lives on, seemingly in defiance to gravity itself.

This violence shows that ideas and dreams threaten material power. The now cliche Medgar Evers quote-turned-slogan "you can't kill an idea" attained popularity because it represents a truth. That truth must forever stand in opposition to "editorializing" like the purges of Stalin or Mao, without ever reaching a certain conclusion. The war of cultures is never-ending, but the rules do change. We are still trying to solve 21st century problems with the 19th century's revolutionary ideas.

In "Invisible Revolution," Chris Hedges wrote, "Throughout history, those who have sought radical change have always had to first discredit the ideas used to prop up ruling elites and construct alternative ideas for society, ideas often embodied in a utopian revolutionary myth." Consciously or unconsciously, rationalized ideology is used as a lever for political power. For instance, subjugation of women isn't inherent to Christian or Islamic symbolism, but the available source material is used to support that outcome.

The editorial ability to make the determining decision of what to cut and what not, and the authorial ability to guide interpretation is central to the codification of power within a social group. There is room for duplicity in this. It seems improbable that all fundamentalist Evangelicals or Wahabists believe the rhetorical interpretation they sell, but either way the purpose of such presentation is the reification of the desired power structure, which almost invariably benefits those most active in selling that interpretation. One acts as if those stated beliefs are true, even if we all cynically knew it was otherwise. This is part of the way that politics works as performance— there is always a certain amount of ambiguity between act and intent. But so much as belief serves as mere smokescreen for action, it doesn't matter if the performance is sincere or not. Much like an actor who can make us feel without actually having those feelings themselves, power accomplishes its aims. Some believe, while still others wink and nod.

> "Power is not a means; it is an end. One does not establish a dictatorship in order to safeguard a revolution; one makes the revolution in order to establish the dictatorship. The object of persecution is persecution. The object of torture is torture. The object of power is power." —1984, Orwell

This echoes Foucault, that truth is little more than a series of differing narratives reflecting existing power relations, and builds on Nietzsche, 'no facts, only interpretations.' This should sound eerily familiar to anyone who has been paying attention to American politics in recent years.

Sociology has wrestled with the dichotomy between state and rebel since its beginnings. In *Ideology and Utopia*, Karl Mannheim diagnosed the structure of the mutual misunderstanding that underlies this conflict. Ruling groups become so concerned with their interests that they can't see anything else. The real condition of society has become completely inscrutable from the top down. Rebel utopian thinking, on the other hand, becomes so fixated on social transformation that it sees the world in black-and-white terms of the obstacles in their path. Perhaps the starkest example is the blood lust that threatened to consume all of Paris in 1793–94.

If this observation is accurate, then the factions in a conflict can become so entrenched in their beliefs that they quite literally aren't interacting with the same world any more. This calls to mind the popular parable of the blind men and an elephant. This has Hindu, Buddhist, Jainist, Sufi, and many other versions, but the gist is this: Several blind men have never seen an elephant, and one day an elephant is brought before them. Each takes hold of a different part, a trunk or an ear or a leg. And each reports quite factually on the experience, yet their stories of what an elephant is don't line up. Only if they confer, might they begin to construct a story that accurately represents an elephant. In Rumi's version, he concludes, "We are like boats dashing together; our eyes are darkened, yet we are in clear water." This may also be analogous to the filter social media and news bubbles we find ourselves in today. Of course, the real question is why it took so long for us to realize we're all part of a collective dream, same as has been recognized for thousands of years within other cultural traditions. Better late than never.

If you wish to maintain civil democracy, the endless conflict of opposites requires a level playing field, a metric for legitimate compromise, a sort of radical Centrism[37] that enacts a *decentered*, nominalist, pluralist program on culture while at the same serving as a political center. Benoist's perspective on this is curious, especially in regard to his seemingly contradictory statements pertaining to national identity. As he says in an interview with The Occidental Quarterly, "Only the advent of a multipolar world will preserve human and cultural diversity and regulate globalization in a way not exclusively favorable to the interests of a single dominant power. I do not believe in Huntington's clash-of-civilizations thesis: Civilizations are not unitary or homogeneous blocs and no miracle will turn them into the principal agents of international relations."

---

[37] Centrism is considered to be the opposite of radicalism in politics. The radicalism is, instead, of a cultural-aesthetic nature.

However, Benoist's contention that cultural enclaves can simply wall off from one another is antithetical not only to multi-culturalism, but also the pluralism can allow for "peace treaties" of tolerance, which is to say a certain amount of good faith to be able to debate within the same framework and to a vast degree live and let live to the extent our cultural and identity norms don't overlap or agree. This "treaty" depends on a robust center—the polarization that is increasingly the norm now is anathema to a functioning pluralistic society. Civility is not a politic of war, it has no true response against obliteration and erasure. How is it that it has become radical to demand tolerance within the range of certain collective norms?[38]

The balance of cultural fragmentation and political center can be a form of resistance against authoritarianism, since fascism is monomythic, and the very manner of extreme reproducibility of simulacra, a lack of central animus, would seem to make the metaphysics of fascism impossible. At the same time, it needs to undermine all identitarianism that seeks to leverage the collective good for the interests of any one world-myth. However, some form of power is required to enforce that center of discourse and enactment of those norms, and this is what liberals seems to forget, time and again. There are many barbarians at the gates, and some of them wear suits. What use is it to point out your chess opponent isn't following the rules when they've put a gun to your head and lit the curtains on fire?

More prosaically, divergent and dissident stories are important. So, too, are the experiences of those with the authorities, though, of course, these are often the most ready at hand. Still, blind anti-authoritarianism is as easy to manipulate as its mirror image. Even more important are the stories of those that have fallen between the cracks, and those that are just trying to get by. We must listen to them all. It is only through mindfulness of the repetition of history, of all the conflicting stories we can get our hands on, that we can awaken from our dogmatic slumber. Yet who has the time for all that?

---

[38] This is still somewhat idealistic in the present climate, because we seem be entering a time of war, where you have to stake a claim on your self preservation, everything else be damned. We have to act along completely different lines when resisting authoritarianism, and this is one of the ways authoritarianism can upend political norms even when it is engaging rhetorically.

THE WAR OF ALL AGAINST ALL

Throughout history there have always been segments of a society that hold views that do not agree with the majority. Common wisdom goes that if that minority becomes a majority, then the tide will turn with it. But social networks, modeled in "topological maps," rarely seem to work in terms of simple minority or majority. Slavery wasn't abolished in the United States the moment 51% were against it.

Consider this study, first published as "Social consensus through the influence of committed minorities",

> Scientists at Rensselaer Polytechnic Institute have found that when just 10 percent of the population holds an unshakable belief, their belief will always be adopted by the majority of the society. The scientists, who are members of the Social Cognitive Networks Academic Research Center (SCNARC) at Rensselaer, used computational and analytical methods to discover the tipping point where a minority belief becomes the majority opinion. The finding has implications for the study and influence of societal interactions ranging from the spread of innovations to the movement of political ideals.

In light of how social media is weaponized, this is a serious concern, as well as a means of leveraging better collective goods. Whether these findings are reproduceable, the analysis of the spread of political ideals always hints at how ideas work as contagion. It should go without saying that no group, let alone nation, is of a single mind about much of anything. Yet we still can't help ourselves. We change our minds more readily than our identities, but the principle is the same.

At the same time, some consideration must be given to what such "contagion models" are actually describing. Manuel DeLanda discussed this in an interview with CTheory,

> All models, by definition, simplify things. Contagion models can be very useful to study certain propagation effects, whether these are fads, fashions or ideas. Can they also be useful to study the propagation of affect? We can't tell in advance. What is important to see is that even if they turn out to be useless to study violence that does not affect their usefulness in other areas. Also, contagion models differ in the detail with which they portray agency, from completely mechanical models with no agency at all (a homogeneously socialized population) to models in which some form of virtual agent is included. But the key problem is that no one agrees what agency is: must it include some form of rational choice, and if so optimizing or satisfying rationality? Should all psychological effects be eliminated and only inter-subjective effects taken into account? How socialized and obedient should we assume agents to be, and should these qualities be modeled as homogeneously or heterogeneously distributed?

This gets back to the considerations given in the first section about the role of psyche and identity within social systems. And we are stymied, to some extent, by the same roadblocks. The concept of contagion is endemic in pretty much all racism and xenophobia. There's an innate element of human social behavior that this rhetoric pings.

But the other side is it's yet another demonstration of how easy we are to troll. "If you had a bowl of skittles and I told you just 3 would kill you, would you take a handful? That's our Syrian refugee problem," read an ad run by Donald Trump Jr. during his father's campaign. For anyone sane enough to recognize that refugees are not in fact skittles, skittles are not in fact poison, and figuratively the analogy is no more coherent—we're not at risk of being taken in by the rhetoric. We aren't the target market. Or are we? In our outrage we're partially responsible for spreading that contagion to those who can be effected by it. So maybe to an extent the "liberal media" is a carrier for the Trump virus. And thusfar, we haven't found an effective inoculant. We can easily be tools for the forces we seek to oppose in our very manner of engagement.

That doesn't keep us from drawing some interesting inferences. We rally behind flags and causes and pretend to wage a war of ideas on a single front. But when it comes to talking about cultural revolutions, it may be more accurate to think of Hobbes' never-ending war of all against all from De Cive: *bellum omnium contra omnes,*

> I demonstrate in the first place, that the state of men without civil society (which state we may properly call the state of nature) is nothing else but a mere war of all against all.

This is a bleak outlook, if we look at it as literal violent conflict. And sometimes it is. Revolutions can erupt amidst too-sudden change. Narratives of hope can gloss over violence, and the ideals that often fuel rebellion are often conflict with the reality of what comes after. The day after the revolution, and the one after that. There may always be people who seek and manipulate via power, they will always consolidate that power, and the ideology of the society will be bent in service of those aims. It always seems to be the story within empires.

All the same, these remain a somewhat staid views of "war," when we live in a social world that is changed more frequently and readily by how we look at ourselves and one another than by tanks and missiles. True, people that look at the world one way can erase another, and do so with tanks rather than diffusion of ideas. But that isn't the only way unpopular and dissenting ideas—the fringe—become commonplace.

Not all revolutions need be bloody, and minorities can dramatically change the face of the future without breaking a single bone. Violence is a sign your revolution may have already failed. State powers often push rebels to violence for this very reason.

In this regard, the State is a protection racket. Inspire people to think in new ways, the State has no idea what to do with you. (Though often they'll lock you up just to be sure). But start popping off an AK-47 in public, they definitely know what to do.

A more typical examination of the intricacies of revolution, gathered from Timothy Snyder's insightful Guardian piece excerpted from "Black Earth," further demonstrates how flawed these common frames can be,

> On the political right, the erosion of state power by international capitalism seems natural; on the political left, rudderless revolutions portray themselves as virtuous. In the 21st century, anarchical protest movements join in a friendly tussle with global oligarchy, in which neither side can be hurt since both see the real enemy as the state. Both the left and the right tend to fear order rather than its destruction or absence.

The "powers that be" are oft maligned on both sides. Nevertheless they serve an important function when the state is doing its job. Because in the complete absence of a state, very bad things can happen.

As he says, "a common American error is to believe that freedom is the absence of state authority." We might conclude the revolutionary mindset needs reframing, because it is often short-sighted, without ample consideration of systemic factors or the plain fact that toppling dictators rarely goes well for anyone. We are constantly juggling the interests of the individual and the group, of change and stability, of revolution and tradition. The pendulum swings endlessly, as different factions push one on the other. There is no end state, there is no rest.

This is the ceaseless war of all against all, waged ever in our minds, whether or not it's ever in the streets.

II. THE LONG MARCH AS PARABLE

THE BLESSED CURSE OF HOPE

"The goal of the revolution is the abolition of fear."— Theodor Adorno, "Letters to Walter Benjamin" 18 March 1936

With revolution still on our lips as we continue into the 21st century, it's worth considering how rarely revolutions have worked in the benefit of the people on the ground.

Let's consider an example from the previous century. When Mao Zedong left Jiangxi province in 1934, he wasn't yet the Chairman of legend. He was tall, thin from the life of a revolutionary, but already inspired a reverence in many of his idealistic followers. This was true, at least for a time, of his lover, He Zizhen. She bore him several children, and was forced to abandon more than one in the long march with the 1st Front Red Army to Shaanxi. They were fighting against the dynastic system on one hand, and the KMT on the other, who represented a mostly urban, classist alternative. They were fighting for the common people, and theirs was a just fight.

Or so they thought. In reality, few came out ahead after the long, soul crushing trek, aside from the figures history remembers, like Mao.

Women of the Long March, by Lily Xiao Hong Lee and Sue Wiles, paints the often bleak picture of the idealism and betrayal of these thirty individuals who, we are led to believe, are indicative of a generation. In the case of all these women, the dedication they felt toward the cause was hardened as much by material need and frustration with the status quo.

It was during this march that Mao was established as the revolution's leader. Red Army soldiers starved, women were frequently abandoned unless they had attachments to important people, having *guanxi*, (connections.) Even this only went so far. He Zizhen was seduced and then quickly marginalized by Mao, but still had what was likely an atypical experience based on her relationship with the ascending leader.

Throughout their journey, which under his guidance was narrativized from a retreat into an inspiring odyssey, she had been nothing more than an occasional shadowy presence. While he became a demigod, she suffered physical and emotional devastation.

It would be reasonable to assume, for it is not recorded, that 25-year-old He Zizhen was not there to share Mao's grand gesture toward history when he sat down at his rickety desk in Wayaobu to write a poem of celebration.

> The Red Army fears not the trials of the Long March, one thousand mountains and ten thousand rivers. The Five Ridges but gentle ripples... Laughter in the thousand li of Minshan's snows and smiling faces when the last pass is crossed.

There is always a danger in turning any individual life into parable or myth, but in a sense we can't help it. Stories are how we understand the world. We must recall that narrative always conceals as well as it reveals, and often both at the same time. So the tale of He Zizhen and the other women that marched out of Southern China is nevertheless instructive, even if a totalising interpretation remains elusive. Were they, in the final reckoning, "brainwashed and suffering in silence," after all? Where is the place for their agency in this narrative? This is one of the challenges of coming to terms with history.

Although there are cultural and historic peculiarities that make their story unique, it is, in a broader sense, a clear example of the true currency of social revolution: propaganda. And this is an economy driven by desperation and hope—the desire, dreams and fears of a people already made desperate by life within the old regime. They didn't suddenly become different people when they started waving a Red flag. What it symbolized merely assuaged a common psychological need, the need to flee the traumas of the past.

People kill one another over the flag that they're waving, but what motivates them to wave flags in the first place is more or less the same. These motives transcend both place and time. Loyalty to those who we've come to see as our own, fear of the Others that might threaten that well-being, most of all, the hope for a better life. When combined with the crushing reality of the present, these things have always provided fertile ground for exploitation. Not that it always took much convincing on the surface. Recruitment was often accomplished with surprisingly little rhetorical flair, as one of the Long March women's amusing recollection of her introduction to the party in 1931 shows:

> 'Are you joining the Communist Party?'
>
> 'What's the Communist Party?'
>
> 'The party of the poor, there are advantages in joining.'
>
> 'What advantages?'
>
> 'Many advantages, later. First, though, you have to bear hardships. If you want to join I'll sponsor you.'
>
> 'OK. I'll join!'

Hope is kindling for revolution. It keeps one foot moving after the other, and blocks those questions that might turn a person about. So the story of Pandora speaks to us still through the ages. *In Human, All Too Human*, Friedrich Nietzsche argued that "Zeus did not want man to throw his life away, no matter how much the other evils might torment him, but rather to go on letting himself be tormented anew. To that end, he gives man hope. In truth, it is the most evil of evils because it prolongs man's torment."

Americans are also unlikely to forget President Obama's campaign of hope in 2008 any time soon. Almost everyone can agree about wanting a better society, a more just society, but translating that hope into reality is complicated. At best, "The trajectory of progress is fits and starts." Consider also the disillusionment that was spun in benefit of the populism that allowed for Trump's rise.

Though no single narrative can be definitive, the stories of the women involved in the Chinese cultural revolution draw a clear picture of the shape and scope of this conflict. It is not having enough rice to get through the grasslands, or sitting for months waiting for instructions. It is believing in the community you've joined so deeply that you can't see how you're being used. Ideas can drive people to fight and kill, by political forces that rarely have their best interests at heart. Hopes and fears may seem rather nebulous until someone gives them a name.

Before it was "the Long March," it was just a bunch of people running for their lives and hiding in the frigid hills. The limit of our conceptual worlds is compounded by how single narratives are used to give us a broader myth. Fiction—whether literary or film—tends to over-emphasize the role of individuals in the construction of a historic narrative, nevermind the actual events silently lurking beneath or perhaps tangentially to that narrative. For instance, Cesar as representative of the "rise of Roman power and at once its own hubris," or even the tale of unfortunate events, such as how the assassination of Franz Ferdinand is said to have "caused" the first World War when it's quite evident that the happenstance of that event is merely how the overall systemic trend unveiled itself, in retrospect. And it's quite hard to say to what extent our unconscious narrative priorities play not only in what stories we tell, but also, how we tell them, especially in the subtle manner of underlying structure and conflict.

In other words, history is also a form of propaganda. Distorted or not, the tales that make us feel that our actions matter, and that they reflect on the nature of the world, never cease to capture our imagination and attention. They can help to give us hope. Heaven help us.

PROPAGANDA IS THE EDITORIAL OF THE MASSES

> It is useless to dream of revolution through content, revolution through form, because the medium and the real are now in a single nebula whose truth is indecipherable. —Simulacra and Simulation, Baudrillard

Propaganda has long been recognized as a tool that key Communists leveraged to rally, or alternatively, excise the people. And much has been written about Stalin's "editorializing," and the power wielded by those that control what we remember, and what we don't. The palimpsest process is often how histories are remade, or erased. The Purge line-edited people as well as ideas. Like the best editors, he even rendered himself invisible, when it served his purposes. All that remained was the iconic image of the "Big Other", a figure that serves as a kind of looking glass for the folk.

> The editor is the unseen hand with the power to change meaning and message, even the course of history. Back when copy-proofs were still manually cut, pasted, and photographed before printing, a blue pencil was the instrument of choice for editors because blue was not visible when photographed. The editorial intervention was invisible by design.

> Stalin always seemed to have a blue pencil on hand, and many of the ways he used it stand in direct contrast to common assumptions about his person and thoughts. He edited ideology out or played it down, cut references to himself and his achievements, and even exhibited flexibility of mind, reversing some of his own prior edits. —"The Tyrant As Editor," The Chronicle of Higher Education

Our memory of a revolution is purpose-built. That recollection transforms into something quite different as that purpose fades away. It's never certain if our vision is clear. Consider the words of Simeon Strunsky, in a 1915 editorial in The Nation, entitled "Muckraking the Fathers,"

> It is all the more curious that the present-day revolutionist should be so merciless to the past when one considers how fatally the same interpretation can be applied to his own case. If the American Revolution was fought for land-grabbing and crooked finance, if the Protestant Revolution was merely an expropriation of the church, if the French Revolution was an assault on ecclesiastical revenues, what will prevent the historian of 2050 from describing the social uplift movement of 1915 as primarily engineered by young men and young women of the middle class in search of jobs as investigators and research directors, and the Socialist party as made up of lazy factory hands, grafting walking delegates, and ambitious lawyers?

The line between historian and propagandist can be a narrow one, as Herodotus knew.[39] The iconography of the group, the very ways we mythologize collective identity, is a powerful tool. When we talk of as "Americans" or "the French" or "Women" or "Palestinians" or "gay men" or "Russians," thinking we speak of these as reference to monolithic categories (Hegel), or beings who share a common essence (Plato), or at best, flail at a recognition of the generalization we're performing.

Real people are rendered into collective fiction with the use of a single world-shrinking, world-unifying label. We imagine we can be retroactively engaged as that single imaginary identity. This bit of essentialist fiction is an often necessary simplification, but it is also the beginning of the dehumanization process that's required to codify any group as an Other, an invasive contagion. This sweeping gesture can even be the result of good intent too, like trying to help "the black community" under the assumption that there is a singular "black community" that needs one thing, or would agree what that thing is.

Our basis for such categorical labels amounts to stories about stories, which makes the term "meta-narrative" seem a bit less jargonistic. Most people speak of groups as if they present a material force, as if they themselves are fixed and certain entities existing in the world in the same way as a chair or tree, because that's the only way many of us have learned to think of group taxonomies. We even speak of totalizing ideologies as if they had agency themselves, or as if we are actually saying anything at all, beyond fabricating a myth from whole cloth. "Christians believe..." "The problem with Feminists..." "Leninists are all..." and so on. This charge can be levied against any group of people that we cluster based on a myth of collective identity rather than individual acts and experience, described collectively.

The atrocities perpetrated by the State far exceed those any one individual could account for, but the will to those ends must be spread through a sufficient collection of bodies for any of them to occur. So the psychology of the individual remains relevant in any work of anti-authoritarianism, following an assemblage theory approach to totalities.

> Let me summarize the main features of assemblage theory. First of all, unlike wholes in which parts are linked by relations of interiority (relations which constitute the very identity of the parts) assemblages are made up of parts which are self-subsistent and articulated by relations of exteriority, so that a part may be detached and made a part of another assemblage.—A New Philosophy of Society, DeLanda

We are one, and yet we are many. Our bodies are an assemblage of cells, of organs. Our societies are composed of physical bodies and their acts, their ideas, a self fragmented into as many pieces as our stories allow. But the moment we reify any of these myths as contained totalities—believing that nations, Gods, or selves are real as concrete entities, existing with absolute,

---

[39] The "father of History," remembered now as the guy who gave Frank Miller the story for 300.

discrete boundaries—we pave a route for fascism or totalitarian collectivism to march into the square. The physicist Schrodinger, now famous for his "cat" thought experiment, said the following, "There is no kind of frame-work within which we can find consciousness in the plural; this is simply something we construct because of the temporal plurality of individuals, but it is a false construction... The only solution to this conflict insofar as any is available to us at all lies in the ancient wisdom of the Upanishad." Yet is it not also true that, though there is no self without a story, there can be a body without a self? How are we at once one, many, and none?

This is an issue that DeLanda himself presents the tools to deal with in *A New Philosophy of Society*, wherein we can take a realist view of the ontology of social categories without resorting to essentialism. However, though Delanda's solution to this problem—based on Deleuze's assemblage theory, to group based on "externalities" which represent in the world differences and similarities, rather than mass fictional "identities" with a common basis —has much to recommend it, it does not readily lend itself to assimilation in conversation.

> What does it mean to affirm the exteriority of relations? As DeLanda explains it, an entity is never fully defined by its rela-tions; it is always possible to detach an entity from one particular set of relations, and insert it instead in a different set of relations, with different other entities. For every entity has certain "proper-ties" that are not defined by the set of relations it finds itself in at a given moment; rather than being merely an empty signifier, the entity can take these properties with it, as it were, when it moves from one context (or one set of relations) to another. At the same time, an entity is never devoid of (some sort of) relations: the world is a plenum, indeed it is over-full, and solipsism or atom-istic isolation is impossible. Put differently, no entity can be absolutely isolated, because it is always involved in multiple rela-tions of one sort or another, and these relations affect the entity, cause it to change. But this is not to say that the entity is entirely determined by these relations. On the one hand, the entity has an existence apart from these particular relations, and apart from the other "terms" of the relation (i.e. apart from the other entities with which it is in relation) precisely insofar as it is something that is able to affect, and to be affected by, other entities or other somethings. On the other hand, what the entity is is not just a function of its present relations, but of a whole history of rela-tions which have affected it. —"The Pinocchio Theory", shaviro.com

To simplify the crux of his argument, collective categories do not refer to entities in the real world. But everyone and everything can be said to have traits, in one degree or another, and without those traits defining the indi-vidual as an identity, they can be considered collectively shared. For instance, if we both have brown hair, we can be said to be people with brown hair. The fiction is that there is such a thing as *a brown haired people* that exists as a single entity, materially or otherwise. We are individually distinct, but quite obviously might be properly described as having brown hair.[40] What happens if for two hundred years a culture re-enforces the collective identity of the "brown haired people who came from the West" through myth? It becomes a historic fact, even a "lived experience". But it remains a myth.

The things that seek to describe us can not be used to prescribe what we are, nor can anything be represented in its entirety through description. We use such labels as matter of practical necessity, and they can become important to us in the sense of historic experience, but we do ourselves and one another a disservice when we cage the world in words. The yet more troubling outcome is when these common traits are used from the outside to define the range of our own possibility, or even our total value as a human being.[41]

The same postmodern cultural factor that led to the disavowal of all labels and categories (as they perpetuate reification that reflects social power structures) has led to embracing labels as fixed and determinative. This only accentuates a sort of endless cultural fracturing, it provides an unintentional accelerant for alienation.

Is it possible for us to use labels without being trapped by them? It requires considerable acceptance of difference to use language but not be used by it, as well as a certain informed distance from the tyranny of the literal.

If this point about essentialism and group identity remains unclear, consider the following quote from Yuval Noah Harari's *Sapiens*,

> Telling effective stories is not easy. The difficulty lies not in telling the story, but in convincing everyone else to believe it. Much of history revolves around this question: how does one convince millions of people to believe particular stories about gods, or nations, or limited liability companies? Yet when it succeeds, it gives Sapiens immense power, because it enables millions of strangers to cooperate and work towards common goals.

Group identity presents a means for propagandistic control. Far from being an exception, splinter groups have been responsible for much of the history of the 19th and 20th centuries that has made its way into the books, whether we are speaking of the rise and fall of Soviet communism, the second World War, or the ongoing strife in the Middle East, and is only likely to accelerate as the Internet further Balkanizes society.

---

[40] This debate about taxonomy goes back to Plato and Aristotle.

[41] Note the uncertainty of the relationship between a label and the thing labelled is not meant to imply that concepts can never describe or carry secondary traits.

Propagandists are a step closer to understanding how to capitalize on hearts and minds when they get people waving the same flag. Myths of collective identity are potent, if oddly retroactive. There is some intentional irony in the apocryphal Alexandre Auguste Ledru-Rollin quote, "There go the people. I must follow them, for I am their leader."

Propaganda is hardly a tool for just any one ideology. The idyllic, pastoral paintings and heroic, yet functionally content-less anthems that characterize fascist art promise essentially the same utopia as those of totalitarian Communism—all the people holding hands, living in harmony through the party, the state, or God. There is an almost comically religious element to the propaganda of even the most atheistic regimes. The rhetoric of hope even appears to us on billboards in Times Square. This rhetoric is so ubiquitous because, as Slajov Zizek discusses with stuttering but still atypical eloquence in "The Perverts Guide To Cinema," it is a blank container. Much space is given for us to project our own hopes and desires up there on the board.

Neither hope nor desperation are exclusive to Communism. Marxism's reputation for anti-modern conservatism is something of a lie by simplification. Alexei Monroe's book *Interrogation Machine* looks at NSK and how they took communist propagandic devices and turned them to new purpose. This is the great strength and danger of such tools of ideology: they can work on us all. And these forces are fundamentally psychological, and personal. According to Wilhelm Reich,

> Today it has become absolutely clear that fascism is not the deed of a Hitler of Mussolini, but the expression of the irrational structure of the mass individual.

The danger of revolutionary hope, taken as such, should be equally instructive for progressives and radicals living within late-capitalist states. So we must be mindful of such grand narratives about rebellion and "fighting the good fight," especially when they're being delivered in our own backyard. Beware the stories we tell ourselves, beware the stories we are willing to believe, because they so often turn our nature against our own best interest. The history of post-Soviet propaganda is lesson in this, a narrative machine so quickly repurposed by the KGB upstart, Putin, to create a truly retrofuturist state.

All of these are potential exploits in the hands of politicians, or anyone that uses rhetoric and ideology from a sufficient platform to direct mass psychology. Movements gain power from ritual that can spread and develop quite organically. Any genocidal fascist has more or less the same hardware as you do. Our nature is in our origins, in our bones. It is in our genes as well as our societies. Looking for the roots of human nature in ideology is all wrong, after all. Ideology arose as the servant of the emotions and rational thought to be sure, but they themselves are *owned* by something else.

Myth are mysterious. They truly are the shadow puppets playing on Plato's wall. We can't escape them. They are ingrained in whatever it is to be human. But they are not what a human *is*.

NARRATIVE**MACHINES**

FEAR IS WORSHIP

III. THE 107 TRILLION DOLLAR GLOBAL SUICIDE MACHINE

THE BLACK IRON PRISON, A LOVE STORY

You get up on your little 21-inch screen and howl about America and democracy. There is no America. There is no democracy. There is only IBM and ITT, and AT&T, and Du Pont, Dow, Union Carbide and Exxon. Those are the nations of the world today. What do you think the Russians talk about in their councils of state? Karl Marx? They get out their linear programming charts, statistical decision theories, minimax solutions and compute price-cost probabilities of their transactions and investments, like we do. We no longer live in a world of nations and ideologies, Mr. Beale. The world is a college of corporations... inexorably determined by the...immutable bylaws of business. The world is a business, Mr. Beale.—Network

Many of our modern myths are based on presuppositions that were ground-breaking when crucifixion was still in style. As Walter Benjamin says in *The Work of Art*, "The destruction caused by war furnishes proof that society was not mature enough to make technology its organ, that technology was not sufficiently developed to master the elemental forces of society." Yes, we have gotten quite smart at building our toys.

We advance exponentially in technological capability, standing, as it has been said, "upon the backs of giants." But our individual capacities have yet to advance in any significant and lasting way since before Babylon.[42] In fact, they are thought to have declined somewhat. Though Ray Kurzweil's predictions about the exponential growth of processing power seems more or less correct,[43] he forgot to realize that such societal "progress" bears no necessary relation to our own internal development. Einstein, Oppenheimer, and many other scientists contemplated just this problem upon the advent of the atom bomb. A tool is only an extension of its maker, and in this regard Prometheus is a cautionary tale. Modern man is an ape with a rocket launcher.

We now face a Great Filter, not in a Firmi Paradox of missing extraterrestrial life, but in the consideration of our own survival on this "pale blue dot," in Carl Sagan's words.

The Earth is a very small stage in a vast cosmic arena. Think of the rivers of blood spilled by all those generals and emperors so that, in glory and triumph, they could become the momentary masters of a fraction of a dot. Think of the endless cruelties visited by the inhabitants of one corner of this pixel on the scarcely distinguishable inhabitants of some other corner, how frequent their misunderstandings, how eager they are to kill one another, how fervent their hatreds. Our posturings, our imagined

---

[42] Corporate egregores transcend any of their apparent agents, and this lends an afragile, nonheirarchical bent to these considerations.

[43] "The Law of Accelarting Returns," Kurzweil.

self-importance, the delusion that we have some privileged position in the Universe, are challenged by this point of pale light. Our planet is a lonely speck in the great enveloping cosmic dark. In our obscurity, in all this vastness, there is no hint that help will come from elsewhere to save us from ourselves.

Now we enter the fourth act of modernity. In a historic sense, America is past its industrial boom, with countries like China and India rushing even more quickly through theirs, with just as little heed paid to the ultimate results of such blind progress. We will soon reach a crisis point wherein these ignitions will either lead to paradigm shifting technologies and a new way of being in the world for all of us, or nature will force that change—the latter route being, most likely, on the heels of a die-out event unlike any we have seen, at least since the bubonic plagues. That's where we are, "interesting times," like the "famous Chinese curse" refers to. The history of purges following revolutions is not a hopeful one. This lends an almost Transhumanist bent to Nietzsche's "self overcoming."

Some consideration still needs to be given to the long arm of history, as this project stretches back far before the memory of modernity. As much as mythic structures like capitalism have accelerated processes, so that we can speak in any sense of "progress," there is at the same time a force that seems to reach to us from the past, and tug at us again and again. The entirety of human civilization could be seen as this long term, public works project, a grand, gnostic experiment to bootstrap our way to godhood. This edifice has allowed for the mutual survival of a growing population. Unlike a structure of stone and earth it is adaptive, it can thrive on a certain burn rate of disaster and chaos as well as construction. It is a modeled ecosystem, an overlay upon reality which seeks to become reality. And over the next 50 or 100 or 200 years, it is going to slit the Earth's throat.

The Global Suicide Machine is fundamentally a construct of cultural technology, a virtualization of relational value, not rendered in 0's and 1's, but in the way our collective illusions can control the material world—a system that needn't be caged in a world of messy animals and unforeseen consequence. Behold, the Leviathan!

THE RIVER FLOWS FOREVER DOWNSTREAM

Due to the invisibility of cultural belief when viewed from the inside, most of us unwittingly act out scripts written by our ancestors. The West was formed by Alexander the Great, by Caesar and Socrates, Newton, Kant, and Picasso, but equally by the lives of billions of unknown cultural sculptors. Their ghosts are all still with us. Many who contributed to the creation of our present were simply serving their role within their own circumstance. Intent is irrelevant in the long-view. After all, it isn't as if Albert Einstein helped pull the curtain off the atom so we could turn around and bomb Hiroshima.

The true horror of the bomb has always been what it signifies, as much as what it can do. An arrow or a gun can be a symbol of death. The Bomb is a symbol for something that transcends even death: utter annihilation.

We have another a similar word, however, that has been in the lexicon since before the Bomb: genocide.

The following passage from *Memories, Dreams, Reflections* is one of the clearest examples of just how complete the "invisibility" of a culture is to those living within it,

> We always require an outside point to stand on, in order to apply the lever of criticism... How, for example, can we become conscious of national peculiarities if we have never had the opportunity to regard our own nation from outside? Regarding it from outside means regarding it from the standpoint of another nation. To do so, we must acquire sufficient knowledge of the foreign collective psyche, and in the course of the process of assimilation we encounter all these incompatibilities which constitute the national bias and national peculiarity.

When speaking with Ochiaway Biano of the Pueblo Indians, this seems to come together most clearly,

> "See," Ochiaway Biano said, "how cruel the whites look. Their lips are thin, their faces furrowed and distorted by folds. Their eyes have a staring expression; they are always seeking something. What are they seeking? The whites always want something; they are always uneasy and restless. We do not know what they want. We do not understand them. We think they are mad."
>
> I asked him why he thought the whites were all mad.
>
> "They say that they think with their heads," he replied.
>
> "Why of course. What do you think with?" I asked him in surprise.
>
> "We think here," he said, indicating his heart.

I fell into long meditation. For the first time in my life, or so it seemed to me, someone had drawn for me a picture of the real white man.... I felt rising within me like a shapeless mist something unknown and yet deeply familiar. And out of this mist, image upon image detached itself: first Roman legions smashing into the cities of Gaul, and the keenly incised features of Julius Caeser, Scipio Africanus, and Pompey. I saw the Roman eagle on the North Sea and on the banks of the White Nile. Then I saw St. Augustine transmitting the Christian creed to the Britons on the tips of Roman lances, and Charlemagne's most glorious forced conversions of the heathens; then the pillaging and murdering bands of the Crusading armies.... What we from our point of view call colonization, etc., has another face—the face of a bird of prey seeking with cruel intentness for distant quarry—a face worthy of a race of pirates and highwaymen.

In Noam Chomsky's essay, "After Pinkville," we find a similar sentiment, which further demonstrates the scope of cultural subjectivity, even, or perhaps especially, in the face of the erasure of an entire world, a People,

Some time ago, I read with a slight shock the statement by Eqbal Ahmad that "America has institutionalized even its genocide," referring to the fact that the extermination of the Indians "has become the object of public entertainment and children's games." Shortly after, I was thumbing through my daughter's fourth-grade social science reader. The protagonist, Robert, is told the story of the extermination of the Pequot tribe by Captain John Mason: His little army attacked in the morning before it was light and took the Pequot by surprise. The soldiers broke down the stockade with their axes, rushed inside, and set fire to the wigwams. They killed nearly all the braves, squaws, and children, and burned their corn and other food. There were no Pequot left to make trouble. "I wish I were a man and had been there," thought Robert."

Technological development also follows the guidance of myths. The concept almost always moves a step ahead of actualization, so it was only after the myth of the atom was born that we could develop technologies that harnessed its power. Underlying the technological history of the Western world is the ever-present myth of progress, which found its crystallization in the Enlightenment and Reformation that defines our memories of the 16th to 19th centuries. This myth presupposes that time moves in a straight line, a teleology with man approaching god-hood by half-steps through the divine providence of reason.

As the industrial revolution progressed, it morphed in deference to the changing needs of industry. This had far-reaching repercussions. Untested myths structure, and continue to structure our grading systems in schools, our politics, our public works, reifying and re-affirming themselves in closed loops. e.g. Our public education system follows the precedent of the machinations of the factory, a regimented process developed to create good workers to tend the machine, sent from task to task by the ring of an alarm bell.

Technology is focused on the utility of the consumer market that supports it. Cost is driven not by the human needs of those working in the supply chain, but rather by "what the market will bear." As Marx recognized, the best interest of this system, in abeyance to some kind of inverted gravity, falls up rather than down.

Technology isn't just *things*, is it? The societies that we live in are the direct result of our collective ideas and understanding of the universe—passed on, misremembered, remembered differently, maybe—and handed to us. Even the linearity of this example is misleading, when in a systems context causes and effects are mutually dependent. Yet it also bears mentioning that there are fundamental differences between machine and organism in terms of what they do, though there are ways organisms are *machine-like*, so we've retroactively applied a lot of machine metaphors to ourselves. Narrative is a machine in whose image we construct ourselves, but we are not, ourselves, machines.[44]

Wittingly or not, for centuries we built a framework for meeting quantifiable growth goals, assessed by partially hidden algorithms and heuristics, a method of virtualizing the world based on shared value that transcends cultural differences. This machine transcends politics. Its OS works equally well under authoritarian or democratic rule. It has established itself as the foundation of a growing, global, social reality. The criteria for success is built into the myths of a corporation, entities with interests as well as their own methods.

The technology we have developed has been "smart" in the terms established within the system, optimization of shareholder profits, for instance. In this sense the virtualization of value is a game, and adheres to game theory, rationally defined as an outgrowth of our wetware, especially if that system is optimized for profit and not long term externalities like quality of life, a thriving commons, clean water, and so on. We fed inputs into this system, and it evolved means of ensuring its survival and reproduction. We are its agents, to It,[45] expendable as an ant in a colony. Egregores are like an AI, constructed by our psychological shadow, over the span of generations. From the bottom up, human behavior can't be rationalized the way machines can. What metrics can be used to collectively evaluate "benefit," and on what time-frame? Capitalism seeks to offset this problem, though this long-view solution is nothing other than the instrument of our collective demise.

---

[44] Unless, of course, machines are capable of autonomous, synthetic experience, in which case, both terms themselves may need re-evaluation. We simply don't know at this point if consciousness emerges spontaneously from sufficent systems complexity, or if there's quite a bit more to it.

[45] And here we must be actually clear, "It" is defined strictly in its behavior as a narrative machine, not in the sense that it exists as an entity, any more than we do, in truth.

"Benefit" "need" and "desire" have all been flattened, even survival is secondary to profit. There is only one concern now: more fuel for the Machine.

Let's consider yet another example. It is hard to imagine that just seventy years ago, there was no real military industry in the United States. The second great industrial boom in America came on the heels of World War II. The war was arguably one of the factors that brought about the industrial demand necessary to pull us out of the depression of the 1930s. In 1961, President (and former General) Eisenhower gave his now famous speech about the military industrial complex that has an almost prophetic air to it.

> This conjunction of an immense military establishment and a large arms industry is new in the American experience. The total influence—economic, political, even spiritual—is felt in every city, every State house, and every office of the Federal government. We recognize the imperative need for this development. Yet we must not fail to comprehend its grave implications. Our toil, resources and livelihood are all involved; so is the very structure of our society. ...Another factor in maintaining balance involves the element of time. As we peer into society's future, we —you and I, and our government—must avoid the impulse to live only for today, plundering, for our own ease and convenience, the precious resources of tomorrow. We cannot mortgage the material assets of our grandchildren without risking the loss also of their political and spiritual heritage. We want democracy to survive for all generations to come, not to become the insolvent phantom of tomorrow.

This is precisely what has happened. Since 1961, the financial demands of this military industrial complex have required the invention of wars-without-end based on what is a faulty concept, even in an economic sense.[46] This is just another instance of how each point in history draws on its past: now we must contend with this complex, and it makes its demands upon us, rather than the other way around. Hammers find nails, and there seems no way to rewind the clock.

Environmental pressures bring out radically different behaviors. There's absolutely no assurance the end results will follow our desired moral arc. It might just as well be an atrocity.

> Our evolutionary past, on the other hand—the period during which psychological mechanisms developed to keep our forebears on their bipedal toes until they had perpetuated their genes— stretches back millions of years. What this means is that the brain that allows humans to write code for iPhone apps is, in many ways, the same prehistoric brain that is finely honed to meet the challenges of daily life on the savanna.

---

[46] Wars may help failing economies recover, at least in the Keynesian model, but they are a drag on healthy economies.

Thus, present-day humans must grapple with legacy systems. These are cognitive routines that were highly adaptive and useful in another time, but that have since become outmoded, clunky and sometimes detrimental—yet they cannot be dumped or over-written because they underlie basic functions of the human machine. One of these legacy systems relates to forming coalitions with other humans. —"Does Evolution Explain Social Antipathy to Refugees", Aeon Magazine

There are divisions and sub-divisions of cultural bias down to the view of each individual, but there is no implicit ethic within reality. Aberrations and norms are the result of accident and statistics, not nature. This is the very kind of cultural relativism that so many academics desperately want to dismiss, for it implies a groundless chaos, but with the revisions of the word "relativism" to "contextualism," it most clearly demonstrates the way our world works, horrifying or not. Human society, taken as a whole, is functionally or dysfunctionally pluralist. Homogeneity is not a form of resilience in the natural world, just ask a farmer about monoculture.[47]

If we look instead to the universe to be our guide, we may be very disappointed. No one lives long enough to see that the moral arc of the universe curves nowhere. There is nothing inherently moral about survival. The war of all against all is never-ending, that in itself provides some of these evolutionary selection processes, or at least, they are a motive force. We have, arguably, demonstrably, seen improvements in our quality of life, and the statistics can stack up very neatly for progress since the close of the last World War. The picture we paint with data is still sadly myopic. 50 years of "progress"—check it out in 10,000. Never think we've won this battle. Time marches ever on, but there is never any assurance to where it inevitably carries us.

> For some advanced thinkers, violence is a type of backwardness. In the more modern parts of the world, they tell us, war has practically disappeared. A litter of semi-failed states, lacking the benefits of modern institutions and modern ideas, the developing world may still be wracked by every kind of conflict—ethnic, tribal, and sectarian. Elsewhere humankind has marched on. ... With the spread of democracy and increase of wealth, these states preside over an era of peace the like of which no has seen.

> ...Talk of state terror and proxy wars, mass incarceration and torture only dampens the spirit, while questioning the statistics is to miss the point. It is true that the figures are murky, leaving a vast range of casualties unaccounted for. But the human value of these numbers comes from their opacity. Like the obsidian

---

[47] This is not said to posit a stance that colonialism or genocide pertains to any particular society of humans and no others. These examples just pose some of the starkest examples of the extreme power of myths as they contribute to cultural bias. If we wish this world be ethical in some specific sense, we have to essentially code that into our societies.

mirrors the Aztecs made from volcanic glass and used for purposes of divination, these rows of graphs and numbers contain nebulousness images of an unknown future—visions that by their very indistinctness are capable of giving comfort to anxious believers in human improvement. —The Soul of the Marionette, Gray

The motivating factor behind our growth to the furthest reaches of our planet, even to outer space, is nothing other than the urge to compete, destroy or multiply. There is no "why," it is what we *are*. Homo sapiens are fundamentally an invasive species. This premise may strike humanists and optimists alike as offensive, but it is grounded in considerable research, as well as a matter of simple deduction, for instance,

In America, thirty genera of large animals—some very large indeed—disappeared practically at a stroke after the arrival of modern humans on the continent between ten and twenty thousand years ago. Altogether North and South America between them lost about three quarters of their big animals once man the hunter arrived with his flint-headed spears and keen organizational capabilities. Europe and Asia, where the animals had longer to evolve a useful wariness of humans, lost between a third and a half of their big creatures. Australia, for exactly the opposite reasons, lost no less than 95 percent. ...The question that arises is whether the disappearances of the Stone Age and disappearances of more recent times are in effect part of a single extinction event—whether, in short, humans are inherently bad news for other living things. The sad likelihood is that we may well be.

According to the University of Chicago paleontologist David Raup, the background rate of extinction on Earth throughout biological history has been one species lost every four years on average. According to one recent calculation, human-caused extinction now may be running as much as 120,000 times that level. —A Short History of Nearly Everything, Bryson

When we consider what we've built, the overarching theme is hard to ignore. The least ethical options may wind up being the most actionable. Will other worlds come to know us as the plague that spreads to the stars, or will future earth species remember us (if they "remember" at all) as the meteor that purges the tree of life of some of its prominent limbs? Only time will tell, but more pointedly, are we actually certain that option A is superior to option B, when we remove our ingrained desire to survive at all costs?

Here too our myths may blind as well as reveal. The desire to "explore" space is only different than conquering of the West because we don't yet know of other life to exploit or eliminate. Pollution, "human assisted climate change," modern diseases both physical and mental, increased consumption of non-renewable resources, these are all seen as evils that can somehow be separated from the boons of civilization, an increase in general quality of life, a decrease of child-birth related deaths, communicable disease and famine. However, when seen as outputs of a single system, this moral equivocation no longer makes sense. We cannot simply paint the Suicide Machine pink and be done with it.

These trends are categorically carried out as if they willed their own annihilation. Short term profits over long term survival. That end is the *real* end of history, the end of its own motivation and desire. This is only confusing when you come at the problem from outside the behavioral logic that our modern societies are unconsciously built upon. No single person ever truly invented an iPhone or a pyramid, much less built one.

Not even survivalists are equipped to deal with the harsh realities that such a dark age would entail. Our population depends on a sort of collectivized social body of knowledge, individually we are domesticated primates without any capacity to thrive or even survive on our own, primarily beneficial to the occult architecture of the system itself. As a social animal, this is ever as it was, but our societies are radically shifting. We are at once atomized, isolated, disenfranchised, and more interconnected than ever before. In a generation, most of us will be *productively superfluous*. Theoretically, this could usher in utopia or dystopia, but either way, it puts us on the doorstep of apocalypse.

> The dissolution of morals leads, in its practical consequences, to the atomistic individual and thence to the splitting of the individual into pluralities—absolute flux.— Nietzsche

Soon, the system we built will itself maintain to the parameters of the system, and machines will build machines. It's just a low hum now, just outside our frequency of hearing. But we can feel it.

There is not, however, a certain inevitability to our doom. We might consider HANDY, a thought experiment developed to analyze sustainability, which concludes, "Collapse can be avoided, and population can reach a steady state at maximum carrying capacity if the rate of depletion of nature is reduced to a sustainable level and if resources are distributed equitably."[48] We could soon have the means available for the first time in human history which allow us to no longer be slave on a field, or forager, or be owned by kings or corporations. But we are liable to turn it into a nightmarish hell instead, because our governing, corporate sentience isn't constructed around collective best interests. When the robots take our jobs, there's no good reason we should be fighting for table scraps or living on the streets as houses sit empty. But there many of us will be, retreating into the past, not building that bridge to our own future.

They will have us starve rather than let the machines cook us breakfast.

---

[48] "Human and nature dynamics: Modeling inequality and use of resources in the collapse or sustainability of societies."

RETRO-FUTUREPOCALYPSE

> The retreat into the forest (Waldgang) is not to be understood as a form of anarchism directed against the world of technology, although this is a temptation, particularly for those who strive to regain a myth. Undoubtedly, mythology will appear again. It is always present and arises in a propitious hour like a treasure coming to the surface. But man does not return to the realm of myth, he re-encounters it when the age is out of joint and in the magic circle of extreme danger. It is not a question therefore of choosing the forest or the ship but of choosing both the forest and the ship. The number of those who want to abandon the ship is growing, and among them are clear heads and fine minds. But it amounts to a disembarkation in mid-ocean. Hunger will follow, and cannibalism, and the sharks: in short, all the terrors that have been reported from the raft of Medusa. Hence it is advisable under all circumstances to stay aboard even at the danger of being blown up. —Der Waldgang, Junger

Our remembrance and recreation of the past in new forms is critically important to how we aestheticize the present—it situates us within that scheme of collective memory which is so key in fabricating a mass myth, for after all aren't we just participants in a collective dream, who forget ourselves and our world upon waking to nonexistence? And what is capitalist mythology but aesthetic stripped of exterior ideology? Clearly we cannot say we have really looked at the forces at play here without also considering the cultural experience of time.[49]

We live with an emphasis on the past, the present, or the future. Many so-called primitive cultures are past-oriented; the focus of their cosmogony, their festivals and rites and so on all relate towards connecting with the time "before," when the world was hewn, when man was taught to work with fire or tools, or so on. Ancestor worship is often a factor here as well, and in such a frame it is the dead who are truly immortal. This is also the operative frame of Traditionalism. Examples of this exist throughout Eliade's *The Sacred and the Profane*, which we have already touched on, as well as Alan Dundes' essay "Thinking Ahead," which we will be turning to in a moment. There are also examples of present oriented cultures, or even models of time that we can't easily frame in any of these contexts, as has been observed in several Australian Aborigine tribes.

We have a need to recreate a sense of connection with the past, it is to the past that many seek to find identity. Yet this fantasy exists within the imaginal field of the future. Without anything but media images of that past to

---

[49] Granted, there is an element to the passage of time that occurs the same regardless of culture, or so we must generally assume; but the way that we process our experience, in relationship to time, is a cultural matter.

envision it in, we invent new aesthetic mythologies, encapsulating identity in a "look" or a "sound". One of the more absurd examples of this can be found in the ketamine fueled retro-futurist visions of Vaporwave, a genre which plays into a form of nostalgia for manufactured memory snippets, a virtualized fever dream glimpsed from elevator music and obscure songs from popular artist—the sounds of generations past merely half-remembered and elaborated on. Trapped within big brother's Windows 95 in a terminal k-hole, we enter a liminal space.[50]

The backlash of nationalism is an instinctive regression against the threat of an alien future, an attempt to escape into a fantasy of the aristocratic class "stability" that preceded World War I. Views of the future are almost always comically painted in the clothes of the present. A fascination with the aesthetics of retrofuturism and Lovecraftian horror lead the politics of the Dark Enlightenment. As theater, it is quite interesting. As anything else, it is a banal reprisal of the atrocities of modernity. Indeed, homogeneity and heterogeneity seem to be one of the central conflicts of the 21st century, and we should expect to see more of the same, as people struggle to find in and out group, and a sense of personal identity in what feels like an ever-shifting chaos. We must also keep in mind that mass movements are the result of subconscious, systemic forces, rather than a prescribed, individual decision. Trumpism is one example of many—it was hard to predict precisely because we rarely recognize mass psychology at work until it latches onto a cause or explicit ideology. That doesn't mean these forces derive from one cause. Quite the opposite.

This is the function of appropriation, for well or ill. With each passage from mouth to mouth, another layer is painted on top, or another element deleted. The apparent acceleration of history will make many of the examples presented seem dated by next week. Herein is the imperative for retro-futurism to stake a claim in the past rather than the present. The past is a known quantity, fixed in time. The present seems to slip by ever faster, because the increase of media output presents a sense of time dilation. The contemporary is so ephemeral that we need to ground it in the past; the present becomes how we re-aestheticize the past.

We—most specifically Americans and those closely tied together through a shared, if imagined "American culture"—live not in the past, but in a vision of the future. This explains the "futurist" re-interpretation of most past "never was" alt-histories. Dundes spells this out very thoroughly in "Thinking Ahead," but a few examples may help clarify the point:

> It is not only the past that is sacrificed for the future; it is also the present. Sometimes it is an unpleasant present which is denied in favor of a reference to a brighter future. "Better luck next time" and "Tomorrow's another day" are examples. In addition, there is

---

[50] We may also incidentally recognize in vaporwave (named after vaporware, a product that never reaches market), the trans-ironic surrealism of Dadaist, futurist sensibilities that give rise to the Fascist Manifesto.

the proverbial cry of baseball fans backing a loser: "Wait till next year." ... But it is not just the unpleasant present which is denied. Americans are so future-oriented they are discontent even with pleasant presents. For the present reality, no matter how good it is, can never be as good as the future might be. ... With Americans and their belief in efficiency, evolution, perfectibility, etc., "The best is yet to come." Whatever one has, one hears, "You ain't seen nothin' yet." The same kind of sentiment is expressed in the American military slogan: "We have not yet begun to fight." Nevertheless, in American culture, one never does catch up with the carrot on a stick in front of the donkey; one never does reach the "pot of gold at the end of the rainbow." (Now there is a compact folkloristic expression of the American worldview!)

Is it any wonder that blind progress has yielded the results that it has? One cannot help but be reminded of the word of the "hungry ghosts" in the *Tibetan Book of the Dead*. For those unfamiliar with this image, Chogyam Trungpa provides a concise summary, "In the hungry ghost realm, there is a tremendous feeling of richness, of gathering a lot of possessions; whatever you want you do not have to look for." We only need to turn to our smartphones to see this at work; after all the Bardo refers not to just the state after death, but psychological realms we must contend with at all stages of existence. He continues,

> ...this makes us more hungry, more deprived, because we get satisfaction not from possessing alone but from searching. ... This is symbolized by the image of a person with a gigantic belly and extremely thin neck and tiny mouth. ... The joy of possessing does not bring us pleasure any more once we already possess something, and we are constantly trying to look for more possessions.

The economic system that we have developed—in accord with our cultural experience of time, in accord with our ideology of progress, and so on—promote the psychological state being described here. The American economy depends on consumption. We are "hungry ghosts," eating food that provides no real sustenance; always hungry, never satisfied, grasping at the simulacra of an emotional, familial, romantic, or personal sacred. Always yearning for a future that is yet to come, and the meaning that it will somehow confer. In America, we marry progress and teleology, almost always. This goal-oriented obsession was strapped to the front of the Manifest Destiny Wells Fargo gravy train, paved over the homes and graves of the indiginous peoples, and then exported to a long list of island colonies who weren't enlightened enough to see we were there to "civilize" them. After thumbing our nose at the Spanish and toward the end of the 19th century for their imperialism and brutality, we did much the same. But we did it for their own good, of course. Not justified by Divinity, at least no more than through His Providence, which allowed for American Freedom to come to an island near you.

In the face of massive ecological and environmental upheaval, it is easy to assume that at some point, people will have to "get woke," and bring about systemic change from the bottom up. This bears a striking resemblance to other forms of millenarianism, another guise of the postmodern End of History, wherein the enlightened progressives can link hands and save the world. Often linked with anti-authoritarian or anarchist political mythologies, it also appears in the capitalistic green movement, which says that if people "vote with their dollars" within the framework of capitalism, and if the vote comes from a majority, it'll force a shift of priorities and may be the only way for a capitalist state to maintain cogency in the face of declining resources (material and human) that cannot support a never-ending increase in profits, even with the addition of technological advance in the mix.

Despite the hopeful optimism of this opinion, there is a fair chance the underlying premise is flawed. We may be able to generate cultural reform from within the system in the way that counterculture attempts, and more rarely, succeeds at doing. But this does not extend far. Consider instead the idea that the ecological and economic pressures are already intensifying, the destratification is already underway, though we have a hard time seeing it because even rapid change in a historic sense may still seem slow to our eyes. The carrying capacity of our population is such that backward movement (to earlier forms of society), or even a momentary lapse in the production chain would lead to nothing short of unmitigated disaster.

What's the result of these pressures? Depression. Wild hope. Fear. Panic. In that order. All of these make people easier to manipulate, not less. We see anger and outrage embodied by the exaggerated posturing of fringe political groups in the United States that have clawed their way into the mass cultural dialog, but it seems fairly impotent in terms of enacting the kind of change that would even improve the standard of living for their own. The new slaves and proles don't build monuments to dying rulers and bloodthirsty Gods, they work in Walmart and McDonalds, and factories in Indonesia and China. The US will become a part of this global factory farm, the process is already well underway. What do corporate egregores care for nations? There is no exit. It is a mistake to assume that at some point mistreated, underpaid, undereducated classes will inevitably rise up in arms in a final glorious Marxist revolution. For thousands of years civilizations have built their empires on the back of a workforce living little better than their livestock.

This has been, if anything, the norm rather than the exception over the past 3000 years.

> Capitalism is a system that is committed to an unbounded increase in production in the name of an unbounded increase in profits. Production, however, cannot be increased in an unbounded way. Freed from the restraints of despots and paupers, capitalist entrepreneurs still have to confront the restraints of nature. The profitability of production cannot expand indefinitely.

> Any increase in the quantity of soil, water, minerals or plants put into a particular production process per unit of time constitutes intensification. It has been the intention of this book to show that intensification inevitably leads to declining efficiencies. That declining efficiencies have adverse effects upon the average standard of living cannot be doubted. —Cannibals and Kings, Harris

This follows from Marvin Harris' general thesis, that the processes of human history shows groups and even civilizations following a pattern of production which, if population is not kept in check through internal or external means, results in a forced movement to another method of production, which often has a decreasing effect on the standard of living. Again based on Harris' research, we see that in plentiful times, effective hunter gatherers have to put in far fewer hours per day than farmers, who have to invest their energies into the entire life-cycle of the plants that they are harvesting, as well as deal with the repercussions of the strain that may put on the environment by vast, fixed populations.

Should this be fundamentally correct, the ills that capitalism produces will inevitably outweigh the boons, and it is unlikely that a transition to a different method of production can occur from within that same system. Furthermore, if we ultimately survive the Suicide Machine in some small numbers, we will never have the 'easy' fossil fuels to rebuild ourselves to our current point. The fat has already been burned. We have one shot to escape the gravity well *en masse* or create true AI or whatever the next step in the civilizational epic will be. The next best option is regression, followed by unmitigated disaster.

What history cannot show us is the end-game of production at its present scale and rate of increase, nor on the concurrent effects of globally intertwined civilizations and economies. But it may not be very hard to guess. This is one of the reasons why the apocalypse myth has so forcefully become the *zeitgeist* of our age, even as capitalism tries to squeeze a profit out of that as well, from Hollywood blockbusters to Televangelists. This is precisely the same as apocalyptic mythic fascinations of the past, but the possible fallout is beyond a scope we can process.

We cannot, on the other hand, escape by regressing into the state of Rousseau's mythic "noble savage." Any successful cultural solution to this problem must take this to heart, as all "escape to the forest," Luddite communes are doomed to failure from the inception in a cultural sense, when founded on an idealized concept of survival truly off the grid.

Thoreau might have been correct when he said "most of the luxuries and many of the so-called comforts of life are not only not indispensable, but positive hindrances to the elevation of mankind." However, it is unlikely that the future of mankind will be lived out in log cabins, and a mass-culture of isolationists seems improbable to say the least. Despite the fact that teleology and progress both condition myths that support their premises, it is impossible to move backwards.[51]

There are other dimensions of this mythic complex to explore, but for now sew a seed in the back of your mind to consider not only through the rest of this assemblage, but hopefully far after you've put it down. At this point, you may be despairing at our predicament. We have thousands of years of history crushing down on our heads; and, if you'll pardon the mixed metaphor, it should be quite evident that any single attempt to change the course of this history will gain little more result than a pebble tossed into a river with the intent of diverting its flow.

However, there is one thing that we might take solace in: as much as our histories are driven by myth, they are a collective product of it as well. The Suicide Machine *is* a mass narrative machine. A machine built blindly, but not without skill. Capitalism turned us all into agents in a virtualized game. That "game" has many knobs and levers, and those means can be put to any end. But where to start?

---

[51] That is to say, that anything is designed with a specific purpose, that a purpose can be abstracted from being, or that the procession of beings moves toward any one particular end.

THE WRITING ON THE WALL

A fundamental difference between humans and our still-living relatives is that our language allows for abstraction, which in turn allows for myth. To many, myth calls to mind outdated images of Zeus or Moses, but as a process, there's very little difference between Zeus and Lexus, or Moses and the capital that a hundred dollar bill supposedly represents. Collective fiction is the realm of art and the occult as well as history.

Myths themselves are a large-scale utilization of the technology of language, which doesn't so much serve as communication device as a medium for cultures to grow in. Other animals communicate, and now extinct homo species probably spoke and may have had some form of symbolic communication—but we're the only living species with this technology on Earth. Art, religion, science, government, money, all depend on the technology of language, abstracted from direct representation. And they all vanish eternally when we do. We've built up an unseen but ever-present cache over the generations, which has created the sense of inevitable and accelerating momentum—history, progress. Despite the untold loss of obliterated knowledge, our retained narratives have allowed us to gather and even improve. This has been the Great Experiment of our Civilization.

> What human beings seek to learn from nature is how to use it to dominate wholly both it and human beings. Nothing else counts. Ruthless toward itself, the Enlightenment has eradicated the last remnant of its own self-awareness. Only thought which does violence to itself is hard enough to shatter myths. Faced by the present triumph of the factual mentality, Bacon's nominalist credo would have smacked of metaphysics and would have been convicted of the same vanity for which he criticized scholasticism. Power and knowledge are synonymous. —The Concept of Enlightenment, Adorno, Horkheimer

In *Sapiens*, this is framed rather more positively as the end result of cognitive revolution. Harari is talking about the point when a system changes suddenly from one state to another. This idea of state change may be more instructive than revolution, as it moves beyond a sense of repetition, or the idea that a state change as from ice to water always requires an act of violence. (Though it's maybe no small irony that "state" can also refer to a regime.) We don't want to carry this metaphor too far, but the energy released or stored as potential in chemical state changes is also worth some consideration. Entropic and ordered states of matter bear similar cross relations with patterns of social behavior, even if there is no truly predictive model for history, even within chaos mathematics.

Yet the nature of this change is fundamentally based in idea,

> There are no gods in the universe, no nations, no money, no human rights, no laws, and no justice outside the common imagination of human beings. People easily understand that 'primitives' cement their social order by believing in ghosts and spirits, and gathering each full moon to dance together around the campfire. What we fail to appreciate is that our modern institutions function on exactly the same basis.

This is expressed rather more laconically by Delanda, in *A New Philosophy of Society*, "...most social entities, from small communities to large nation-states, would disappear altogether if human minds ceased to exist."

When we act as if our myths—the corporate or divine Will they appear to make manifest—are the center of the universe, a strange thing happens. The entire word spins around that new point. We have a long history of ideological exceptionalism. Whether seeing the Earth as the center of solar system, or seeing humans as the end result of a long evolutionary history—all of history and pre-history occurring so that we could exist. Yet the current of scientific discovery keeps tugging at the self satisfaction of ideology. We find that in evolutionary terms we occupy some distant branch, we are displaced, insignificant. And yet we must also question if this sense of displacement too is some form of ideology? Even in our frail solitude we find ourselves somehow unique.

The root of ideology can nevertheless be found in what we are. A hairless primate, with incredible adaptations that have allowed us to bloom like algae in a pond. This is, of course, far from an outlier observation. Evolutionary psychology, for all its faults—especially when exaggerated or used reductively—works on this premise that our so-called hardware has a structural effect on our software, as do various models of developmental consciousness, from Gurdjieff to Robert Anton Wilson.

We will adding some observations to this idea, without pretending to replace or supersede it. What does our biology have to say about human nature? Unsurprisingly, it's complicated. "Biology enables, Culture forbids," Harari observes. He continues,

> Biology enables women to have children—some cultures oblige women to realize this possibility. Biology enables men to enjoy sex with one another—some cultures forbid them to realize this possibility. Culture tends to argue that it forbids only that which is unnatural. But from a biological perspective, nothing is unnatural. Whatever is possible is by definition also natural. A truly unnatural behavior, one that goes against the laws of nature, simply cannot exist.

Instead of a singular, inborn will to power, we seem to be the result of a collection of selection forces—personal, cultural, historic, and genetic. And each of these factors can play into the specific course of development of the others. So there is only so much we can draw from kinship. But it is much more than many are comfortable with, for after all, all these individual factors are themselves conditioned by the others, not just at this moment but throughout all of the past. The fear of anthropomorphizing may have a reverse effect when the animals actually are rather like us. And the animals most closely related, bonobos and chimps, are both social animals. Nevertheless, we take socialization to a whole new level, and this is thanks to the technology of language.

> Bonobos, chimps and humans shared a single common ancestor from about 6 million years ago, Prufer said. Chimps and bonobos shared the same common ancestor until about a million years ago, when the Congo River formed. Then the bonobos developed on one side of the river, the chimps the other. They became different species, even though scientists didn't realize that until about 90 years ago.

> Though biological commonality is a curious subject. One of the most startling facts about life on Earth is that it is all related. If you go back far enough, we share a common origin with a fern. "Wherever you go in the world, whatever animal, plant, bug or blob you look at, if it is alive, it will use the same dictionary and know the same code. All life is one," says Matt Ridley. That doesn't mean we can look to ferns to decode human behavior. —"You Share 98.7 Percent of Your DNA With This Sex-Obsessed Ape", Mother Jones

Sapiens are even closer related to one another. Researchers believe this was the result of a prehistoric disaster that nearly wiped out the early human population. Whatever the cause, we can safely say we share a common range of experience and behavior. And further, our "nature" must share much in common with both chimps and bonobos. It has been only a few million years since we shared ancestors with our primate cousins.

> No matter the languages we speak or the color of our skin, we share ancestors who planted rice on the banks of the Yangtze, who first domesticated horses on the steppes of the Ukraine, who hunted giant sloths in the forests of North and South America, and who labored to build the Great Pyramid of Khufu. [And] within two thousand years, it is likely that everyone on earth will be descended from most of us.—Joseph T. Chang, professor in the Department of Statistics at Yale University

This was never factored into the early political and moral theories that have built up our biases about these things, even as research has long since changed.

"Darwin was right," said Frans de Waal during his "Morality and Primate Social Behavior" presentation to a capacity-filled room at the recent 2007 Sheth Distinguished Lecture. De Waal, director of the Living Links Center at the Yerkes National Primate Research Center and a C.H. Candler Professor of Psychology at Emory, agreed with Darwin's emphasis on continuity with animals even in the moral domain: "Any animal endowed with well-marked social instincts . . . would inevitably acquire a moral sense or conscience, as soon as its intellectual powers had become as well developed, or nearly as well developed, as in man."

Contradicting this theory are the beliefs of 19th-century philosopher Thomas Henry Huxley. De Waal noted that Huxley believed that humans are selfish and competitive, and human morality is nothing more than a facade. This "veneer theory," as de Waal calls it, suggests human morality is a departure from nature and humans are essentially bad to the core. —Emory Report

An array of primatologists and anthropologists agree that we have conflicting impulses in regard to cooperation and competition. On the one hand, chimps have been observed committing startling acts of violence, though that isn't to say cooperation doesn't also considerably factor into their socialization. Then, as if to aid in creating an easy to grasp dialectic, the bonobo gallantry struts into the picture... And promptly gets distracted by the lure of group sex and honey on a reed straw.

The origin of human aggression and warfare remains hotly debated. Until now, this debate has been dominated by what chimpanzees do and how this compares with our own species. It is little known, however, that we have an exactly equally close primate relative, the bonobo. This species makes Hobbesians very uncomfortable, so they do everything to marginalize it. One anthropologist seriously suggested that we should ignore bonobos, because they are close to extinction, not realizing that by the same token we should also ignore "Lucy," "Ardi" and all those other ancestors that bit the dust. Others treat bonobos as a wonderful afterthought, a great curiosity, but irrelevant to where we come from. —"Frans de Waal on the human primate", Scientific American

De Waal's central thesis is that our morality, and the ideology it informs —"human nature"—is rooted in our biological origins. While not identical to other primate group behavior, it is still a variation on the same theme, likely with more complexity.

To account for speciation, he thinks it is necessary to bring in environmental and ecological factors: natural catastrophes that wipe out large numbers of species, like the dinosaurs, leaving room for others, like the mammals, to flourish; geological movements that separate sub-populations of a single species and, by preventing them from interbreeding, allow divergence through differential environmental selection, and so forth. In other words he argues that natural selection has to be understood as operating in interaction with facts about the surrounding world, and that ethics as a condition for group stability is not surprising when the environment doesn't change radically, or when populations can migrate to stay in an environment to which they are adapted. There isn't an ethical *terra firma* within the world, but there are a variety of ethical solutions that allow us to live on the earth more or less successfully within the context of that specific environment. *That* place, *that* time, and no other.

The basic issue isn't one of primacy—social divisions are commonly grounded in myth before reality. Our ancestors evolved the ability to conceive of kings and money, yet as is already pointed out, kings and money don't exist, at least not in the sense that a table or a monkey exist. Myths allow groups that have never even met one another to interact—myth is the intermediary. The problem comes in when we start to codify the surface message—Joseph Campbell returns to this idea again and again throughout his career, what he calls the "concretization of myth".[52] And he took it to its logical conclusion, that if we want to find any ground for the myths we make, we have to look at their ground, as well. For him, that was to look to the implicit metaphysics of Jung. But in the context of political behavior, Reich's *Mass Psychology of Fascism* is a less murky starting point for mass psychology than the collective unconscious, insofar as it is clear that the organizing and power principles of a society also takes charge of our individual psyches. Man, woman, and child.

> The structure of fascism is characterized by metaphysical thinking, unorthodox faith, obsession with abstract ethical ideals, and belief in the divine predestination of the führer. ... however, the intensive identification with the führer had a decisive effect, for it concealed one's real status as an insignificant member of the masses. Notwithstanding his vassalage, every National Socialist felt himself to be a "little Hitler."

Taking this more broadly, outside Reich's intended meaning, the will to power and dominance is fulfilled by a variety of narratives, but they don't supersede their underlying impulse—in other words, they are a variety of answers to the same question. We only need to look at chimp and bonobo socialization to get some sense of the range of possibilities available to us.

---

[52] e.g. from his interviews with Bill Moyers, "When I was a little boy and was being brought up a Roman Catholic, I was told I had a guardian angel on my right side and a tempting devil on my left, and when it came to making a decision of what I would do, the decision would depend on which one had most influence on me. And I must say that in my boyhood, and I think also in the people who were teaching me, they actually concretized those thoughts. ... It *was* an angel. That angel is a fact and the devil is a fact, do you see; otherwise, one thinks of them as metaphors for the energies that are afflicting and guiding you."

We can find new answers, but without fundamentally changing what we are, we can't find a new question. If we're developing a myth of human nature, we need to look not into the content of our ideology or political theories as ends in themselves, but also to the psyches and bodies that produce those ideologies and mythologies—in the systemic conditions that behavior arises in—and frame them within a nonlinear systems-theory / historical context to better understand what may be at work beyond the veil of our myths. Consider again the idea presented in Chapter 1 of mythic "phase spaces", the range of possibilities afforded by nature, inflected or interpreted by culture. There is no sense of speaking of nature and nurture as separate things. They instead present a complex matrix of the possible states within the interior relationships of a closed system.

We can gesture in the direction this may occur in the remainder of this chapter, though certainly not exhaust it.

NATURE OF THE BEAST

We can look outward at the social structures that support the growth of the authoritarian tendency in our own nature, the tendencies against which we should be vigilant if we don't want to live under the yoke of such restriction. These types are supported not only by American or European monoculture, but also by the vast majority of state-cultures in recorded history. This is not merely a Western phenomenon, for surely we can look to the history of China or Japan and see the same pattern of power manifesting itself in some totalitarian manner. The will to power is not a provincial cultural peculiarity.

There are of course many ways to frame this narrative. One quintessential example is the debate between Hobbes and Rousseau. For Hobbes, man's natural state is miserable, nasty and fearful; that is why, he has needed to found some institutions for self-protection. However, for Rousseau, this is not a valid argument because he firmly believes that man was much happier in his early natural state.

Hobbes' Leviathan gives an essentially pessimistic view of human nature, often used by conservatives as the reason that the state needs to keep us in line. Hobbes felt that it was the purpose of a controlling state to protect man from himself, whereas Rousseau saw the state itself as the likely root of evil, and certainly the source of inequality. This is, in a nutshell, the argument about whether human nature is fundamentally "good" or "evil." The idea of raising the mask of civility to find a beast underneath is not a new one. Rousseau criticized Hobbes for asserting that since man in the "state of nature . . . has no idea of goodness he must be naturally wicked; that he is vicious because he does not know virtue."

On the contrary, Rousseau holds that "uncorrupted morals" prevail in the "state of nature" and he especially praised the admirable moderation of the Caribbeans in expressing the sexual urge. (*Discourse on Inequality*, Rousseau).

This argument serves as the backdrop for nearly every revolution of the 19th and 20th centuries, as well as the core ideological schism between America's Right and Left.

Regardless of how we are raised or who we are, the truism goes, "absolute power corrupts absolutely." The full quotation,

> Power tends to corrupt, and absolute power corrupts absolutely.

> The one pervading evil of democracy is the tyranny of the party that succeeds, by force or fraud, in carrying elections.

> Opinions alter, manners change, creeds rise and fall, but the moral laws are written on the table of eternity.

Yet if we open our history books, we'll see that the future has never been a march in a single direction. Our ethics aren't graven in the tablets of time.[53] This has significant repercussions for the social outcomes of science. In the 1970s Harry Harlow conceived of a horrific experiment, which he literally called "The Pit of Despair," although its technical names was the "vertical chamber apparatus." (Which is possibly even more ominous.)

He tortured rhesus macaque monkeys to determine if this would make them depressed. We may owe something to Harlow in the fact that we now take this for granted, but the now-obvious result of these tests was that environmental factors could, indeed, produce depression.

Especially if those factors involved unending torment. The key difference between feral, abusive primates and nurturing, loving ones resides in the treatment they themselves received. Primates will often choose affection or even the illusion of it from a soft surrogate stuffed 'mother' than food itself. "Not even in our most devious dreams could we have designed a surrogate as evil as these real monkey mothers were," he wrote.

This points us toward a key, if somewhat premature question. The history that goes in the books—genocide, torture, war, revolution—is this the history of abuse, especially of children, and generational trauma, lived and lived again? We are all chased by phantoms—an intergenerational legacy haunting our dreams. This is where myth originates in one sense: with our ancestors.

> Children may absorb parents' psychic burdens as much by osmosis as from stories. They infer unspeakable abuse and losses from parental anxiety or harshness of tone or clinginess—parents whose own families have been destroyed may be unwilling to let their children grow up and leave them. ... Researchers are increasingly painting a picture of a psychopathology so fundamental, so, well, biological, that efforts to talk it away can seem like trying to shoot guns into a continent, in Joseph Conrad's unforgettable image from Heart of Darkness. By far the most remarkable recent finding about this transmogrification of the body is that some proportion of it can be reproduced in the next generation. The children of survivors—a surprising number of them, anyway—may be born less able to metabolize stress. —"The Science of Suffering," New Republic

The societies we grow up in have a definite effect on what we make of them, and so the idea of a pure "human nature", which all the old models of social contract are based upon, is further muddled by the fact that it's based on essentialist notions and fictional concepts.

---

[53] What "table of eternity"? This is a central flaw in progressive ideology. Aside from its fractiousness, it is prone to Hubris, because it seems to think progress moves of its own accord inexorably forward in one direction. This sense of inevitability is shared within progressivism, more than collective goals—the cry "Forward!" As if everyone in a population of 318 million actually agrees about what direction "forward" is. "Politics is performance" is essentially a restatement of the abbreviation "war by other means," and it points to the fact that surface appearances and rhetoric don't actually determine which direction you're headed. They're just as often a form of misdirection.

We may also consider the idea that history is fundamentally psychological, and so the psychology of power bears consideration if we ever want to break or at least alter the revolutionary cycle of king deposed by upstart turned king deposed by upstart ad infinitum, in Foucault, and in another way, in Deleuze.

> Foucault challenges the idea that power is wielded by people or groups by way of 'episodic' or 'sovereign' acts of domination or coercion, seeing it instead as dispersed and pervasive. 'Power is everywhere' and 'comes from everywhere' so in this sense is neither an agency nor a structure (Foucault 1998: 63). Instead it is a kind of 'metapower' or 'regime of truth' that pervades society, and which is in constant flux and negotiation. Foucault uses the term 'power/knowledge' to signify that power is constituted through accepted forms of knowledge, scientific understanding and 'truth': 'Truth is a thing of this world: it is produced only by virtue of multiple forms of constraint. And it induces regular effects of power. Each society has its regime of truth, its "general politics" of truth: that is, the types of discourse which it accepts and makes function as true; the mechanisms and instances which enable one to distinguish true and false statements, the means by which each is sanctioned; the techniques and procedures accorded value in the acquisition of truth; the status of those who are charged with saying what counts as true' —"Foucault, Power is Everywhere"

Power prunes the leaves of the tree that it thinks won't yield the fruit it wants, but how does it determine its wants? The scientific method bears no connection to ethical or social imperatives, and on its own, like any human social mechanism, it is prone to the same bugs. If we must speak of Human Nature at all, it is writ large in such networks, and its effects are already factored in. The way that these improvements are used—and funded—and indeed what counts as "improvement" in the first place, is determined by the ideologies prominent in a power hierarchy that supports the scientific process. Science served the Nazis fully as well as the Allies.

Let the previously stated consideration stand in the way of any idea that this essay is a unilateral attack upon the methods of science. The misuse of science in the name of blind progress as profit without end, much as the misuse of religion in the name of tyranny in years before, is a trend in need of attention, at least in the form of massively increased budgets for independent research with Church and State like boundaries.

The solution of growing hot-house flowers in academia has not been nearly sufficient. The deficiency is societal, it is structural. At the same time, science is besieged by a cultural war that it is not prepared or designed for.

We should remember that the scientific method was born with one foot still in the occult, but grew to adulthood within a culture with an increasingly industrial, corporate mythology. Nothing in society truly occurs within a bubble. We may hold on to anxieties about a supposed conflict between science and religion—though scholastically the necessity of that antagonism was done away with during the Renaissance, by and large—because industry and science came to adulthood together, just as the imaginary monoliths of gods and kings were beginning to crumble. We also hold many myths about the actual practice of science, as well as the objectivity and even efficacy of the scientific process as it plays out in a literal rather than theoretical capacity. Jonah Lehrer's 2009 Wired article "Accept Defeat: The Neuroscience of Screwing Up" looks at this quickly but closely,

> The reason we're so resistant to anomalous information—the real reason researchers automatically assume that every unexpected result is a stupid mistake—is rooted in the way the human brain works. Over the past few decades, psychologists have dismantled the myth of objectivity. The fact is, we carefully edit our reality, searching for evidence that confirms what we already believe. Although we pretend we're empiricists— our views dictated by nothing but the facts—we're actually blinkered, especially when it comes to information that contradicts our theories. The problem with science, then, isn't that most experiments fail—it's that most failures are ignored.

The scientific method is ill-equipped to deal with the psychological dimension of myth, the logically unknowable which Wittgenstein referred to as "the metaphysical." As he famously said, "That about which we cannot speak clearly, we must pass over in silence." Scientism is an ideology worthy of philosophical critique. But the method of science has either bootstrapped us to a future of near divinity, or an early oblivion. We have no choice but to see this through. Philosophy has a lot to offer scientists on this matter, though many public scientists like Neil DeGrasse Tyson, Bill Nye, etc. seem unwilling to accept the offer. On the other hand, most political problems are a reframed or inverted commentary on Plato's Republic. Sweeping assumptions about human nature have been the purview of philosophers for centuries, but this speculation was based on nothing more than ideology and grand narratives. This work, too, isn't absolved of this criticism, and so we see here the paradoxical and antagonistic relationship between the so-called "humanities" and "science", which show no sign of vanishing anytime soon.

Plotkin said the outcome was unexpected. "It's surprising because it's within the same framework—game theory—that people have used to explain cooperation," he said. "I thought that even if you allowed the game to evolve, cooperation would still prevail." The takeaway is that small tweaks to the conditions can have a major effect on whether cooperation or extortion triumphs. "It's quite neat to see that this leads to qualitatively different outcomes," said Jeff Gore, a biophysicist at the Massachusetts Institute of Technology who wasn't involved in the study. "Depending on the constraints, you can evolve qualitatively different kinds of games." Chris Adami, a computational biologist at Michigan State University, contends that there is no such thing as an optimal strategy—the winner depends on the conditions.

Indeed, Plotkin's study is unlikely to be the end of the story. "I'm sure there will be people who look at how the result depends on the assumptions," Hilbe said. "Perhaps cooperation can somehow be rescued." —"Game Theory calls Cooperation into Question," Scientific American

History seems to support the premise that the end result of any over-reaching state is either collapse, domination by another state, or totalitarianism. This is the traditional narrative of state and revolution. But—to dodge what would otherwise easily become a long dissertation on world history—we are missing the full picture if we make an evaluation based only from results, even if they have been repeated time and again. A human nature of power and dominance is enmeshed in circumstance, opportunity, and evolutionary selection processes that favor certain dispositions. There is no one "fittest", it is a constantly running heuristic based on a changing world, in which the decisions made themselves enter into future equations. The defining characterists of power are not fixed. No outcome or dynamic is a given, it's not "*a* human nature"—as a fundamental change of the social mechanisms themselves would change that nature. Our nature isn't innate in an intrinsic sense, even if the propensity for such behavior clearly exists in our biology. Biology and circumstance provide variable probability, our chances of getting a certain cancer, for instance. If our ethical behavior is grounded in our biological heritage, as de Waal proposes, then why should it be any different?

The first revelation came from Dr. Nassir Ghaemi of Tufts University. In his recent book, "A First-Rate Madness," he went beyond merely restating the old adage that anyone crazy enough to run for public office probably shouldn't occupy that office. Instead, the book sheds light on what Ghaemi calls an "inverse law of sanity," whereby tumultuous times like these actually reward and promote political figures who are "mentally abnormal (or) even ill." —"Study: Wealthy Stockbrokers More Dangerous Than Psychopaths," Alternet

The global financial elite probably pose more of a menace to society than known psychopaths. In the immediate sense to those of us in the United States, President Trump shows all the signs of a Dark Triad malignant narcissist. Beyond the "failure" of a political system that has put such a person in control of the world's most destructive arsenal, we need to entertain the thought that this is instead a natural output of the system that we have built, in a context far broader than politics. It is a manifestation of what our society privileges. We all need to take a long hard look in the myth-mirror.

The problem isn't necessarily that power "always corrupts," as it could be equally true that those obsessed enough with power to pursue it with monomaniacal fixation may be thereby artificially selected to be fucking bonkers. See also: Captain Ahab. A causes B; B causes A. Dictators, from Stalin and Mussolini to Hitler or Ganghis Khan, provide a cherry-picked list of those that are consumed by the drive to take power.[54] Their rise to power depended on an amplification of that nature amongst the collective psyche of entire nations or the ethnic myths that preceded them. They were like the final word of a sentence, or even the period that followed it. Then consideration of dictatorial power becomes a study on the mythology of authoritarianism, not universal human nature writ large.

Our social structures don't work on account of a political overlay, in deference to simple ideology. This idea is as outdated as 19th century concepts of genetics. It is telling to look at how other group structures—living cells, schools of fish—actually behave.[55] The economists Richard Nelson and Sidney Winter espouse an evolutionary theory of economics based on the idea that once the internal operations of an organization have become routinized, the routines themselves constitute a kind of "organizational memory." When an economic institution (e.g. a bank), opens a branch in a foreign city, it sends a portion of its staff to recruit and train new people; in this way, it transmits its internal routines to the new branch. Thus, institutions may be said to transmit information vertically to their 'offspring.' We are narrative machines, and information is our way of reproducing ourselves socially.

---

[54] None of this is to say that the society we live in is the direct result of conscious planning on the part of a government, or some secret Illuminati or Masonic order. Though there are surely sociopaths at the helm of many major corporations, this Suicide Machine does not require any conscious malice to run its course. Even the best intentions, when rendered within the framework of this system, will yield the same results so long as you follow its definition of success and progress. Everything that we have discussed has been set in place and kept in motion by mass psychological factors.

[55] Of course, behavioral analysis is popular over at the NSA. "Who watches the watchers" is always a problem that haunt such enterprises.

It should surprise no one that the nature of our modern political process, and even more to the point, of today's casino economy, inherently self-select for certain kinds of traits. We're not building a very good future for ourselves.

In the University of St. Gallen study, the researchers "pitted a group of stockbrokers against a group of actual psychopaths in various computer simulations and intelligence tests and found that the money men were significantly more reckless, competitive, and manipulative." Even more striking, the researchers note that achieving overall success was less important to the stock speculators than the sadistic drive "to damage their opponents."

These selection processes (or their results) can make it seem that "absolute power corrupts absolutely," but what we're seeing is a systemic effect, not a purely innate one. So, the salient question then becomes whether we can create sustainable social and economic systems that self-select for the traits that we actually want in our leaders and fellow citizens. How do we game what we are, systemically, to become what we want to be, what we need to be, for our mutual well-being and survival? We would need to reverse-engineer our social (and possibly machine-learning) mechanisms from this model, rather than the lowest common denominator of our collective brain stems. There is a real catch 22 here, as the environment and society that is conducive to this end goal needs to take hold sufficiently for it to become self re-enforcing. Mutual re-enforcement is a matter of systems theory, not just fuzzy feel good personal values.

Otherwise, we will be doomed to repeat the same narratives time and again, and it won't matter if its source is innate or conditioned. Debate rooted in ideology always leads back around to that ideology. It's self validating. It sounds overblown to say this, but it is true: there is nothing more crucial to our development or even survival in the next century than this, if we give climate and ecosystem stability any consideration at all.

We may come at this from many vantage points, and in fact, we absolutely must. From "Leverage Points: Places to Intervene in a System" by the late Donella Meadows,

> 12. Constants, parameters, numbers (such as subsidies, taxes, standards).

> 11. The sizes of buffers and other stabilizing stocks, relative to their flows.

> 10. The structure of material stocks and flows (such as transport networks, population age structures).

> 9. The lengths of delays, relative to the rate of system change.

8. The strength of negative feedback loops, relative to the impacts they are trying to correct against.

7. The gain around driving positive feedback loops.

6. The structure of information flows (who does and does not have access to information).

5. The rules of the system (such as incentives, punishments, constraints).

4. The power to add, change, evolve, or self-organize system structure.

3. The goals of the system.

2. The mindset or paradigm out of which the system—its goals, structure, rules, delays, parameters—arises.

1. The power to transcend paradigms.

Matter and myth are not interchangeable, but they are in a sense symbiotic, and in various ways condition a mutual phase space. We can glance across many domains at once, and find congruent forms as well as patches of discontinuity of hetero- and homogeneity within larger groups across multiple domains; however, it stands to reason that the layer that contains genetic and biological patterns should be considered to structurally determine the arrangement of the other strata, even if this demonstrates a shard of conceptual hierarchy into what is clearly a series of non-linear systems.

How can we deal with the infinite expansion or contraction of scale (cosmos, culture, individual, cells, atoms—) without giving primacy to one scale and seeing the others as beholden to that privileged center? By understanding the structure of our narratives as the chief process through which we come to know both the self and the world; much as that might seem irrelevant to the macro- scale that emphasizes flows, mesh-works, and all other processes that condition the flow and adoption of information, within emergent systems the parts are interwoven with the system, not apart from it, as input or output, but embedded in it.

When contemplating humanity as a "hive brain," we should consider the metaphors presented by nature. Schooling and flocking behaviors are restricted to large groups of individuals from a single species, but self-organizing properties operate even at the level of multi-species ecosystems. Vegetation on arid soils will, for example, arrange itself into groups with plain soil between them: the plants in the groups all benefit from their mutual ability to help rare rainfall penetrate the ground. And in simple experimental microbial communities (not, in fact, different species, but yeasts genetically engineered to have different metabolisms that can co-operate to use environmental nutrients), the different types of individual self-organise. Many ecologists believe that large-scale ecosystems of co-operating organisms, for example trees and fungi, show similar self-organizing behavior, without need for reference to ideology or political party. These relationships are complex, and our ideology reduces the apparent available options.

If we continue to see myth as collective narrative, as the material that both structures and destratifies society, then maybe the first glimmer of an integration of myth, mind and matter, *mythos* and *logos*, might begin.

THE TWO APOCALYPSES

What do contact with extraterrestrials, the return of Jesus Christ, apocalypse, and revolution all have in common? In a sense, they are all imagined redemptions—epic reset buttons for humanity. Onto these we can pin our heartbreaks and frustrations with the world as it is, with all its suffering, mire and messy details. Any of these redemptive apocalypses can serve as the X that solves the daunting problem of our sense of impotency. This messianic X— this unknown and imaginary seismic intervention—might help us to hold onto a kind of hope despite overwhelming evidence of a hopeless reality. Somehow, someday, something will occur that stops the madness, and we will be able to begin anew. —"The Danger of Fetishizing Revolution," Waging Nonviolence

We speak of apocalypse with increasing frequency and urgency. It has seeped into nearly all forms of popular media. Yet when was it otherwise? To the people living in the age of the Black Death, or drowning in mud at Verdun in 1916, or certainly the survivors of Hiroshima, the future must have seemed irreparably shattered, an impossibility.

But apocalypse isn't truly about scrying a future doom (remembered by us, in advance, since there will surely be no one afterwards to bear a candle in that darkness.) Apocalypse literally means "lifting the veil." (Greek: Apokálypsis.) We use the more modern version—absolute destruction, a meaning conferred quite literally by the nearly invisible but pervasive presence of the atom bomb—but maybe not without a hint of the possibility for great transformation in times of uncertainty and turmoil. We are not static, there is always opportunity for transformation. This is the only answer we can give, when beset by the reality of a world bereft of the sacred. Beauty requires no point. Meaning is our burden to bear in isolation, within a world that truly has no use for it. The absence of the sacred, the death of myth's positive dimension, is its own apocalypse, and we are already living through it. This apocalypse is the secret identity of modernity.

Moments of revelations most often occur at the points when all previous expectations have been utterly destroyed. Immanuel Kant hints at this with his aesthetics, a formulation which includes the sublime. The sublime could be the beatific vision, but at the same time, it includes the powerful, horrific forces of nature and the psyche. This may have been his place to stuff the irrational, an early precursor to Wittgenstein's "Whereof one cannot speak, thereof one must be silent." A monster is merely that which cannot be explained, it doesn't fit inside the frame. So apocalypse is any massive rupture in our understanding of ourselves or the world.

The history of all hitherto-existing societies is the history of monsters. Homo sapiens is a bringer-forth of monsters as reason's dream. They are not pathologies but symptoms, diagnoses, glories, games, and terrors. —Thesis on Monsters, Mieville

The rupture either creates an ouroborous, so that the currents of the past can re-shunt into the future, or it provides a true break in which an entirely new process can begin. A galaxy can whirl about itself in seeming harmony for billions of years, and then "collide" with another in such a way that the stars therein don't collide, but the two galaxies mutually annihilate as individual structures, sending some stars whirling off into the void while others remain to start a new show. This is in our own distant future, as Andromeda and the Milky Way approach their death-dance. Everything moves in cycles, until it doesn't, and state change does happen. So we can't deny possibilities that transcend the boundaries of our frameworks.

The apocalypse is not in the explosion, the rupture, it is not the initial catastrophe but rather what exists in the silence afterwards. Apocalypse is that revelation—some temporary, some final. In our present case, this is an apocalypse of the sacred. This amounts to a crisis wherein the rupture between what something is and what it signifies has occluded all else. All messages are propaganda, and truth has died. Yet this is merely a revelation of what has already long been the case. The method of deriving the latter from the former has always been ideological, and Nietzsche's proclamation of the death of God is over a century old.[56]

Another example comes to mind, which incidentally and eerily fits the Tarot imagery of the Blasted Tower. After the World Trade center was leveled to the ground, many in the States, certainly many in New York, witnessed something interesting. In the weeks that followed, we looked at one another with new eyes. We were snapped awake, startled as if out of a dream, and though frightening, there was also a sense of possibility, even hope, in those new eyes, and in seeing our old neighbors in new ways. Of course, the predominant culture over the years that were to follow fell into a myth of fear and hate, and that rhetoric shrouded over any internally transformative apocalypse that could have been. If anything, in terms of mass psychology, it was regressive. At times of crisis we are forced to transform, but the actual nature of that transformation is not certain. Trauma can lead to healing, even to new breakthroughs, but it is not medicine.

The juncture arises in the times during our lives when we think things are a certain way, and we operate under the mandates of that myth, and suddenly we are shown in a stark and often painful way that those illusions will no longer suffice. We move from one dream into another. However, if you

---

[56] "With the collapse of the onto-theological order, the foundations of the Western and Middle-Eastern worlds collapse. Concomitantly, though they continue to persist, the politics, ethics, and virtues founded on the Abrahamic traditions also lose legitimacy. Thereafter, the phenomenon of nihilism arises, but it is a stage that humanity must pass through. Since, as Nietzsche observes, the shadow of the dead God may continue to engulf us for thousands of years, the war between Dionysus and the Crucified—a war that is between two philosophical modalities—remains to be fought; the shadow in all its manifestations must still be vanquished, again and ever again into the future, just as nature must undergo de-deification and, in order to restore it to its original condition, humanity must undergo naturalization. For, to shoot one of Nietzsche's arrows: "It is by being 'natural' that one best recovers from one's unnaturalness, from one's spirituality."" —The Sacred Conspiracy: The Community of the Accursed Share.

can brave the passage with your eyes open, for even a split second, you will be offered the opportunity to see the emperor without his clothing, before we again begin wrapping the world in new mythic fabric.

The possibility of apocalypse also presents itself in our perception of time. While, from a scientific standpoint, time is a sort of grid within which events occur at discrete intervals—$x1$, $x2$, $x3$, ...—without qualitative distinction, from an apocalyptic and mythic standpoint, time is measured by the ruptures that identify different eras. So, from the Christian standpoint, we live in a time defined chronologically from the chaotic moment of Christ's birth until the point of his return. (Interesting that it should be from his purported birth and not death, since much of their symbolism is based around his crucifixion.)

It may be easier to grasp this concept if we view it from the perspective of our personal life, as we identify "eras" by the institutions that rule us for periods of time, such as during high school or military service, or when our intimate relationships change. These transitions are deeply traumatizing, most of all in how they challenge our sense of identity. The very characteristic of our experience during one period may be qualitatively different than the next, so that we might ask "who was I?" when we look back upon a past "era" from the privileged perspective of the present.

This would seem to highlight an event that demarcates those points in time. But in an apocalyptic sense, they are characterized most of all by that point when a previous historical framework was destroyed to produce the new one. Every invocation is a banishment, and each step toward one thing is a step away from something else.

For as much as myths can bring us close to the blood of life, it is less of a mystery how they can be used to distort, to deceive, to fabricate. The tarot symbol of the Magus (and Hermes, the God most cognate with the symbolism of that card) can lead us into greater understanding of both sides of this bi-valent truth. It is with *logos* rather than *mythos* that the Magus creates the illusions that form the world, but it is nevertheless *world from word*. The most primal and fundamental magic.

This bi-valence is intrinsically linked to what Horkheimer and Adorno called "the dialectic of Enlightenment." They were speaking more specifically of the rise of Nazism when they said "Myth is already enlightenment, and enlightenment reverts to mythology," but it was nevertheless to this truth that they were speaking, that myths create false histories, they support the very sort of premises that served as justification for the now famous genocide that happened in factories of death such as Auschwitz and Dachau.

It shouldn't be surprising that if the Eschaton would be immanentized, it would happen at the fundamental lowest common denominator of consciousness: the ravening id unleashed in an endless procession of hanger-ons, sycophants and narcissists, all hoping to take advantage of the chaos sewn by the mad charge forward. The Enlightenment was, after all, a scam, designed to transform us into Gods through the application of transcendental Reason. It was a scam that transformed our world, and for a time saved countless lives and aimed for the gnostic invention of an intelligent deity within ourselves, to contrast the blind cruelty of the Demiurge. It is a scam that almost works, but in the final act the charlatan is always uncovered. The Magician is just the crowned and conquering fool, returned transformed from his Hero's Journey. This transformation remains an illusion, for the Magus is the illusionist *par excellance*. The power of the logos is so easily revealed by hubris as spectral phantasm. The illusion fails, the Fool topples down the cliff. Enlightenment was a myth that worked so long as the hierarchy was in place and we turned a blind eye to the lie that there's any single organizing principle in the universe, save incalculable Black Time.

Now we again stand at a precipice. Do we turn back to find unity and comfort in the zombie mythologies of past atrocity—the false unity of nationalism, traditionalism, and evangelism—or do we embrace difference, ambiguity and paradox, and... then what?

Why is the rapture of revolution the only alternative we can imagine to imminent annihilation?

> ...Man is a rope, tied between beast and overman–a rope over an abyss. What is great in man is that he is a bridge and not an end: what can be loved in man is that he is an overture and a going under. I say unto you: one must still have chaos in oneself to be able to give birth to a dancing star. I say unto you: you still have chaos in yourselves. Alas, the time is coming when man will no longer give birth to a star... —Thus Spake Zarathustra, Nietzsche

PROPAGANDA

There is the story of the American in the train who saw another American carrying a basket of unusual shape.

His curiosity mastered him, and he leaned across and said: "Say, stranger, what you got in that bag?"

The other, lantern-jawed and taciturn, replied: "Mongoose."

The first man was rather baffled, as he had never heard of a mongoose. After a pause he pursued, at the risk of a rebuff: "But say, what is a Mongoose?"

"Mongoose eats snakes," replied the other.

This was another poser, but he pursued: "What in hell do you want a Mongoose for?"

"Well, you see," said the second man (in a confidential whisper) "my brother sees snakes."

The first man was more puzzled than ever; but after a long think, he continued rather pathetically: "But say, them ain't real snakes."

"Sure," said the man with the basket, "but this Mongoose ain't real either." —Magick in Theory and Practice, Crowley

DESIRE IS THAT WHICH KNOWS NO BOUNDS.
AND SO MORALITY IS UNBOUNDED.

NARRATIVEMACHINES

WWW.MODERNMYTHOLOGY.NET

I. NIGREDO

THE PORNOGRAPHY OF CRUELTY

> Alchemy is thus a form of chemical research into which unre-
> solved psychic elements were projected. The alchemical nigredo,
> the initial phase of the operation which produces "black blacker
> than black," is also an internal experience of melancholia, an
> encounter with the shadow. —The Alchemical Tradition in the
> Late Twentieth Century, Grossinger

Several months after the atrocities at Abu Ghraib were first reported, a porn was produced, somewhat unsurprisingly, based on the events that took place there. Some of the copy accompanying the video read:

> I'm sure you've seen the news where they had those prisoners on
> top of the box with electrodes and a hood on the person's face,
> and if they fell off they would get a zap? Well we did just that.
> We put her up on the box with the electrodes on her fingers and
> hood on her head and did everything imaginable to her in her jail
> cell.

Play this movie in an art gallery, and some of its meaning—doubtless entirely unintentional on the part of the crew—might become more clear. In other words, as a porn, the movie is crass and in bad taste on so many levels. But it just might be decent art. Not that this particular pornographic arti- fact has any value on its own ground, but its underlying impulse shows us more about ourselves than we might like to see. Nor is vicarious participa- tion in sado-masochism quite as simple an act as one may assume.

We have a neurological response to what we see on a flickering screen or in a theater, same as we would to the real deal.[57] Aristotle knew this as well as our modern neurologists, though in different terms. Our narratives—the stories we construct that explain to us what things are—are often built in relation to what we see on screens. Movies are exciting precisely because signified and signifier become muddled. Despite that, most of us can make a distinction between a production of Antigone and a real mass homicide.

This is the conundrum, which grows increasingly charged as media sub- sumes all our referents for ideology and even identity. How we're liable to behave as a reaction to violent images is still mostly determined by how we were already predisposed to behave. Horror movies aren't likely to create any mass murderers. But identity is also always a form of play-acting. When we look at the rationalizations of murderers, we don't see their motive: we see the hidden architecture of their ego. Rationalization has always been a useful psychoanalytic tool.

---

[57] Even when it appears fictional, media intersects with the real—to the extent that "the network of artificial signs will be inextricably mixed with the real." (Baudrillard.)

Consider Maria Abramovic's performance art piece "Rhythm 0," when she stood still for 6 hours and offered herself as an object, to be used as people desired, using a selection of preserved "tools": a razor, a gun, and so on. Most journalistic commentary seems to focus on this as "the Heart of Darkness," a sort of aestheticized version of the Stanford Prisoner Experiment. But it may be more fruitful to see it as a pedogogy of violence, how trauma teaches us that the only "tools" available are things that hurt us, and wilfully priming others to engage with us in a way that deepens that cycle of trauma.

Our often casual relationship with fictional violence, even our vicarious excitement, has inarguably problematic implications. Doubly so when that fiction mimics reality, as it always must. But "problematic" only gets us so far, and moralizing is not necessarily the same as morality. The things we know that we know—analysis of rationale—is never enough for us to understand ourselves.

LIVING VICARIOUSLY

The Abu Ghraib pornography is a simulacra of reality, based on actual rape and abuse, which itself doubtless didn't have the self awareness to recognize the power of its inadvertent satirization. Let us consider it unintentional art of the sort that accompanies this volume, and see what we find.

The need for vicarious violence can be considered passive participation in the crime, whatever it is.

> There is some commotion. But no, [the victim] does not move anymore. He does nothing anymore... The other apes break off their fights and come to take a look. A circle is formed around the deceased. Silence... Time after time, the same happens. There is total disorder, a lot of aggression and violence; and suddenly... someone is killed. Violence stops, and everybody comes to take a look at the deceased... Suddenly, disorder disappears and an ordered structure comes into being: a circle around the deceased. Moreover, disorder and violence do not return immediately. The circle dissolves, and the apes take up again their daily routine. Rest has come back in the group.—Violence and The Sacred, Girard

Casual cruelty we can recognize, but it does not at once reveal its identity. Instead, we come to the dark side of the moon, psychologically, which is never revealed to us unless if we ourselves go there. As Nietzsche rightfully recognized, this is not a safe exploration, you can't do it entirely from behind a windshield; the "abysses we look into also look back into us." This porn as art would seek to bring about confrontation with fascist idealizations as a means of demonstrating their opposite. It is a realm that does not just accidentally lead to misunderstanding, it provokes it. It demands an interrogation. Following is a long quotation from the introduction to *Interrogation Machine*, which makes this point elegantly:

> In his reaction to the photos showing Iraqi prisoners tortured and humiliated by US soldiers, made public at the end of April 2004, George Bush, as expected, emphasized how the deeds of these soldiers were isolated crimes which do not reflect what America stands and fights for: the values of democracy, freedom, and personal dignity. If this is true, how, then, are we to account for their main feature, the contrast between the "standard" way prisoners were tortured in Saddam's regime, and the US army tortures? In Saddam's regime, the emphasis was on direct brutal infliction of pain, while the US soldiers focused on psychological humiliation. Furthermore, recording the humiliation with a camera, with the perpetrators included in the picture, their faces smiling stupidly alongside the twisted, naked bodies of the pris-

oners, is an integral part of the process, in stark contrast with the secrecy of Saddam's tortures. When I saw the famous photo of a naked prisoner with a black hood covering his head, electric cable attached to his limbs, standing on a chair in a ridiculous theatrical pose, my first reaction was that this was a shot of the latest performance-art show in Lower Manhattan. The very positions and costumes of the prisoners suggest a theatrical staging, a kind of tableau vivant, which cannot but bring to mind the whole scope of American performance art and theatre of cruelty.—Interrogation Machine

This is not only an American issue, it is a re-occuring psychological motif, which has throughout history played its role in the definition of in-group and out-group—initiation and all other rituals which bring us into the social circle, or which thrust us from it—the enactment of taboo, by which societies define their relations to one another and the world around us. In other words, the debasement of the "sacrifice" is not merely, as the quotation would imply, an expression of our dark half. It is a rite of initiation, though the victims may not be the ones who are being initiated.[58] It is an expression of the fundamental power structures. Violence, ritualized and sublimated or literal, remains a primary method that human social hierarchies are formed and re-capitulated.

To continue with the quotation,

> ...It is in this feature that brings us to the crux of the matter: to anyone acquainted with the reality of the US way of life, the photos immediately brought to mind the obscene underside of US popular culture- for example, the initiation rituals of torture and humiliation one has to undergo in order to be accepted into a closed community. Do we not see similar photos at regular intervals in the US press, when some scandal explodes in an Army unit or on a high school campus, where an initiation ritual goes too far and soldiers or students get hurt beyond a level considered tolerable? ... Abu Ghraib was not simply a case of American arrogance toward a Third World nation: in being submitted to these humiliating tortures, the Iraqi prisoners were effectively initiated into American culture. They got a taste of its obscene underside, which forms the necessary supplement to the public values of personal dignity, democracy, and freedom.

> ...In march 2003, none other than Donald Rumsfeld engaged in a little bit of amateur philosophizing about the relationship between the known and the unknown: "there are known knowns, There are things we known that we know. There are known unknowns. That is to say, there are things we known we don't know. But there are also unknown unknowns. There are things we don't know we don't know." What he forgot to add was the

---

[58] And this raises many difficult questions, if not them, than who, the soldiers, or all of us, as we participate by viewing? How is this relationship changed by fictionalizing and fetishizing violence? How can we engage our fascination without participation?

crucial forth term: the "unknown knowns," things we don't know that we know—which is precisely the Freudian unconscious—the "knowledge which doesn't know itself" as Lacan used to say. If Rumsfeld thinks that the main dangers in the confrontation with Iraq are the "unknown unknowns" the threats from Saddam which we do not even suspect, the Abu Ghraib scandal shows where the dangers are: in the "unknown knowns," the disavowed beliefs, suppositions, and obscene practices we pretend not to know about, although they form the background of our public values. ... So Bush was wrong: what we get when we see the photos of the humiliated Iraqi prisoners on our screens and front pages is precisely a direct insight into "American values," into the very core of the obscene enjoyment that sustains the US way of life. (ibid)

What better example of our unknown knowing is there than a brutal re-enactment of the Abu Ghraib incident, shown on a porn website as a form of entertainment, for people to masturbate to from a safe distance—safe from the potential shame of participation, but allowed to engage with it by proxy, like drivers rubbernecking at an accident? What else is the bulk of our news watching, in truth? Sympathy porn, torture porn, grievance porn. Nothing could be more to the point than this vicarious violence, enacted upon the degraded subject of our (supposed) desire. What better demonstration of precisely what is hidden behind our collective cultural mask of civility, or the outstretched hand of our "foreign diplomacy"? What better way to see it than in something so awful, so absurd?

Even this kind of analysis of such a subject is, in its way, nothing more than a farce. Atrocity can have an unintentional element of the surreal, even the comedic. At our worst moments, many of us find, to our own horror, that our reaction is to laugh rather than cry. This is how life ends, as a joke that forgets itself before the punchline. We might bookend Milan Kundera's literary career with this observation, *The Joke*, his first novel about the tragi-comedy of Communism, and *The Festival of Insignificance*, quite possibly his last work, dealing in an elliptical sense with the narcissistic insignificance of our lives. Jung, also, seemed to want to lead patients in this direction. The alchemical process deals with the unification of the dark and the light, of the transformation of the dross, of base materials, to a more refined form. Shit to gold.

In the aggregate, we re-visit the same blind brutality on ourselves again and again, one generation after the next. Who wouldn't want to get off this awful carnival ride? But we must stay a while longer, for it is not the monster that peeks through at us, but merely our own banal mirror image.

When those same powers who enmonster their scapegoats reach a tipping point, a critical mass, of political ire, they abruptly and with bullying swagger enmonster themselves. The shock troops of reaction embrace their own supposed monstrousness. (From this investment emerged, for example, the Nazi Werwolf program.) Such are by far more dreadful than any monster because, their own aggrandizements notwithstanding, they are not monsters. They are more banal and more evil.—Thesis on Monsters, Mieville

On a personal level, before it can be transformed, it must be identified. That process does not mean we should support the horrific, it does not mean condone it; it means that we must identify the roots of cruelty in ourselves, peel back its shroud so that it recognizes itself, look into its eye, and laugh. The Jungian observation holds true: he who is illuminated with the brightest of lights will have the darkest of shadows. The alchemical process calls for opposites to be brought back into contact, so they can balance one another, rather than cleaved in two, so they can redouble their animosity. Dark humor is kind of a tacit recognition of the bleakness of existence, a celebration to our imminent frailty and failure, but also the fact that recognition is shared, if we can laugh together. Laughter in the face of meaninglessness, futility, cruelty is an expression of being beyond their grasp.

The absurd is the point of the sword. But we must beware, because, in being a sort of inoculation against negativity, it can allow us to come so close to it that we think we have come home.

If one considers the dangerous tensions which technology and its consequences have engendered in the masses at large—tendencies which at critical stages take on a psychotic character—one also has to recognize that this same technologization has created the possibility of psychic immunization against such mass psychoses. It does so by certain films in which the forced development of sadistic fantasies or masochistic delusions can prevent their natural and dangerous maturation in the masses. —The Work of Art, Benjamin

We shouldn't also forget: myths act through us even when we are unconscious of them.

THE THEATER OF ULTRA-VIOLENCE

"Violence is never just abstract violence… violence is a kind of brutal imposition of the real." –Zizek

Unconscious vengeance, the establishment of social hierarchies through hazing and bullying, and the blurred lines between known behavior and unknown motive—all these are distinctly human. Violence underwrites these transactions, in one way or another. Mass shootings seem to be the more explicitly American expression of this psychology.

And this process can be effectively reversed. Obscene enjoyment comes back to bite us in the slick marketing of ISIS, which uses our relationship to media as fiction to sell real world atrocity. So we see Facebook "performances" of real beheadings followed by denouncement, and their historical revisionism and execution of scholars are all a form of calculated "PR." It is awful, and yet unsurprising that we see even this flipped again, for instance with HSBC corporate training videos including "spoof" beheadings as some form of perverse team building.

The amount of scare quotes required to write that paragraph is excessive, but if we do away with them, it might get lost which is real and which is "real." Can we even tell the difference anymore? Trump's three ring circus of a campaign was the height of demagoguery, a farce against reason itself which depended quite centrally on the flattening of the real. A malignantly narcissistic reality TV host leading a mish-mash of apocalyptic cultists into the White House—if the plot had been pitched twenty years ago for television it would have been dismissed as unrealistic. Now it is our reality. The proliferation of ISIS or Sandy Hook conspiracy theories may be an expression of this very problem. The juxtaposition of the two creates the perpetual sense of the surreal that seems to permeate modern life. Uncertainty is the new normal. And violence seems to bring this to the fore. A common refrain during Aurora Colorado theater shooting, and throughout the aftermath, was that it seemed like a movie.

Consider the strange alliances formed through enemies in such circumstances. ISIS has released brochures detailing the strategy of the "grey zone," and their need to radicalize moderate muslims.[59] With the United States now closing its borders and hunkering down, all they need is a few more "performances" and the government might substantiate internment

---

[59] "The grey zone, for Daesh, is a state of hypocrisy, existing not only in the West but in the Arab world. In the minds of its leaders, their declaration of a "caliphate" instantly imposed on all Muslims everywhere the obligation to join their cause. "No Muslim has any excuse to be independent of this entity waging war on their behalf," says Dabiq. "A stance of 'neutrality' would doom him." And this is what the world needs to understand about Daesh. Its goal in the West is to destroy the grey zone, and make it simply impossible to be a Muslim in the West." —"Islamic State Wants to Divide The World Into Jihadist and Crusader," Telegraph.

camps. It's a synergistic if not mutual relationship between those who would be the Crusaders and those who would be the Jihadists. Overtly you fight your enemy, covertly you are creating mutually beneficial chaos by establishing an oppositional narrative.

When Theodore Dalrymple's wrote his review of "A Clockwork Orange," "A Prophetic and Violent Masterpiece," Aurora and Sandy Hook had yet to happen, and ISIS was still gestating. But in it we see him wrestling with some of the issues raised by these events. He begins,

> When, as a medical student, I emerged from the cinema having watched Stanley Kubrick's controversial film of A Clockwork Orange, I was astonished and horrified to see a group of young men outside dressed up as droogs, the story's adolescent thugs who delighted in what they called "ultra-violence."

> The film had been controversial in Britain; its detractors, who wanted it banned, charged that it glamorized and thereby promoted violence. The young men dressed as droogs seemed to confirm the charge, though of course it is one thing to imitate a form of dress and quite another to imitate behavior. Still, even a merely sartorial identification with psychopathic violence shocked me, for it implied an imaginative sympathy with such violence; and seeing those young men outside the theater was my first intimation that art, literature, and ideas might have profound—and not necessarily favorable—social consequences. A year later, a group of young men raped a 17-year-old girl in Britain as they sang "Singing in the Rain," a real-life replay of one of the film's most notorious scenes.

Contrast that with another point of view. In Zizek's "The Pervert's Guide to Ideology," he proposes that violence originates in and must be turned against ideology, rather than externalized. When it cannot be, violence is a possible result.

> ...Exactly the same holds for the terrifying bouts of violence Anders Behring Breivik's murder spree in Oslo. Exploding a bomb in front of the government building and then killing dozens of young members of the social democratic party in an island close to Oslo. Many commentators tried to dismiss this as a clear case of personal insanity but I think Breivik's manifesto is well worth reading. ...It's exactly like Travis Bickle's killing spree at the end of the Taxi Driver. When he is there, barely alive, he symbolically with his fingers points a gun at his own head; clear sign that all this violence was basically suicidal. He was on the right path, in a way, Travis of the Taxi Driver. You should have the outburst of violence—and you should direct it at yourself in a very specific way, at what in yourself chains you, ties you to the ruling ideology.

As he explains in an earlier scene, "even the most brutal violence is the enacting of a certain symbolic deadlock." This struggle—fictionalized in John Nada's struggle with his friend to put on "critique of ideology glasses" in "They Live," to look past ideology by putting them on; or the suicidal outburst of Travis Bickle in "Taxi Driver," where his lack of self knowledge and projection trap him in a destructive script—becomes a real world outburst precisely when it can no longer articulate itself.

Our inability to wrestle with these conflicts internally results in irrational physical outbursts. Violence is an expression of what we haven't otherwise been able to process, and violent media is both a way to act that through without actually harming people, or a way of immersing ourselves further in violent impulses. It can serve as invocation or banishment, purgative or costive.

In either event, evil is as unsatisfying an answer of motive as any other. Ideology explains how underlying impulses express themselves. But neither ever fully reveal their source. When we level the playing field and see all narratives as equivalent *qua* myth, many of our ethic-aesthetics become coherent: for instance, the American love of anti-heroes. We love the rebel, the under-dog. Tony Mantana from "Scarface" or "Dirty Harry." The outcast has a strange role to play in the U.S.. They were misunderstood and abused, but through an often furious outburst, *they proved them all wrong*. This comes through clearest in the self-narratives of mass murderers. How many heroes and anti-heroes are defined most of all by their kill count? How many real-world mobsters and killers see themselves as a fusion of Dirty Harry and Elvis?

The dichotomy is hard to come to terms with. It's troubling. It *should* be troubling. But the last thing we should do is brush what troubles us out of sight. It is liable to breed in that darkness, like the rise of Trumpism as Freudian "revenge of the repressed." Instead, we must be able to hold multiple contradictory ideas simultaneously, such as the quotations from Zizek and Dalrymple, and recognize that the constant wrestling of one against the other—without any final solution—is how we can improve anything at all, without enforcing one set of values above all others. We may find cognitive dissonance deeply uncomfortable, but it may be one of our greatest tools for transformation. In this we can find the first inkling of what an artist and art movement must do, or at the least, where they must begin. As discussed in *Interrogation Machine,*

> "Coincidentia Oppositorum" is a key alchemical procedure with acute mystical connotations. ... Alchemical and ideological processes (both often referred or alluded to by NSK) produce subtle and intangible mystical effects that surround the combination of opposites, as in the case of Orwell's "Blackwhite" concept. ... Deleuze and Guattari argue that Kafka's work reveals the secret architectures of power—the internal workings of a system. NSK's repeated intensive combination of "public" opposites reveals "secret" connections: between Nazism and Stalinism,

science and mysticism, nationality and postmodernity, popular music and social control, and so on. These combinations interrogate and undermine the public image and self-image of institutions and ideologies, and refer to deeper, "universal" levels of underlying reality that conflict with contemporary postmodern relativism.

When we shut down contradiction simply because it's problematic, we move further away from the truth. When we try to force the world to conform to a single moral frame, we can deceive one another and ourselves. This is how fundamentalism commonly expresses itself, enforcing its monoculture by eliminating difference.

None of this lessens the brutality of violence, or the pervasive challenges of trauma, nor does it mean we need to agree in any sense with the perspectives we entertain. Alexei Monroe's repeated use of the word "interrogation" (popular in many other cultural theory books as well) is not just allusion to the book's title, it denotes a posture of artistic engagement with ideas, so that even what we say or portray within this mode allows for ironic distance. This use of irony has been quickly adopted by various subcultures online as a means of avoiding moral culpability, which is a mistake on several levels. But it does serve to instruct us in how we relate to media, through a confrontation with its roots in ourselves. We only know how we feel about something once we have played it out. Children's games of imagination are quite instructive, as they demonstrate a mental process that continues throughout our lives, only in a more subtle and hidden form. So watch that war atrocity on TV. Play a character or explore a train of thought you're deeply uncomfortable with. *Lolita* wasn't meant as a glorification of pedophilia, after all.[60] Just be conscious of what you're doing, and remember that all public performances ultimately re-enter the real. Ironic distance can grant new perspectives, but it does not keep us from reaping the repercussions of our actions. We may also consider Keats' Negative Capability.[61] Yet it is only the aesthetic impulse which provides a means of transfiguring abomination into the sublime.

As Heinlein recognized, man is a creature that laughs at wrongness. Does this laughter transform? Does tragi-comedy relieve us of complicity? Perhaps not, but it does allow us to approach it without fear of being taken in by it, and this proximity allows for further transformation to occur. Only then can we change. Only then can we change others.

---

[60] Though it's worth considering how she was sexualized in Kubrick's and all subsequent film adaptations. This has even seemed to have a retroactive effect on the book cover designs, and Lolita has become near synonymous with femme fatale in mainstream consciousness.

[61] "...at once it struck me, what quality went to form a Man of Achievement, especially in literature, and which Shakespeare possessed so enormously; I mean Negative Capability, that is when man is capable of being in uncertainties. Mysteries, doubts, without any irritable reaching after fact and reason."

Taboos and the divine are opposed to each other in one sense only, for the sacred aspect of the taboo is what draws men towards it and transfigures the original intention. The often intertwined themes of mythology spring from these factors. — Taboo and Transgression, Bataille

THE FLATTENED EARTH

For beauty is nothing but the beginning of terror which we are barely able to endure, and it amazes us so, because it serenely disdains to destroy us. Every angel is terrible. —Rilke

The flattening of aesthetics into ethics has had repercussions that not only span the past century, but help define it. In 1936 Walter Benjamin wrote that Europe was a society whose "self-alienation has reached such a degree that it can experience its own destruction as an aesthetic pleasure of the first order." He concluded, "all efforts to render politics aesthetic culminate in one thing: war." Our postmodern panopticon is only a continuation; it should be considered a part of a historic continuum, rather than an aberration. Under all this remains a pervasive anxiety about the nature of reality, and the simulacra we invariably reproduce in an effort to get at The Truth.

Benthem's utilitarianism, far from the "punishment" of Foucault's interpretation, depends merely on the externalization of social value. This presents a curiously efficient measure of social control, as,

> The self-enclosure of utilitarian social structures led Foucault and many who have seen the force of his account of disciplinarity to suggest that schools and workplaces have come to resemble actual prisons, and that modern society has come to resemble a universal prison. And those who are anxious about the dangers of regimented social structures are not entirely mistaken. The dangers are obvious in the historical accounts of "ordinary Germans" who were prepared to commit murderous acts merely in going along and the psychological accounts of ordinary individuals who are prepared to torture other people merely on someone else's say-so. It is clearly part of the power of utilitarian regimented structures that they make values apparent by virtue of treating themselves as powerful indexes for values. *While our characteristic way of talking about aesthetic judgements is to say that their value can only be indexed to single individuals, utilitarian structures encompass a number of individuals within their embrace.* ... If the Benthamite project is to replace metaphysical accounts of morals with utilitarian structures, the motive is not to eliminate morality *tout court* but to give morality a new language—not that of remote moral maxims but that of *representations* of perceptible choice. —Pornography, The Theory, Ferguson

We order and valuate the world based on an implicit aesthetics. This ordering appears at once personal—born from our sense of how things are, or rather ought to be—and cultural, for we are taught how to see the world, and it is from this picture that we construct our worldview. Our aesthetics are inculcated and determine not only what we see, but how we want to be seen. Our organs of sense provide merely raw data that is ordered and interpreted before we are made aware of that interpretation—and find ourselves within in. And yet for all that, this aesthetic is not merely whatever we have been taught, nor is it only a reproduction of our organs of sense and the billions of years of evolution that stand behind them. There is an ongoing synthesis or dialog between these various factors. Aesthetic is the result, an ideal, or at least a *field of idealized possibilities and desires*, composed among other things of what we want to see and how he want to be seen. All our ethics might amount to the attempt to make that ideal real. Most of this occurs behind the curtain, which is why the very idea is so offensive if it is properly understood.

Might the terror of beauty be truth peeking through the clouds? We can at least pretend, because art can teach us how we turn the world into a life-affirming lie. Art is the pedagogy of aesthetics, it teaches us as we approach it with an ear to receive, which is something philosophy can never claim. This is why all art is either an experiment, or a product. The true *felix culpa* is when it can be both.

Aesthetics are nevertheless seen to exist somehow on the surface,[62] "beauty is only skin deep," so we are want to dismiss art as superficial. We would do well to remember the basis of Nazi attacks on modernist art as degenerate. The persecution of Jews was based atop the idea that "degenerate" abstract philosophy, cultural criticism, and modernist art was a direct attack on German tradition.[63] The Nazis hated the Weimar decadence, and it was only a step further to pin this to a mass racial character. Should we doubt the power and value of art, we need only look to how quickly it is controlled under authoritarian or fascist rule. They realize the cultural power of the mass image, the very Platonic ideal of aesthetic mythology. Yet for all of that, in the time since the second world war, artistic value has been eroded to the point of serving as propagandic entertainment, or not at all. And Benjamin's observation is equally well taken, "the logical outcome of fascism is an aestheticizing of political life."

What is the meaning of slogans? What about the poetic nonsense of the best rock lyrics? The messages may have meaning, but meaning was never the point. It's as if a nation stands in attendance in front of a television but the screen isn't on. It is through aesthetic that political ideology can first assert itself. For instance, David Bowie's poetic nonsense remains open

---

[62] Maybe finding its basis in the Kantian correspondence theory of truth, the epistemic frame of correlation between image (representation) and fact.

[63] Nevermind how relatively new Germany was as a nation then. So much the more cause for anxiety about collective identity

ended, transparent enough to receive multiple meanings, and yet containing none in itself. This is the logic of myth, and it was constructed as a participatory ritual, beginning with "Man Who Sold The World" and "Ziggy Stardust." This theme—and the ironic effort of playing at becoming a rock God and thereby having it happen retroactively as if by magic—was elaborated on quite consciously by the time of "Diamond Dogs" and "Station to Station," though it fell to the wayside until it arose as a more theoretical, postmodernism on "Outside," and then again, finally, in "Blackstar."

Bowie was never a fascist but he explored this idea as well, which caused quite a stir in the 70s, when he ranted to Playboy about how Hitler was a rock star. He was primarily concerned with the mass psychology of fascist aesthetics, how it could fascinate and even mesmerize those who found the ideology monstrous. After all, fascism may be an art movement gone horribly wrong; that doesn't mean artists can learn nothing from fascism. As we've explored, if it wasn't for our collective fictions, our myths, humans never could have developed beyond small roving bands. That collective technology is a potent art. So, Bowie's idea of using collective fictions as a rock star, a "superman"—which seemed to be his central artistic obsession at least up until the mid- 70s—isn't really that out there after all. And in this specific regard, Hitler *was*, in fact, a rockstar.

> Turn and turn again
> The screw
> Is a tightening Atrocity
> I shake
> For the reeking flesh
> Is as romantic as hell
> The need
> To have seen it all
> The Voyeur of Utter Destruction
> As beauty
> —"The Voyeur of Utter Destruction," Bowie

The implicit relationship between beauty and social value is impenetrably problematic. We should be suspicious of the "Everyone is beautiful" slogans, unless that virtue-performance aesthetically appeal to us itself. Beauty can create economies of desire and shame, as in women's magazines, but the push-back narrative wants us to say it's just random chance that all the dudes Michelangelo sculpted look like they could bench press a house. Neither the mainstream sale of homogenized aesthetics, the reductive narratives of evo-psychology nor the feel-good posturing of "white feminism" actually engages with the inherent reality of beauty. Its utter horror, its inscrutability.

We may consider Yukio Mishima's body of work on this account, "True beauty is something that attacks, overpowers, robs, and finally destroys." In any event, these reactions can be built into the structure of ad campaigns; their opposition is already prepared for, often, it is a part of the distribution method. Outrage is an effective amplification device.

Aesthetics can pose as ethics and vice versa. We read who we read, or vote for who we vote for because of what that image represents to us. All social behavior is manipulative in this sense—because we have come to understand that our society is entirely based on economies of relational value. It is often a means of reinforcement of our own self images—"they are a good person who cares" can be a narrative that we want others to have, and so we perform it. Give the homeless man $5 because it fits the image you have of yourself, or just as likely, because it counteracts the possibility of its opposite. (No one wants to be seen as a "bad person," especially by themselves. Though many Americans hold to the opposite aesthetic, that the downtrodden are distinguished by some innate flaw, like the mark of Cain). Even the rush of believing you have been understood is a form of manipulation. Even a baby's cry is a crowbar—a form of social leverage.

This point is well demonstrated in *Interrogation Machines*. Fascination emanates from ambiguity, specifically the ambiguity between aesthetics and ethics/politics. That ambiguity can be left simply as it is, which Laibach mostly does—they don't seem particularly interested in resolving that internal discord. Creatively, it is what seems to be of interest. But ultimately that ambiguity seeks some kind of resolution in the real. Even nihilistic irony and the aesthetic of fascism, (as performed by Laibach, or Rammstein, or Death in June, or Milo Yiannopoulos) could theoretically further any end goal, any potential ethic. That same fascination runs through many horror or Nazi movies. We might consider "Inglorious Basterds" in this sense as a call for critical engagement with cinema, and our own complicity in fascist ideas. Generally that appeal is just used to capitalistic ends, but there's an open question as to what ideological effects that fascination otherwise renders. One can be drawn by taboo or carnival spectacle and not have it resolve as armbands and death camps. As a tool, aesthetic is not unipolar. Like "progress," it can move in any direction, and we should at once find ourselves reassured and horrified, freed and constrained by this realization. So the real question is how broad are the end uses of a single aesthetic?

We know there's a dangling carrot when it comes to social interaction— social media, marketing, video game design—they all count on it. The digital ecosystems we've built are just mirroring and optimising our hardware and all its biases back at us. You get that little hit of reward to know you've been heard, because we're wired for it.

In our mirror image in the mythic, there may appear a phantom on the other end that lures us on—to be heard, to be understood, to have our existence acknowledged. But whatever legitimacy this seems to have beyond behaviorist button pushing, seems to be very quickly leaving the ring.

Will the future be like a Reality TV show where we compete to have human rights? Will you be popular and relatable enough to successfully crowdfund your healthcare?

Tune in 20 years hence and find out.

NARRATIVE**MACHINES**

WE ARE PARTS OF A VAST SELF-REGULATING MACHINE THAT SPRAWLS INTO AN **INFINITE VOID**

II. LIFE IN THE CLOUD

VIRTUALIZATION OF THE REAL AND OMNIPRESENCE OF THE VIRTUAL

"The television screen is the retina of the mind's eye, therefor the television screen is part of the physical structure of the brain." — Videodrome

According to Guy Debord, only the spectacle is real, only the performance of identity is a real identity. Only that which is recorded and presented has presence. He wrote this before the time of social media, but seemed to be writing with this sort of future in mind, much as Baudrillard with his *Simulacra and Simulation.*

This is the inversion of Walter Benjamin's "aura" of authenticity which individuals and the sacred are said to possess—a quality that cannot be reproduced. Modernity is based upon utter reproduceability, and so we find that our identities, so much as they can be said to exist at all, are merely commodities. To the Suicide Machine we are only meat, and shouldn't be so surprised to find ourselves in a factory marching slowly toward the killing floor when our use can no longer be fulfilled.

Being shut offline has a different significance now than it did even just 10 years ago. Our digital simulacra are the very things we'd need to delete to disappear from the world. What lies under the anxiety that would drive us to "delete ourselves" from our virtual societies? If deletion silences the real, can we finally say the one has subsumed the other—or more accurately, can we rather say that virtual and real has been shown as they truly are, a false binary?

PICS OR IT DIDN'T HAPPEN

irl is an Internet neologism, "in real life"—though not so new, really, in a world where last week is ancient history—that we'll be using mostly because rather than implying some "realer reality" in our bodies and minds, it defines our relationship with the so-called digitized virtual society. In other words, irl is all that is *not* a digital Other. Neither more nor less real, just a different way that we interact with the world and one another. The irl world seems a sea of strange faces floating by as we huddle aboard a subway car, illuminated by the lights of their phone screens—the "real" world mirrored back, and mediated by the true symbol for the self, not our body but the device in your hand. (Because all symbols lie in the intersection of signifier and sign). The real, then, is under your fingers, not just behind your eyes. That is, of course, assuming we can speak seriously any more of *reality*.

The "return to irl" is not a Luddite fantasy, a "nature" that has been corrupted by the digital. When we shut ourselves offline, we do not regain some unity with the silent heart of the world. We are, instead, increasingly barred from the village.

We have to recognize the significance of this process, which is so easily rendered banal—like water to a fish. We live at least partially inside a distributed network, where identity is performance and history is forever forgetful of itself. We have started a process of expanding and offloading our consciousness into the net. Before you write this off as nonsense, consider just how deeply Google and other info giants have entangled themselves in our memories, our identities, our most personal and inner thoughts.

Online, if you don't speak, you vanish. For many of us, ties and boundaries and identities sculpted by long histories have already been cut. We have already started the process of irl disappearing. Forgetting always happens as minds are erased, but stories can keep these things alive—what I want, what you want, and why. We've come untethered, and this is yet another guise of the end of history. Let's call it, instead, a death. After all, you will be forgotten and disappear into a silence that is not even itself remembered. That void is the true face of all our frenetic, virtual performance. Identity is now both performance and commodity, or it isn't anything at all. Now the virtual seeks to usurp the manifest.

DO YOU EVEN IRL?

Can a People define themselves by the memes they remember from their childhood? Maybe they can, but it doesn't bode well for the content of that communal memory. Bronies demand recognition of their culture, Jedi demand religious protection. Commoditized mythologies, utterly fungible and replaceable. Cults that can be bought and sold.

Sometimes we all get the urge to delete every virtual sign of ourselves we can—to run from it and try to create some bastion of irl reality, something with the feel of bedrock under it. "Get off the Internet for good, it's been co-opted anyway".

If you flee it all, delete what you can and reclaim the material, what have you done but lock yourself away from the rest of the world? Maybe a cell is also a form of freedom, in such a topsy turvy world. But what will you do there, exactly? Modern life demands, if nothing else, constant distraction and dissociation. The Internet is well wedded to that, even if it wasn't purpose built. "Don't worry," they say, when you shut off your Facebook the 12th time. "They'll be back."

We yearn for something we can never fully satisfy—an immanent reality that can be controlled and curated like the virtual can. Instead, we find ourselves scribbling messages in bottles, without any real expectation of their being opened. Fragments of identity bob along like flotsam, friend and stranger mean nearly the same thing. (We especially mean the tracts of signifier and sign that we have strewn over a lifetime across the Internet—a curated identity and history that is not the life we've lived, not quite an echo or even a reflection, but something quite else. The virtual self as counterculture-corporate cargo cult.) Barthes probes in this direction with his essay, "Death of the Author." We might not wonder at our intentionality with our texts, when we recognize that by building an assemblage (such as a book, or a twitter timeline) we are building *sense*. Writing and recording is compulsory because it is the only way we know to fight meaninglessness. We try to cocoon and thereby save what in ourselves can ever be saved. It is a play-fight, and one we always lose in the end. Once adrift in that ocean, the problem remains, and in a sense, heightens the anxiety.

(—And here we speak to a generalized kind of anxiety that many of us seem to be experiencing, a culture in a state of ruptured self-relation, more than a personal or particular sort.)

Walk around a city these days and you might find it strangely similar to the experience of wandering around Second Life in 2007. Amidst a random assortment of malls, casinos, and nightclubs, you see avatars mulling about, frequently freezing in place as the human behind the screen does something at their terminal, or heaven forbid, irl. Now our places have been reversed, we stop in place with the screen in our hand.

This speaks to our desire to get the goose out of the bottle and not only imagine a new world but *inhabit* it, yet lacking both the imagination and ability to do anything other than reify our world, our society, our identities in a hall of mirrors. A real relationship can happen in this sea of avatars and screen names. But what relationship do those doubles share with our inner life, and how do either compare with the bumbling idiots we encounter in ourselves and one another should we chance to meet irl?

What do we actually gain by accumulating likes in Facebook or on Instagram? The more you drill down into it, the more it might re-enforce a kind of movement toward "hygiene"—by removing all desire not at the root of desire, but at the point that desire is projected onto the Other. Digitization has yet to allow us to flee our material origins. Expect various fads involving cassette tapes and handicrafts to continue.

That very hunger that ceaselessly seeks something in the world to reflect our own image back at us is meat on the hook for Silicon Valley. "Who am I now? who am I now?" we ask our collected pantheons of branded media, and hear nothing in reply except the far off sound of a cash register dinging. We need one another to convince ourselves that our nonexistence is existence, and that something in this has meaning. It is a game we play. "I tell you that you are real, and you do the same for me." We can't possibly do this for ourselves. A person alone on an island survives, but they become, at least for a time, no longer entirely human.

If you are aware that identity is a manner of performance, it is at best a seduction—two lies told to create one shared truth, at least for tonight— then you can continue, even though you recognize it will vanish on light of day. Ultimately, the urge to delete all our doubles and vanish into the wilderness tends to pass, not because "it gets better," but because it wouldn't actually change anything. Without even the facsimile of a community, a common referent that goes beyond shared pop-cultural reference, our masks are just chattering at one another, repeating forgotten histories for no one. Underneath, we find nothing except more signs. If you return to the village, it has fallen in on itself, the windows cracked and soot-stained. It is eerily silent, with not even the sound of coyotes howling in the distance. Performance is not only play, it is an obligatory part of our existence. Even the gesture of nihilism remains a performance that defines our personal brand.

"Seems," madam? Nay, it is; I know not "seems."
'Tis not alone my inky cloak, good mother,
Nor customary suits of solemn black,
Nor windy suspiration of forced breath,
No, nor the fruitful river in the eye,
Nor the dejected 'havior of the visage,
Together with all forms, moods, shapes of grief,
That can denote me truly: these indeed seem,
For they are actions that a man might play:
But I have that within which passeth show;
These but the trappings and the suits of woe.

This line of thought gives lie to the conclusion of that famous stanza. Cease performing, and you cease existing. Even if you find Enlightenment in your LSD visions, the body still needs to pee. The heart beats on. What then?

NARRATIVEMACHINES

WWW.MODERNMYTHOLOGY.NET

REALITY IS A FALSE FLAG

III. WE CAN WEAPONIZE FICTION,
BUT HOW DO WE MONETIZE TRUTH?

THIS IS NOT A GAME, THE ALTERNATE REALITY GAME OF THE REAL

I n modern political performances," writes Richard Sennett in *The Culture of New Capitalism*, "the marketing of personality further and frequently eschews a narrative of the politican's history and record in office; it's too boring. He or she embodies intentions, desires, values, beliefs, tastes —an emphasis which has again the effect of divorcing power from responsibility."

Consider this in contrast to the scheme presented in "They Live," where there is one true reality that underlies all the messages that we are bombarded with. Nada puts on the glasses, and those covert messages are rendered overt. OBEY. CONSUME.

Reality, of course, is far more confusing. All messages are "in code", every collection of data points can be fictionalized in any number of ways. And we must ask, to what purpose? All fictions stand in for the truth as they are repetitively performed. This is the central fallacy behind pop-cultural re-interpretations of enlightenment, getting #woke, or taking the Red Pill. Wake up Sheeple, there is no one truth hidden beneath propaganda. The rise of conspiracy news should not be mysterious in light of this. One does not step out of ideology, one switches one pair of glasses for the next.

We may find no better presentation of the crisis of the hollowness of appearance than Baudrillard's *Simulacra and Simulation*—the surface has subsumed the imagined possibility of an essence. The anxiety here is that without some sort of neo-Platonic ground to rest on, an immoveable point to hang Foucault's Pendulum from, the whole world will come undone. And people are right to feel anxious, though the fear is ultimately baseless. As Umberto Eco writes,

> ...even the Pendulum is a false prophet. You look at it, you think it's the only fixed point in the cosmos, but if you detach it from the ceiling of the Conservatoire and hang it in a brothel, it works just the same. And there are other pendulums: there's one in New York, in the UN building, there's one in the science museum in San Francisco, and God knows how many others. Wherever you put it, Foucault's Pendulum swings from a motionless point while the earth rotates beneath it. Every point of the universe is a fixed point: all you have to do is hang the Pendulum from it.

All being is ungrounded. That central assertion of existentialism—that existence precedes essence—is not one that we'd like to challenge. Much of Baudrillard's book seems to react directly with today's headlines, of the collapse of 'consensus reality' (or the sense that there is one), into the event horizon. Consider this rather lengthy passage,

> The impossibility of rediscovering an absolute level of the real is of the same order as the impossibility of staging illusion. Illusion is no longer possible, because the real is no longer possible. It is the whole political problem of parody, of hypersimulation or

offensive simulation, that is posed here. For example: it would be interesting to see whether the repressive apparatus would not react more violently to a simulated holdup than to a real holdup. Because the latter does nothing but disturb the order of things, the right to property, whereas the former attacks the reality principle itself. Transgression and violence are less serious because they only contest the distribution of the real. Simulation is infinitely more dangerous because it always leaves open to supposition that, above and beyond its object, law and order themselves might be nothing but simulation. But the difficulty is proportional to the danger. How to feign a violation and put it to the test? Simulate a robbery in a large store: how to persuade security that it is a simulated robbery?

There is no "objective" difference: the gestures, the signs are the same as for a real robbery, the signs do not lean to one side or another. To the established order they are always of the order of the real. Organize a fake holdup. Verify that your weapons are harmless, and take the most trustworthy hostage, so that no human life will be in danger (or one lapses into the criminal). Demand a ransom, and make it so that the operation creates as much commotion as possible—in short, remain close to the "truth," in order to test the reaction of the apparatus to a perfect simulacrum. You won't be able to do it: the network of artificial signs will become inextricably mixed up with real elements (a policeman will really fire on sight; a client of the bank will faint and die of a heart attack; one will actually pay you the phony ransom), in short, you will immediately find yourself once again, without wishing it, in the real, one of whose functions is precisely to devour any attempt at simulation, to reduce everything to the real—that is, to the established order itself, well before institutions and justice come into play.

This wry observation about politics as performance jibes all too well with what we've seen happen in the states throughout 2016, and echoes, in another way, Roger Stone's Rules, "Politics isn't theater. It's performance art. Sometimes, for its own sake", as well as Putin's former "Grey Cardinal's" rhetoric and acts over the past decade,

In today's Russia, ...the idea of truth is irrelevant. On Russian 'news' broadcasts, the borders between fact and fiction have become utterly blurred. Russian current-affairs programs feature apparent actors posing as refugees from eastern Ukraine, crying for the cameras about invented threats from imagined fascist gangs. During one Russian news broadcast, a woman related how Ukrainian nationalists had crucified a child in the eastern Ukrainian city of Sloviansk. When Alexei Volin, Russia's deputy minister of communications, was confronted with the fact that the crucifixion story was a fabrication, he showed no embarrassment, instead suggesting that all that mattered were ratings. "The public likes how our main TV channels present material, the tone of our programs," he said. "The share of viewers for news programs on Russian TV has doubled over the last two months." The Kremlin tells its stories well, having mastered the mixture of authoritarianism and entertainment culture. The notion of 'journalism,' in the sense of reporting 'facts' or 'truth,' has been wiped out. In a lecture last year to journalism students at Moscow State University, Volin suggested that students forget about making the world a better place. "We should give students a clear understanding: They are going to work for The Man, and The Man will tell them what to write, what not to write, and how this or that thing should be written," he said. "And The Man has the right to do it, because he pays them."

Postmodernism has shown itself as a tool for art or annoyance in the hands of the Left. In the hands of the Right, these principles are a heavy rock, itching to be hurled at your head. Without any intent to contribute further to the new Red Scare that seems to have started in the US Press, we still need to open our eyes and ask what exactly is going on. On the 26th of November this year (2016) The Intercept ran a justifiably scathing piece of the Washington Post's apparent citation of an anonymous group with opaque methods as a trusted source on Russian propaganda,

> ...the individuals behind this newly created group (PropOrNot) are publicly branding journalists and news outlets as tools of Russian propaganda—even calling on the FBI to investigate them for espionage—while cowardly hiding their own identities. The group promoted by the Post thus embodies the toxic essence of Joseph McCarthy, but without the courage to attach individual names to the blacklist. Echoing the Wisconsin senator, the group refers to its lengthy collection of sites spouting Russian propaganda as "The List."

Compare that with something Adam Curtis said on the BBC in 2014,

> Surkov is one of President Putin's advisers, and has helped him maintain his power for 15 years, but he has done it in a very new way. He came originally from the avant-garde art world, and those who have studied his career, say that what Surkov has done, is to import ideas from conceptual art into the very heart of politics.
>
> His aim is to undermine peoples' perceptions of the world, so they never know what is really happening. Surkov turned Russian politics into a bewildering, constantly changing piece of theater. He sponsored all kinds of groups, from neo-Nazi skinheads to liberal human rights groups. He even backed parties that were opposed to President Putin.

But the key thing was, that Surkov then let it be known that this was what he was doing, which meant that no one was sure what was real or fake. As one journalist put it: "It is a strategy of power that keeps any opposition constantly confused."

The sky is falling. Or maybe this is just more of the same, multiplied by states, corporations, and rich individuals starting to realize how technology and social media can be leveraged to wage a ghost army culture war in our heads. If this poses a return to the yellow journalism of the previous century, it is at least not unprecedented. We are not merely in a post-factual world, we are in a period where narratives are being weaponized, and we're free to pick our truth, like it's a question of personal preference, vanilla or chocolate ice cream. For instance, might PropOrNot be forwarding a narrative from the Russian Government themselves, directly or indirectly? Maybe, maybe not. It hardly seems to matter. Us calling that into question shows just where we are, in terms of trust. Once we trust no one to deliver even the basic facts, the mission has been accomplished—even if it turns out we did it to ourselves.

A war in the virtual needn't be relegated to hacking attacks, or perhaps better stated, the ultimate target is the human behind the machine. After all, if the Russians did affect the U.S. elections in 2016, it wasn't by "hacking the election" directly. It was through the oldest exploit in the book. And they weren't the only ones who are turning in this direction. One may look just as much at Cambridge Analytica, a company that supposedly used psychometrics to help manipulate the Brexit and Trump elections at the source.[64]

> In the 1990s you couldn't use administrative structures [to rule];
> we had to work through the reality we created instead. Politics in
> Russia is not just a form of theatre. You have to build the theatre
> as well. —Gleb Pavlovsky, a former Putin spin doctor (2007)

These methods of propaganda amount to a reverse engineering of conspiracy theory thinking. All the arguments engaged in for holocaust denial, the moon landing, and so on, provide a kind of template, which are built into memetic munitions with the assistance of postmodern theory. So much for its supposed self-referential uselessness. In "Matters of Fact, Matters of Concern" Latour says, "Of course conspiracy theories are an absurd deformation of our own arguments, but, like weapons smuggled through a fuzzy border to the wrong party, these are our weapons nonetheless. In spite of all the deformations, it is easy to recognize, still burnt in the steel, our trademark: Made in Criticalland."

Though we are want to call them new in the West, as "fake news" became a buzzword toward the end of 2016, this process has been quite active since before even the annexation of Crimea, and indeed back through modern history. Those in the Ukraine also frequently speak of having a sense of

---

[64] "The Data That Turned The World Upside Down," Vice Magazine.

premonition about what is now happening in the West, as they have lived through it, without coming out the other side.

The methods used in creating alternate realities is also quite familiar to anyone with a background in Alternate Reality Games, which arose in the early net and zine culture of the 80s and 90s at the hands of people such as Joseph Matheny. However, and this is absolutely essential, the intent of these works was to broaden the scope of creative possibilities, and was never in any sense to further political objectives. Here is what he said in "Transmedia: Who Invited the Lobsters Anyway?",

> As one of the developers of the literary style now referred to as Transmedia, and it was started as a literary style, regardless of how Johnny-come-latelys and interlopers may attempt to spin it these days, I am here to tell you that it was never intended as yet another marketing gimmick. Hands down, no exceptions, not part of the plan. Transmedia and its immediate predecessor, Alternate Reality Gaming are hybrids of traditional literary narrative, video game story arc, web enabled interactivity and real-life role playing games like LARPs. The original intention was to broaden and open up the storytelling process to mediums outside of the traditional publishing platforms, i.e. text/images. It was part Borges, part George Coates, part The Game (the move with Michael Douglas) and part other things.

ARGs are generally seeded by playing characters online and generating a self-consistent world of media that support this "alternate reality." As we have seen time and again, method is ethic-agnostic. All methods can be appropriated. This isn't to say that Putin's media network consciously co-opted ARGs, (though it's not outside the realm of possibility), but rather that ARGs were a response to changing mediums, which gov-corp media machines have also adapted to. Consider this excerpt from the New York Times report "The Agency," in 2015,

> The Columbian Chemicals hoax was not some simple prank by a bored sadist. It was a highly coordinated disinformation campaign, involving dozens of fake accounts that posted hundreds of tweets for hours, targeting a list of figures precisely chosen to generate maximum attention. The perpetrators didn't just doctor screenshots from CNN; they also created fully functional clones of the websites of Louisiana TV stations and newspapers. The YouTube video of the man watching TV had been tailor-made for the project. A Wikipedia page was even created for the Columbian Chemicals disaster, which cited the fake YouTube video. As the virtual assault unfolded, it was complemented by text messages to actual residents in St. Mary Parish. It must have taken a team of programmers and content producers to pull off.

> And the hoax was just one in a wave of similar attacks during the second half of last year. On Dec. 13, two months later a handful of Ebola cases in the United States touched off a minor media panic,

many of the same Twitter accounts used to spread the Columbian Chemicals hoax began to post about an outbreak of Ebola in Atlanta. ... Again, the attention to detail was remarkable, suggesting a tremendous amount of effort. A YouTube video showed a team of hazmat-suited medical workers transporting a victim from the airport. Beyonce's recent single "7/11" played in the background, an apparent attempt to establish the video's contemporaneity. A truck in the parking lot sported the logo of the Hartsfield-Jackson Atlanta International Airport.

The inventions of our times reflect in great part on the spirit of those times. After all, Bowie and Boyd's fabrication of an artist probably wouldn't have played outside the insular art world, but today it can be done entirely virtually.

I invented a dead American "artist" I called Nat Tate and wrote his biography. Then the team at Modern Painters and 21 transformed the text into a small, beautifully made and copiously illustrated artist's monograph. However, there's absolutely no denying the fact that it was Bowie's participation in the eventual hoax that gave it media heft. He published the book, he organised the launch party (on April Fool's Day, 1998) in Jeff Koons's studio in Manhattan – Koons was a friend of Bowie – and it was Bowie who read out extracts of the book, absolutely deadpan, to the assembled New York glitterati. The clincher was his statement in the blurb that he was convinced that, "The small oil I picked up on Prince Street, New York, must indeed be one of the lost Third Panel Triptychs. The great sadness of this quiet and moving monograph is that the artist's most profound dread—that God will make you an artist but only a mediocre artist—did not in retrospect apply to Nat Tate." —"William Boyd: how David Bowie and I hoaxed the art world," The Guardian.

Much as fictional / pseudonymous artists can be invented, so can entire events, as Russian State (and segments of U.S.) media have discovered. Insular digital social networks can incubate similar myths on an even broader scale. Given ample dissemination points, and a narrative people are already inclined to confirm, and the tail wags the dog all on its own.

Many of Matheny's most popular transmedia narratives, such as Ong's Hat and El Centro, were active parodies of conspiracy thinking, at most raising the specter of all the fictional possibilities posed by the "unknown unknowns," yet they were often quickly adopted by conspiracy theorists, much to his consternation. People still hunt the pine barrens of New Jersey for the fictional Ong's Hat. As anyone who has tried to argue with conspiracy theorists know, an endless procession of cherry-picked stats, "whataboutist" counter-examples and attempts at moral equivalence await. ("Yes, but what about the bad things Zionists have done," "Sure the Gulags weren't great but consider the US prison system, ...") These all serve merely as smokescreen. The ideology may at times be toward racism or nationalism driven by fear or yearning for sacred origins, but even more instrumentally, all the motivating factors we are seeing today have an anti-authoritarian flavor.

This presents one of the key ironies of recent social developments online: the 4 quadrant model of political ideology, always a loose sketch at best, has come totally unmoored. All corners have become anti-authoritarian, even when it is done in interests of an authoritarian regime. The only exceptions may be the moderate anti-authoritarian Left who suddenly find themselves in the impossibly confusing and rather self-hypocritical position of arguing in defense of institutions such as the CIA. Meanwhile, their former anti-authority icons like Assange have become valorized by the newly forming, strange-bedfellows coalitions of the Right.

> ... the far-right and authoritarian left hold similar priorities and sneer just as glibly at "globalism" is often derided as "horseshoe theory": the idea that extremist views all tend toward the same totalitarian horror and truth lies in the sensible centrist middle ground. This is a misunderstanding. The common thread is not extremism but authoritarianism. All authoritarians promote closed societies and esteem them more than open ones because all authoritarians benefit from being able to insulate people from subversive outside influence, denying access to novelty and exploration. Freedom is inherently caustic to nation and tradition. They all intuitively recognize this, and that is why they get along so well. —"Understanding Richard Spencer's Holodomor Denial", Center for a Stateless Society

These are topsy turvy times in even the most literal sense, so this can only serve as an instructive example. These situations could flip in a matter of days or minutes. If the US government wasn't as fully committed to this game of asymmetrical cultural warfare as much as the Russians, it was purely because their relative might made these tactics seem unnecessary. And we better believe they will be now. The future is likely to include yet more layers of fictional narrative, not less. Who knows what tomorrow will bring?

WE ARE THE MONKEY FLOWERS

"Politics, religion and law work their magic on us through images and symbols, costume, and ceremony." —Pretentiousness: Why It Matters, Fox

Within the context of modern markets, we are taught to think of media (articles and editorials, podcasts, books, movies, music, etc) not much different than any other commodity for sale—a sandwich, a car, or a book. This misses the function—it is primarily fungible socially.[65] Memes are produced through exposure to a medium, rather than the container or vessel that merely serves to propagate the content in a material world. We may need to reconsider "the medium is the message" in this light. A book is dead trees, glue. A CD or hard drive is petroleum. There is an art to the container, the beauty of the hand constructed book, of paper or inks that are rendered by hand, constructed conscientiously, carefully. Regardless, to the extent that the art is in the content, containers are designed to attract us to what in many cases cannot be reduced to the object itself. Again we return to the role of aesthetics and political and personal life. Art is an act, in the way speech is an act; the container is a carrier vehicle, a Trojan horse for myths. Even in terms of profit, the real motive lies in what happens when those soldiers slip past the gates. Star Wars made considerably more on merchandizing, after all. The movies baited the trap.

So, a better metaphor than those following from ideas of consumption and commodity might be found in the relationship of flowering plants and the insects that help them spread. Imagine that pollen is cultural information. Flowers generate pollen and passively make themselves attractive to the insects that lap up the nectar, in the process carrying pollen from one flower to the next.

What sweet nectar and bright colors will lure in the unwitting insects? That's the question advertisers and political strategists are bound to ask. The market is strictly concerned with selling the container, the surface. A random breath of wind also plays its role in disseminating this genetic material, but for the most part, this substance is carried along with the bees, who have no personal interest in its distribution.

We imagine bees are blissfully unaware of the pollen. They are drawn by the flower. The same is true in advertising. Countless dollars have been spent researching customer reaction to different colors, configurations of symbols and patterns. Certainly, much of this plays into the cutting edge of UX design, which is increasingly driven by neurological research to produce the desired results.

---

[65] Money can deliver messages to receptive minds, which has a far greater value as social capital than in terms of immediate hard profits. In practice, this often comes about through an internal war between journalists, artists, and producers on one side, bean counters on the others, and absentee owners, patrons, or board of directors that still manage to have their big picture interests served by the narratives supported by an outlet or publication,.

To an extent we all serve the function of "bees" (memebearers) or "flow-ers" (nexus points, which can be codified within books, movies, or really in whatever container seems most appropriate to the nature of the narrative.) We may be lured in by the narrative, or some other element, but what we take in and carry on are the mythemes embedded within it, which may very well have been placed there completely unconsciously by the author, or built into the architecture of the system. Myths are like narrative genetic codes, and few of us are consciously aware of our genes.

We are all attracted by different ideas and aesthetics, and politics, which themselves in a virtual space remain primarily performative. Political per-formance online can have real world effects, to be sure, but it remains in that context performance art.

So much of what drives us to click, and our immediate response is a learned reaction driven by basic biological and psychological forces. Women's magazines most clearly capitalize on this approach almost singu-larly, triggering insecurity and competition to drive sales, by directly leveraging these biologically and culturally re-enforced mechanisms. But so do magazines constructed around any other market. It is a question of the psychological jujitsu involved in constructing an aesthetic rapport with the viewer. This is why the colossal amount of marketing data available now to companies is significant. We give it to them for free, and they are increas-ingly better able to provide a "better customer experience." Nearly everyone is aware of this, or that sex is used to sell just about everything from deodorant to cars. What's being sold is the representation itself. Pollen that does not impregnate may as well be sterile.

> Consider that the market itself is subject to a sort of evolutionary and genetic model. "…[I]t becomes clear that interactive species in an ecosystem have the ability to change each other's adaptive landscapes. This is just another way of saying that in a predator-prey arms race there is not a fixed definition of what counts as "the fittest." —1000 Years of Nonlinear History, Delanda.

We may also consider the various relationships which may arise in the context of pollination. For insurance, monarch butterflies are lured by the nectar of milkweed plants, but so as to lay its eggs on the underside of leafs. These hatch, and quickly go about eating the plants, which are their only source of food. However, the plants have evolved a defense, a kind of latex that leaks out and suffocates the monarch young. Those that survive, how-ever, cut the vein that supplies this resin, and then eat in peace—until they finally cocoon and emerge as butterflies. At this point they are lured again by the nectar, and in the process pick up pollen, only then to fly off and con-tinue the cycle. Considered metaphorically, this demonstrates one of many sympathetic antipathies which might exist in an ecosystem.

A market is essentially a conceptual domain mapped on top of the pre-existent ecosystem, so ecological and evolutionary dynamics are more like causal agents within that system than the formal rules of many traditional economics theories which, based on various logical presuppositions, have shown themselves demonstrably false. And how systems theory style analysis of social webs is coming along,

> I want to propose a new metaphor for the world as it is—a Narrative Machine—where macroeconomic reality is still understood as a cybernetic system, but where the translation of "reality" (all of those economic fundamentals and if-then statements of the Economic Machine) into actual human behaviors and actual investment outcomes takes place within a larger Machine of strategic communication and game playing. ... How do we observe an invisible network of social interaction? How do we touch the intangible? —"The Narrative Machine," Salient

What we're seeing is a system optimized on what people want to see more of. It has no connection to truth. That simply isn't part of the metrics and won't be unless truth can be monetized. We say we want the truth in news at the least, but the media ecosystem we've built doesn't demonstrate that. And there's little chance of that cloud of unknowing vanishing anytime soon. The "Post Truth Age" is nothing new, information has merely been amplified and accelerated. If we want to monetize truth we have to have a quick heuristic to determine it, and we don't have that either.

This simply exposes an existing problem in our "hardware," because we aren't optimized for this purpose. Our biases are a feature not a bug. The work of Donald Hoffman, a cognitive scientist at the University of California, explores this in more detail,

> "We simulated hundreds of thousands of random worlds and put organisms in those worlds that could see all of the truth, part of the truth, or none of the truth," explained Hoffman. "What we found in our simulations was that organisms that saw reality as-it-is could never outcompete organisms that saw none of reality and were just tuned to fitness, as long as they were of equal complexity." The implication, Hoffman said, is that an organism that can see the truth will never be favored by natural selection. This suggests that literally nothing we can conceive of can be said to represent objective reality, not even atoms, molecules, or physical laws. Physics and chemistry are still inside the umwelt. There's no escape. "If our perceptual systems evolved by natural selection, then the probability that we see reality as it actually is, in any way, is zero. Precisely zero," said Hoffman. —"Questioning the nature of reality with cognitive scientist Donald Hoffman," YANS podcast

...A COST-BENEFIT ANALYSIS OF TRUTH?

The debate about "truth" between various corporate and political interests and their platforms over the past year calls into question the imagined bedrock of our own journalistic ethics and practices, or has, at the least, demonstrated to us in painful detail that the Emperor has no clothes. Bias has always been an accepted dirty secret of journalism, but that has fundamentally changed in just a few short years. (Or it at least appears to be so, which once again, is effectively the same thing.) The assumption has been that the citizens can think for themselves. Trying to jury rig our distribution networks to compensate for bias is Orwellian, the fact that we might need it, incredibly depressing. At the end of the day, a click is money in the bank, whether the content is Badiou's Republic, a new #pizzagate hot take, or a puppy being shot in the head.

Ethics are judged on intent and effect, but aren't meant to replace veracity. It matters if you killed someone truly by accident, or if it was premeditated, or done out of passion. It matters still more that you killed someone in the first place. This is an uncomfortable observation for journalists but that makes it no less true, since the real isn't what we'd like to be the case. Simply telling the truth isn't always enough—and yet, and this can't be understated—this is the argument commonly used by regimes to legitimize disinformation. In practical terms, truth is a statement not of epistemological certainty but rather social power, which is an observation Foucault would probably find appealing.

Any kind of social factor (money, power, prestige) that you try to optimize along with the truth results in a bias at scale—you end up with something that doesn't resemble truth at all.

Consider what happens if you decide to pursue the truth and then only publish what brings money/prestige. You end up with a situation akin to another recent crisis of confidence, this one in experimental psychology, where spurious positive results were considered god's whole truth because the many similar studies with negative results were never published.

If you do it the other way around (purely pursue financial interest but then publish only what's true) you get a similar result: nobody bothers to falsify anything.

Effective propaganda often works the same way. You publish only verifiable, fact-checked narratives that also correlate with the message you want, and if you can manipulate the incentives well enough then nobody will ever notice that it's not the whole truth.

We're left to guess at intent based on the apparent interests that a publication has. The effect is maybe more apparent after some time has passed— but this distancing is never enough to remove us from our own interests.

Our cognitive biases are increasingly easier to weaponize, and our need for the truth has never been harder to monetize—or even justify. And if we're left to guess, we're left to project our own worldview in relief. If we are prone to believe one narrative over another, to what extent is that viridity in the narratives, and to what extent is that in us? Epistemology in this way always seems to loop back around to literature. We can't get the human out of the human.

So, we have to take a hard look at how things are, rather than how we might like them to be, and ask ourselves what truth *does*, what it's *worth*— how that can be monetized within the context of infotainment today. The unpleasant alternative is that this problem continues and grows, and we never again have a consensual basis of even the most basic facts. Narratives drive our engagement with the news, not facts or figures, except inasmuch as they help us feel more connected to those myths. A good myth that gets us going, that's as good as cocaine. Anyone that's tasted religious ecstasy knows that. And woe betide those who try to convince them in the grips of it that it's not *real*.

> The essential characteristic of fascist propaganda was never its lies, for this is something more or less common to propaganda everywhere and of every time... The essential thing was that they exploited the age-old Occidental prejudice which confuses reality with truth, and made that 'true' which until then could only be stated as a lie.—The Seeds of a Fascist International, Arendt

IT WAS ALL A DREAM

NARRATIVE**MACHINES**

WWW.MODERNMYTHOLOGY.NET

IV. ARTWAR

COMMODIFY YOUR DISSENT

"Every anarchist is a baffled dictator." —Benito Mussolini

E very American seems to want to be a rebel. But it's not entirely clear what that means. Does it take camo- pants? A Che T-shirt? A guitar? A cowboy hat? Is it just doing the opposite of whatever your parents did? "Be an individual, a rebel, innovate," so many advertisements whisper. They'd have us believe that True Revolutionaries think different. They use Apple, or drink Coke. We signal our dissent to one another with the music we listen to and the cars we drive.

There's something peculiar going on here, something elusive and possibly even perverse. In the 1997 book, *Commodify Your Dissent*, Thomas Frank laid out a thesis that may appear common sense to those that have watched or lived in the commodified subcultures of the 90s, 00s, and beyond. A New York Times review comments,

> ... business culture and the counterculture today are essentially one and the same thing. Corporations cleverly employ the slogans and imagery of rebellion to market their products, thereby (a) seizing a language that ever connotes "new" and "different," two key words in marketing, and (b) coaxing the young effortlessly into the capitalist order, where they will be so content with the stylishly packaged and annually updated goods signifying nonconformity they'll never so much as consider real dissent— dissent against what Frank sees as the concentrated economic power of the "Culture Trust," those telecommunications and entertainment giants who, he believes, "fabricate the materials with which the world thinks." To have suffered the calculated pseudo-transgressions of Madonna or Calvin Klein, to have winced at the Nike commercial in which the Beatles' "Revolution" serves as a jingle, is to sense Frank is on to something. (After reading Frank, in fact, you'll have a hard time using words like "revolution" or "rebel" ever again, at least without quotation marks.)

The urge to rebel fuels the same system they ostensibly oppose. Whether it's in arms trade, or less ominously, manners of dress and behavior, there are dollars to be made fighting "The Man." And maybe making money isn't always an altogether bad thing. But it is certainly a complication, especially for those espousing neo-Marxists ideals.

As Guy Debord observed, "revolutionary theory is now the enemy of all revolutionary ideology and knows it." Rebel movements are a counterculture, regardless of what they call themselves.

REBELLION IS COOL

We'll begin with a quintessential icon of the branded, shiny counterculture, the Matrix. We've probably all seen it. Even as an example it's a cliché, and that's part of the point. Here's a framed sketch of the first movie: when it first ran, it was a slick take on the alienation most suburban American Gen Xers felt, packaged within the context of the epistemological skepticism Descartes wrestled with in the 17th century. Taken out of the cubicle and into the underworld, we witness the protagonist "keeping it real" by eating mush, donning co-opted fetish fashion, and fighting an army of identical men in business suits in slow motion.

The movie superimposes the oligarchic and imperialist powers-that-be atop Neo's quest of adolescent self-mastery. A successful piece of marketing —you can be sure no one collecting profits or licensing deals let their misgivings about "the Man" keep them from paying the rent.

This is not to point an accusatory finger, but rather to show the essential dependence of the counterculture upon the mainstream, because countercultures are not self-sustaining, and every culture produces a counter-culture in its shadow, just as every self produces an other. *Any* counterculture. Punk, mod, beatnik, romantic, hippy, psychedelic, straight edge, occult. Even the early adopters of Internet culture started as a group of outsiders that shared a collective vision. In this, we must acknowledge the key part played by the messy collision of table-top games, computer hacking, law enforcement overreach and cyberpunk science fiction by the 1990s,

> On January 17, 1980, FBI agents descended on a small business in Wisconsin to investigate a plot against the life of an American business executive in Beirut, Lebanon, named William Weatherby. The tip came to local law enforcement from a concerned citizen who had chanced on a written description of the conspiracy, which the police duly handed over to the FBI. When investigators arrived at the offices of this company, TSR Hobbies, they learned that William Weatherby did not exist: he was a non-player character in a new espionage role-playing game called Top Secret, which TSR was playtesting. This was easily demonstrated to the satisfaction of all parties, and the whole incident would certainly be forgotten today—except that it inevitably became part of TSR's promotion for Top Secret. It was a spy game so realistic that even the FBI thought it was real. ... The computer enthusiasts who could only dream of an open, global network in 1990 would go on to staff the dot-coms of the next decade. The closed networks that once guarded forbidden knowledge quickly fell by the wayside, and curiosity about computers could no longer be imagined a crime. —"Your Cyberpunk games are dangerous," Boing Boing

Shadow Run, another popular cyberpunk RPGs of the 1990s, presented one of the more seemingly-improbable of cyberpunk futures, where you could play a freelancing mutant scrambling to survive in an ecosystem of headless corporations connected through cyberspace. Sound familiar? The Matrix just represented the final translation of these and similar fringe narratives into the mainstream.

Future vision has some effect on future reality, both in the identities we imagine for ourselves and the technologies we choose to explore. They almost always have unexpected consequences. Now we carry the networked planet in our palms, granting near instant communication with anyone, anywhere and anytime, and our friends aren't always the only one listening.

We shouldn't be surprised by this feedback loop. Without laying the material, mythic, and social groundwork for a new society, counterculture cannot be a bridge; it almost invariably leads back to the mainstream, though not necessarily without first making its mark and pushing some new envelope. This is the way minorities effect the mainstream, but it shouldn't be forgotten whose interests the ultimate appropriation always serves: those with the most power in the first place.

This even presents something of a false dichotomy—that old models of business can't themselves be co-opted by countercultural myths. Yesterday's counterculture is today's mainstream. What better way to understand the so-called revolution of iPads or social media?

Our cultural symbols and signifiers are never static. Psychedelic and straight edge can share the same rack in a store if the store owner can co-brand the fashions, and people can brand themselves "green" through their purchasing power without ever leaving those boxes or worrying about the big picture. AdBuster's "Buy Nothing Day" capitalized on that "rebel dollar."

Rebellion is cool. "Cool" is what customers pay a premium for, along with the comfort of a world with easy definitions and pre-packaged cultural rebellions. This process itself isn't new. The rebel or nonconformist is probably a constitutive feature of the American imagination: original colonies were religious non-conformist, the country was founded by rebellion, the frontier, the civil war, the swinging 20s, Jazz, James Dean, John Wayne, Elvis, the list goes on. The non-conformist imagination is as paradoxically and problematically American as cowboys and indians, apple pie and racism.

The territory between aesthetic and ideals, in social movements is blurry at best. But the most well-known expression of this trend in recent history is the now somewhat idealized 1960s, a clear view of which has been obscured through a haze of pot-smoke and partisan politics. Though this revolution certainly didn't start in the 1960s, there we have one of the clearest instances of what good bed-fellows mass advertising and manufacturing make when branded under the *zeitgeist* of the counterculture. In a sense, the only revolution that lasted was the one that *was* televised. When people bought those hip clothes to make a statement, whose pockets were they lining? It's a revolving door of product tie-ins, and it all feeds on the needs of the individual, embodied in a sub-culture. The moment that psychedelic culture gained a certain momentum, Madison Avenue chewed it up and spit it back out in 7up ads. That interpretation of what it meant to be a hippie, a revolutionary, became an influence on the next generation. The rise of Rolling Stone magazine could also be seen as an example of this—a counterculture upstart turned mainstream institution.

While advertising and counterculture get along just fine, authenticity and profit often make strange bedfellows. But they aren't necessarily diametric opposites, either. As movements gain momentum, they present a market, and markets are essentially agnostic when it comes to ideals.

There are many examples of how troubled that relationship can be. The Grunge movement in the 90s began as a bunch of poor ass kids playing broken ass instruments in the Pacific Northwest. This was the very reason it struck disenfranchised youth—the relationship between those acts and the aging record industry in many ways seemed to reflect the relationship of adolescent Gen Xers with their Boomer parents. They retained that common desire to "drop out," as Timothy Leary had preached to the previous counterculture generation of Laguna Beach and Haight Ashbury, but without the mystical optimism of "tuning in." Hunter S Thompson maybe presaged this transition in that quotation from Fear and Loathing In Las Vegas that's now rendered famous to the kids of 90s thanks to Terry Gilliam's film adaptation,

> We are all wired into a survival trip now. No more of the speed that fueled that 60s. That was the fatal flaw in Tim Leary's trip. He crashed around America selling "consciousness expansion" without ever giving a thought to the grim meat-hook realities that were lying in wait for all the people who took him seriously... All those pathetically eager acid freaks who thought they could buy Peace and Understanding for three bucks a hit. But their loss and failure is ours too. What Leary took down with him was the central illusion of a whole life-style that he helped create... a generation of permanent cripples, failed seekers, who never understood the essential old-mystic fallacy of the Acid Culture: the desperate assumption that somebody... or at least some force —is tending the light at the end of the tunnel.

It's no great stretch to imagine the suddenly-famous bands of the Grunge era as a part of this same legacy. Alice In Chains or Nirvana songs about dying drugged out and alone weren't oracular prophecy, they were journal entry. And it became part of the allure, because it too was "authentic." The greatest irony of all was that the tragic meltdowns and burn outs that followed on fame's heels became part of the commodity. (Not that this vulture economy is new to tabloids).

Our narratives about authentic moments of aesthetic expression or innovation often depict them like volcanic eruptions: they build up and acquire force in subterranean and occluded environments, before erupting in a momentary and spectacular public display. It is telling that this quote from

On The Road has become so popular, very likely cited in the papers and journals of more rebellion-minded American teens than any other from that book, "… The only people for me are the mad ones, the ones who are mad to live, mad to talk, mad to be saved, desirous of everything at the same time, the ones who never yawn or say a commonplace thing, but burn, burn, burn like fabulous yellow roman candles exploding like spiders across the stars."

Hendrix, Joplin, Morrison, Cobain… the 27 Club is big. And quite a few more could be added if it was "the 20-something club." Are the public self-destructions of so many young, creative minds informed by this myth, or do they create it?

Maybe a bit of both. The Spectacle, in the sense Guy Debord uses it, disseminates its sensibilities, styles—a version of the truth. The particular moves ever toward the general, as facts gradually turn to legend and, eventually, myth. Mainstream appropriation is the process in which aesthetic movements affect broader society and culture. The ideals need a pulpit to reach the people, even if invariably it is fitted with guillotines for the early adopters once that message has been heard.

YOUR FATASS DIRTY DOLLAR

"Cultures are virtual realities made of language." –Terence McKenna

Capitalism survives so well, in part, because it adapts to any message. A message is a commodity, or it is obscure. If we instead think counterculture is an ideal that exists somehow apart from plebeian needs like making money, then countercultures will forever hobble itself. It doesn't matter that these ideologies have little in common. It is the fashion or mystique that gets sold. Anti-corporate ideology sells as well as pro-. When all an ideology really boils down to is an easy to replicate aesthetic, how could they not?

Where do we draw the line between idealism and profit? The question is how individuals utilize or leverage the potential energy represented by that currency, and what ends it is applied to. Hard nosed books on business by the old guard, such as Drucker's *Management: Tasks, Responsibilities, Practices* say exactly the same thing, in a less epigrammatic, Yoda-like way: profit is not a motive, it is a means. This much, at least, doesn't change with the changing of the (sub)cultural tides. Within our present economic paradigm, without profit, nothing happens. Game over.

Those who position themselves as extreme radicals within the counter-culture framework just disenfranchise themselves through an act of inept transference, finding anything with a dollar sign on it questionable. To this view, anyone that's made a red cent off of their work is somehow morally bankrupt. This mentality generally ends one way: howling after the piece of meat on the end of someone else's string, working by day for a major corpo-ration, covering their self-loathing at night in tattoos, and body-modifications they can hide. That is, unless they lock themselves in a cave or try to start an agrarian commune. None of this posturing is in any way nec-essary, since business rhetoric itself has long since co-opted the countercultural message. For instance, this passage from *Commodify Your Dissent,*

> Dropping Naked Lunch and picking up Thriving on Chaos, the groundbreaking 1987 management text by Tom Peters, the most popular business writer of the past decade, one finds more philo-sophical similarities than one would expect from two manifestos of, respectively, dissident culture and business culture. If anything, Peters' celebration of disorder is, by virtue of its hard statistics, bleaker and more nightmarish than Burroughs'. For this popular lecturer on such once-blithe topics as competitive-ness and pop psychology there is nothing, absolutely nothing, that is certain. His world is one in which the corporate wisdom of

the past is meaningless, established customs are ridiculous, and "rules" are some sort of curse, a remnant of the foolish fifties that exist to be defied, not obeyed. We live in what Peters calls "A World Turned Upside Down," in which whirl is king and, in order to survive, businesses must eventually embrace Peters' universal solution: "Revolution!"

Growth on its own is never a clear indicator that the underlying ideals of a movement will remain preserved. If history has shown anything, it is that successful movements mutate from ethic to aesthetic, as with most musical scenes and their transition from content to fashion; or reverse polarity, so that core of collective identity is so emphasized that the meaning within is lost to literalism, as we can see in the history of the world's major monotheist religions, though it is not a cultural trend specific to only religion. One version of early Christian Gnostic history—of "love thy neighbor," "all is one," and scurrilous rumors of agape orgies—were replaced by the Roman Orthodoxy and the authority provided through the ultimate union of State and Religion. The hippies traded in their sandals and beat up VWs for SUVs and overpriced Birkenstocks. The counter-history of Communism when viewed against the backdrop of Marxist ideals is perhaps equally insightful.

Enantiodromia, the tendency of things to turn into their opposites, is as much sociological observation as psychological. It oftentimes seems that succeeding too well can be the greatest curse to befall a movement. When the pendulum swings far in one direction, it often turns into its opposite without having the common decency to wait to swing back the other way.

As we've seen, this was part of the supposed downfall of counterculture in capitalism: "suits" decided they could deconstruct an organic process and manufacture it. They could own it from the ground up.

But this isn't necessarily so. The branding of projects such as Cirque Du Soleil points toward a third option—arts movements will be dissected in the jargon of marketing, and they must succeed on those grounds to be taken seriously or accomplish anything. But the question for the artist is to what end? Art can and should use the methods of propaganda to spread itself. Artists need to be cultural scavengers, using whatever tools are at hand to attain their goals.

Burning Man isn't suddenly opening its gates to the wealthy. Yacht Communism has been a part of that movement ever since it gained some mainstream appeal, likely before. Seen as an arts and cultural movement, it has been vastly successful. Seen as an example of how to create a true egalitarian society, it would be an utter failure. But that was never the point. Two weeks at Burning Man might be fun, even transformative, but spend two years there and you'd find out what hell is like.

The ideals of various vibrant (if generally short-lived) countercultures seem to have much in common with one another, independent of the markets they depend on to survive—unfettered self-expression, freedom from externally imposed social boundaries, irreverent humor, an element of egalitarianism mixed liberally with pirate capitalism, maybe even a sense of pragmatic community.

The future of a counterculture is either obsolescence, to be co-opted, or to manage to outrun the transition from one to the other, if you can manage to surf that edge, and don't mind living on the fringe forever, while those behind you cash in.

We could quibble about the details, but that'd only distract from the war zone of ideology that rages from one culture of rebellion to the next. This is a conundrum. History shows that these ideals are often lost or at least utterly transformed in such movements as soon as they gain a true pulpit.

But it is also those ideals that can live to fight another day.

WE ARE THE PRODUCT

> The original meaning of the word "prestige" was an illusion or conjuring trick, from the Latin praestigium—a delusion. The delusion is in ever-deferred promises of personal betterment through acquisition. It's there in advertising campaigns that use the radicalism of a previous era in order to market the products of today—the absorption of transgression and dissidence into just more categories of consumer values. "Because you're special." "Because you're worth it." Aspiration is the sense of dislocation between our present state and what we hope will make life easier, more tolerable. To close this gap, we play roles that might help us feel we are living a more ideal life. We might close that gap with a hobby, the way we present ourselves on social media, a way of dressing, or in the food we eat. Pretentiousness defines a degree of dislocation between our circumstances and the image we are trying to project. —"In Defense of Pretentiousness", The Guardian

Countercultures can accomplish a great deal of good as a counterbalance of the mainstream. But this ends at the water's edge. Fringe and niche markets demonstrate how this tends to go. As demand for organic products grows, companies will meet that demand. Though the proliferation of yoga, organic food, specialty food products, high quality imports, the artisanal and local food movements and the like are being supplied to an increasing degree by the "evil empire," it is often argued that these are a sign that consumers have much more power in their hands than they realize. Change the world with your "green dollar." In fact, within a market framework, this power only stretches so far as the paradigm which supports it. And it costs a lot of money to be ethical these days.

Zizek's criticism that this "Starbucks activism" approach doesn't engender real change is a legitimate one. The movie "Czech Dream" by Vít Klusák and Filip Remunda also explored this quandary of identity and value,

> Two students from the Czech Film Academy commission a leading advertising agency to organize a huge campaign for the opening of a new supermarket named Czech Dream. The advertising campaign includes radio and television ads, posters, flyers with photos of fake Czech Dream products, a promotional song, an internet site, and ads in newspapers and magazines. Will people believe in it and show up for the grand opening?

They wait in long lines with such excitement for the grand opening, but it is a facade. It's just the surface of a store, with no content inside. The surface is the thing, and the value is in the illusion that serves the interests of profit and unmitigated "progress" at any cost, so long as that cost is not felt in the boardroom. Ethical value is not to be seen in the message, but rather in its social effects. Until we see the actual force and effect of a message, and unless we actually understand its intent, it remains morally ambiguous.

Products themselves have become secondary, as symbols have overtaken the things they symbolized. "Fight Club" parodied this tendency as the "Ikea nesting impulse."

This is a challenge of modern life, but it's hardly a singular observation. Guy Debord's *Society of The Spectacle*, now a standard text amongst neo-Marxists and counterculturists alike, deals with this matter in nearly aphoristic style,

> The first phase of the domination of the economy over social life brought into the definition of all human realization the obvious degradation of being into having. The present phase of total occupation of social life by the accumulated results of the economy leads to a generalized sliding of having into appearing, from which all actual "having" must draw its immediate prestige and its ultimate function. At the same time all individual reality has become social reality directly dependent on social power and shaped by it. It is allowed to appear only to the extent that it is not.

We live in a culture where symbols of success matters more than the things they represent, and so it is little surprise that we may have a hard time actually making this distinction. We are what we seem. When Ludwig Feuerbach wrote the introduction to the 2nd edition of his *The Essence of Christianity*, he was speaking to Hegel and Marx's world, the rapidly industrializing 19th century. But he may as well have been speaking of the present, "But certainly for the present age, which prefers the sign to the thing signified, the copy to the original, fancy to reality, the appearance to the essence ... illusion only is sacred, truth profane."

The sports car, the expensive watch, the designer suit are all, from a functionalist perspective, equally or even less valuable than items half their cost. Though luxury items such as these are said to cost more because of increased craftsmanship—which may well be true—the customer is still buying them because they are symbols of wealth and success. To have either of these on their own is not enough; the symbols are of greater value. We are performing wealth at one another.

Though this seems harmless enough in itself, a common indulgence of the upper class, it is the same mis-match of value (weighing the symbol over what is represented) that characterizes the ennui of our lives. Nihilist Arby's quite simply wouldn't make sense as a joke if we didn't grasp this on an implicit level.

As eluded to in the previous section, the social dynamics of "have" and "have not" polarize—and thereby power the ecology of an identity-driven economy. Vast inequalities and the asymmetrical power structures that results have been a nearly universal blight on the quality of individual human lives. But that doesn't mean it doesn't serve a social function.

In Capitalism, this inequality is not an unfortunate by-product, it is an essential constituent. What American doesn't hope they too might one day be rich, or famous? How many in the American working class want to go to their tedious job every day without that dream of success to keep them going? These hopes are the carrot, and crushing debt is the stick.

Nor is it just wealth that we perform in this way. Our identities are a sort of curated consumption. Otherwise, how could Facebook and Google analyze your online behavior—your "likes" and purchases, the books and movies you consume, who you talk to and what about—to create profiles that are of any value to marketers? (And the government.)

This is a fairly common observation amongst cultural analysts and theorists like Zizek and Debord, but the connection to countercultural is rarely made. Countercultural identity plays perfectly into this engine. It is a part of it, especially for youth culture. Here too, we are performing for one another, it's just that the currency is changed. Rather than sports car or diamonds as symbol of success, we have fashion symbols of rebellious identity. As counterculture scenes grow and enter the marketplace, they grow ever-readily defined, simplified, commodified, and ultimately made replaceable.

The signifiers of a culture that can be commodified are ultimately all dead shells. Yet it is reductionist to imply that aesthetic or fashion-based signifiers are therefore empty and can't transmit vibrant ideas.

Rather, the implication is that these signifiers of identity—and the styles, genres, etc. that go along with them—are constantly undergoing a process of invigoration, appropriation, and death, until they can be re-appropriated into yet another vintage mashup. The rate of this process continues to speed up, almost as an obvious corollary of the rates of media and other exchange. We've, of course, reached peak "personal brand." But even if the phrase has jumped the shark, we still do it, curating and culling our digital personalities to match the labels we want to affiliate with, signaling our subcultural milieu in increasingly self-referential ways.

Ancient religious texts were often composed to distinguish between the charlatan and the true. The Didache warns against "false prophets" who prophesy for money, and Buddhist writing has frequently addressed a similar problem among exploitative monks. Total commodification is something like a necessary consequence of total skepticism, or of refusing all distinction between the fungible and precious, the extraordinary and the banal, or the sacred and secular.

How can we decrease the "commodification of empty signifiers"? We can continue to build spaces, both virtual and material, that can be utilized by people who share common goals. We can avoid over-identification with easy to replicate symbols of identity. Our interests and digital footprint aren't who we are. Don't let your identity become a commodity. Don't let yourself be encapsulated by simple data points. Learn critical thinking but be just as wary of anti-authoritarianism as authoritarianism. Our job as artists, above all others, is to confound expectations. We mustn't let the map of our identities—personal, social, or political—become the territory. But the border skirmishes on that map are never ending.

The mixed countercultures of the future are always already being born and remaking themselves.

> We're suckers for simplistic, captivating pictures, mostly because we don't even realize that we're being sold a "frame"; we think we're just seeing "the way things are," when, in fact, we are buying into a paradigm. That's why, all too often, while trying to talk our way out of a problem we only dig deeper holes.
>
> ... Now imagine the picture holding us captive is a conceptual map that carves up the boundaries of ideas and disciplines, charting the course of intellectual history. A faulty map is the kind of captivating picture that is bound to mislead us. In that case what we'd need is a therapeutic cartography.— "A Therapeutic Cartography," Los Angeles Review of Books

Simple narratives help us make sense of the world, but also hem us in, this limiting process is what situates us within a conceptual domain. Our minds, our selves, do not end with us. We sprawl outwards, nearly touching at all the points our mythemes overlap.

AUTHENTIC SUPERFICIALITY

We have an odd relationship with the things that we buy—both through and with our iPhones and cars, and soon enough, our sex robots. More broadly, we identify ourselves and each other through the consumer choices we make, or even the ones we don't make. This is often called signaling, and it's an important part of nonverbal and implicit social communication. That's what the lifestyle brand is all about—integrating consumer choice with our lives, becoming grinning robots in some Orwellian-hellscape dumpster fire, and so forth.

Thankfully that's not entirely how it plays out. Theories about the pervasiveness of brands and media brainwashing fall short of reality. Nothing is quite so simple as the behaviorist "image in, behavior out." We may signal our queerness or our religion through what we wear and buy, but that isn't all we are. We still have inner lives, and an experience that can't enter into this marketplace, and our identities and beliefs are shifting landscapes more than fixed, binary wastelands. The complexity of the real world can also save us from the simple rigidity, the certain "thusness" of our stories.

The idea of *qualia* refers to the irreducibility of this inner life. The world of surfaces may be superficial, but there may be something lurking somehow beneath all of that, that's somehow authentic. Erwin Schrödinger, creator of the famous living/dead cat thought experiment, said the following in "What is life?: The Physical Aspects Of The Living Cell",

> The sensation of color cannot be accounted for by the physicist's objective picture of light-waves. Could the physiologist account for it, if he had fuller knowledge than he has of the processes in the retina and the nervous processes set up by them in the optical nerve bundles and in the brain? I do not think so.

But this way also points toward reductive either-ors. If we're going to distinguish between the commodifiable "dead shells" referred to in the previous section and some kind of deep seated, internal identity, what is that identity? How do we know it's authentic? We are wandering dangerously close to a schema of the false and replaceable versus the fixed and true, which is always the point at which the poets are banished (or jailed). This has become a common sense distinction for most of us: surface and interior. Fake hipsters, and real trendsetters, patriots and traitors. But the distinction itself is superficial.

To refer back to section 1, there is an absence of the sacred that seems to penetrate secular society, this mad scrambling for something to pledge our allegiance to. It is through an internal paradox within our culture that the profane has become the sacred in a significant way—the movie star, the porn star, the rock star—that even in the artifice of propaganda we can find the keys to divinity. It is in this intermediary zone that the sacred can still occur for us, which may be the crypto-Dionysian appeal of festival cultures.

Another way of contrasting the idea of real and false self, the figurative and literal, is through mimesis. Here we must challenge the tyranny of the literal,

> In 'Realism,' the opening chapter of J.M. Coetzee's most recent novel Elizabeth Costello, the eponymous heroine, a successful Australian novelist, gives a speech in which she ironically likens herself to a talking ape from a short story by Franz Kafka. The story's ambiguities lead her to reflect on this historical loss of certainty, the way it seems to have undone the very possibility of direct communication and unproblematic representation. There was, she argues, 'a time when we knew':

> We used to believe that when the text said, 'On the table stood a glass of water,' there was indeed a table, and a glass of water on it, and we had only to look in the word-mirror of the text to see them. But all that has ended. The word-mirror is broken irreparably, it seems. ... There used to be a time, we believe, when we could say who we were. Now we are just performers speaking our parts. The bottom has dropped out.

> Her speech is not well received. Elizabeth Costello spends most of Coetzee's novel acting the role of a celebrity writer. She travels the world making appearances, delivering lectures, fielding questions about the meanings and motivations behind her writing. It is not something she enjoys. Often her appearances do not run smoothly; her ideas tend to provoke dissent and dissatisfaction. ... The audience wants literal confession; but Costello's aim is to keep 'her true self safe.' Or so her son John believes; for Costello the issue cuts deeper than this. She has come to doubt the very existence of such a thing as a 'true self.' The word-mirror is irreparably broken, yet she is compelled to appear before an audience. Inevitably, what she presents them is 'an image, false, like all images.'

So, we are drawn to question the authenticity of *both* surfaces and interiors. Immanence is a recognition that everything manifest is surface. There is nothing else, and so, the myth-mirror itself becomes the closest that we have to any kind of certainty—as the image and its reflection can both be called into question, and it is the symbol that both depend on if we are to construct a narrative of meaning. Thus, all domains are conceptual maps, the outer and inner one and the same, even the inscrutable, uncertain, and ultimately implicit world of *qualia*—of dreams, of delusions...

A MAP OF OUR SELVES

We have to contend with tension between surface and interior, and amongst all the principalities thereof. Many of us struggle against these seemingly geological forces, without even knowing what we're struggling against.

The self and society as landscape is a frame suggested by Structuralism, and later by post-structuralism when written in relief. Both position history as structure composed of geological flow rather than events; this was done, in terms of the latter, because the very structures imposed by theory could reify imperialist "grand narratives."[66]

The tension of surface appearance against deeper identity, and the constant anxiety that there is such a thing as a central or deep identity, drives the tectonic forces between what we'll refer to later as cultural borderlands and centers. We needn't know which is authentic, but merely recognize the tensions between these principalities. This might still seem a baroque metaphor, even if it's far from unprecedented in the social sciences, but it's nevertheless apt. Dynamism in the self or the state arises from difference, conflict from too sudden changes; often arising where one identity abuts another, and all are also ever changing.

This is borrowing from the frequent use of geological and even carto-graphic metaphor in such works. These metaphors are essentially impersonal, even when they refer to parts of personal psychology. For this reason, they have been vastly preferred within post/structural analysis, over the earlier *mythopoeia* of Freud or Jung, for instance, which paints all inner experience as personal, in reaction to a mythologized external world.

As we've seen, *A Thousand Years of Nonlinear History* is possibly the penultimate example of this sort of device. In fact, the entire book is con-structed as a series of geological, biological, physical-psychological-historical metaphors (even if he is insistent that it is not a metaphor but rather an "engineering diagram"),

> We live in a world populated by structures—a complex mixture of geological, biological, social, and linguistic constructions that are nothing but accumulations of materials shaped and hardened by history. Immersed as we are in this mixture, we cannot help but interact in a variety of ways with the other historical constructions that surround us, and in these interactions we

---

[66] This was the fundamental observation of structuralism. Whether that narrative is "fiction" or "non-fiction," it is a narrative, with underlying literary structure. Post-structuralism attempted to move beyond the limitations and power structures of single or hierarchical perspectives implicit in such narratives through decentering, the multiplicity of "lived experience," conflicting or divergent narratives—the problem of "truths" that don't agree—and even hyperbolic critique, but this approach too reaches a limit, and beyond that limit it has exhausted itself. The excess of structuralist thought lies in thinking that, this being the case, the entire world itself can be reduced to concrete language and meta-language.

generate novel combinations, some of which possess emergent properties. In turn, these synergistic combinations, whether of human origin or not, become the raw material for further mixtures. This is how the population of structures inhabiting our planet has acquired its rich variety, as the entry of novel materials into the mix triggers wild proliferations of new forms. ...

And so on. It's important to recognize that all the structures on these maps ebb and flow, empires rise and fall more less the same as colonies of coral might. More prosaically, just as one might stand on the Pacific rim and hundreds of millions of years later, they might spy a new continent on the horizon, a 19th century American Republican might find more in common with many of today's Democrats. Our labels are not what ultimately defines us. Nothing is fixed. Baudrillard tried to take us further than this in the 1980s, though many were not yet ready to hear it,

> Today abstraction is no longer that of the map, the double, the mirror, or the concept. Simulation is no longer that of territory, a referential being, or a substance. It is the generation by models of a real without origin or reality: a hyperreal. The territory no longer precedes the map, nor does it survive it. —Simulacra and Simulation

A map does not provide a certificate of authenticity—as so many counterculturists are bound to point out, "the map is not the territory." Without it, we can't begin to track our way out of the shifting hinterlands. We cannot properly understand society, or ourselves, until we've charted the surfaces of our own hyperreal, symbolic fault line. But we mustn't find ourselves limited by the names, labels, and borders that happen to be written in to describe this fleeting moment, as now the best maps are constantly being updated, revised, shuffled and re-ordered.

BORDER ZONES AND CENTERS

It is undeniable that there has been cultural value in a fringe, in an underground, in the paradox of an anarchist community. Even in a concrete way, such ever-changing, forward thinking movements provide something valuable that any so-called mainstream culture at large could not do without—they challenge the status quo, they bring in new ideas from the outside and most importantly, they create and adapt new myths that can invigorate a society, until those messages too have become outmoded,

> The unknown quality of the "other side of the border or frontier" simultaneously generates curiosity, promise, threat, and fear. It is this combination of reactions brought on by approaching unknown and often uncontrolled territory, peoples, or ideas that is the key difference between frontiers and borderlands on the one hand and a border or boundary in the conventional sense on the other. ... The combination of mystery and danger accompanied by promise and curiosity seems to be at the root of the popularity of the use of frontier (and less frequently borderlands) as a metaphor. —"Borderlands Borders and Global Frontiers—Borderlands And Frontiers As Metaphors"

Thus, rather than counterculture and mainstream, a better model for this relationship might be border zones and urban centers. Not that such maps are always quite what they seem. Those that just don't fit in, the underclass or outcast, those of the periphery, the counter-culture, serve a contradictory centralizing force,

> Peripheries are often border zones where peoples or things are thrown into unexpected contact, hybrid spaces yielding new possibilities for social and cultural organization.
>
> Think of the musical genres, poetic innovations, and linguistic creoles of the Caribbean; or think of the social "margins" or the "queer periphery," where disenfranchisement and stigmatization give rise to relatively free experimentation in social practices and cultural life. Though centers may seem more advanced or more privileged than peripheries, decisive change and innovation often begin at the fringes. Yet the very tendency toward difference and transformation out on the margins often meets with a violent reimposition of norms from the center: Soviet tanks rolling into Prague, or the Janjaweed and Sudanese military sweeping through Darfur, or the police descending on Stonewall. —Penn Humanities Forum

There must be a place where this deviant power can serve its role as alchemical catalyst, without fearing a backlash from those who would be the center; after all it is often the demigod who descends to the underworld that doesn't want the keys to the kingdom. "You can have it!" they cry, but the dispossessed nevertheless seek solace in the company of other "beings of both worlds". A less metaphysical formulation is available in many places, and it is a perspective that can be put to nearly any use. It is a concept, for instance, that has frequently appeared in the context of the New Right. Dugin utilizes it as a metaphor in his *4th Political Theory*, and in an interview with Le Monde, Alain de Benoist said,

> The ideas of "Right" and "Left" are no longer pertinent when it is a question of describing the content of major works appearing today. As far as the realm of ideas and the work of thought go, the Left-Right paradigm seems increasingly to have been replaced by a break between the "center" and the "periphery." The former corresponds to a dominant ideology which is to legitimate the market system and the latter includes all those who, no matter what their own itinerary, challenge the axiomatic content of interest and blend of economism, productivism and utilitarianism to which liberal society has led. Fruitful dialogues are possible in this "periphery."

So the virtue of the periphery needs to be balanced against statements in this Guardian piece adapted from *Black Earth*,

> The Nazis knew that they had to go abroad and lay waste to neighbouring societies before they could hope to bring their revolution to their own. Not only the Holocaust, but all major German crimes took place in areas where state institutions had been destroyed, dismantled or seriously compromised. The German murder of five and a half million Jews, more than three million Soviet prisoners of war, and about a million civilians in so-called anti-partisan operations all took place in stateless zones.

This observation is no less viable than the characterization of border zones as a habitat for free and creative exchange. Certainly, stateless and border zones can be host to atrocity as well as freedom. As Carl Sagan observes in the Cosmos episode "The Backbone of Night," far away from the centers of civilization, many ideas could grow and cross-pollinate that may not have taken hold in any of those centers. Without this creative freedom, he surmises, the scientific revolution may not have even happened. At the least, it wouldn't have been there and then, in ancient Ionia.

But the relative lawlessness of border zones like the Barbadian aisles also gives rise to piracy—to which we must make a strong distinction between flouting copyright law, and literal rape and pillage—and served as a staging ground for slavery. Pirates may have become popularized by Disney movies, but they aren't exactly exemplars of the best in humanity.

In a virtual setting, the dichotomy remains nevertheless equally real,

> Like the pirate republics of the 18th century, this virtual underworld mingles liberty and vice. Law enforcement and copyright-protection groups such as the Digital Citizens' Alliance in Washington, DC, prefer to emphasize the most sordid aspects of Tor's hidden services—the sellers of drugs, weapons and child pornog-

raphy. And yet the effort to create a hidden internet was driven by ideology as much as avarice. The network is used by dissidents as well as dope-peddlers. If you live under an authoritarian regime, Tor provides you with a ready-made technology for evading government controls on the internet. —"The Dark Leviathan," Aeon.

This conflicted legacy allows us to return to that old argument about the nature of the State and humanity, between Hobbes, who claimed in *The Leviathan* that humans are essentially evil and need the state to keep us in line, and Rousseau, who claimed humans are essentially good in nature when left free, and are corrupted by the state. This much we know for certain: the State is formed of factions and principalities (no matter how they're codified) much as the Self is. Invariably, the ways we look at human nature seem to presage our views of the state, and vice versa.

It's as of yet unclear in the final reckoning if this is an entirely valid equivalence. Scientific study of how we work from the vantage point of social networks is advancing rapidly, but without working out the broader implications. Other interesting corollaries can be drawn between research of networks, and its implications for topological metaphors. For instance, in research done by Damon Centola in 2015 at the University of Pennsylvania, it's been indicated that,

> ...breaking down group boundaries to increase the spread of knowledge across populations may ultimately result in less-effective knowledge sharing. Instead, his research shows that best practices and complex ideas are more readily integrated across populations if some degree of group boundaries is preserved.

This seems to point toward the importance of a "geography" that includes multiple centers and peripheries, rather than utopian removal of all cultural signaling, or authoritarian emphasis of mass identity. We might in the future extend these metaphor to distinguish the different layers (e.g. igneous, sedimentary, metamorphic), or processes (e.g. weathering, earthquakes and volcanism), that exist in any particular society. What's important is that we can apply these metaphors as a kind of thought-tool to make descriptive distinctions about individuals, who as a mass would otherwise be an amorphous blob, that we at best carve up along antiquated prescriptivist and essentialist notions of nation or ideology.

BRANDING A MOVEMENT

The patron saints of the countercultural idea are, of course, the Beats, whose frenzied style and merry alienation still maintain a powerful grip on the American imagination. Even forty years after the publication of On the Road, the works of Kerouac, Ginsberg, and Burroughs remain the sine qua non of dissidence, the model for aspiring poets, rock stars, or indeed anyone who feels vaguely artistic or alienated. That frenzied sensibility of pure experience, life on the edge, immediate gratification, and total freedom from moral restraint, which the Beats first propounded back in those heady days when suddenly everyone could have their own TV and powerful V-8, has stuck with us through all the intervening years and become something of a permanent American style... The Gap may have since claimed Ginsberg and USA Today may run feature stories about the brilliance of the beloved Kerouac, but the rebel race continues today regardless, with ever-heightening shit-references calculated to scare Jesse Helms, talk about sex and smack that is supposed to bring the electricity of real life, and ever-more determined defiance of the repressive rules and mores of the American 1950s—rules and mores that by now we know only from movies. —Commodify Your Dissent, The Baffler

The myth of the artist as unique and individual creator, slaving away in solitude is romantic, but it doesn't square with history. Nevertheless, it seems to be this myth that inspired Kerouac, in part, to try to write in a secluded cabin at Big Sur. But this conflict underwrites the book written there. It doesn't make a whole lot of sense for a movement to happen in a hermitage.

It is true that the unique perspective of irreverent outsiders is part of what gives countercultures like the Beats their teeth. American cultural "revolutionaries" listen to their experience, everything else be damned. But the necessary compromise comes in learning how to play well with others without putting a pair of scissors in their eye. Art is not a solitary endeavor. No one "makes" it alone, no one is truly "self made." You'd best believe every lone cultural figure that's become a success had friends or collaborators you never heard of that helped spread a message that became immortal.

The very myth of there being a particular movement, such as the Beats, is a kind of sleight of hand. Like a corporate entity or any other egregore, this movement develops a brand identity by virtue of its motility and dispersion. Love them or hate them, you probably know about the Beats as a concept. It's become ubiquitous—in modern parlance, "viral". Most people aware of American art or literature have at least a vague sense of what the Beats were.

Yet here were separate artists, living separate lives. Sure, they may have been friends, and they influenced one another. But this idea of "the Beats," that was effective branding—regardless of the history, or how the mytheme perpetuated itself. It may be coined intentionally, announced with manifestos and a movement, as André Breton did with Surrealism, or it can happen later, a convention for the benefit of journalists that need to name something, as seems to have been the case with Gonzo. Retroactive or intentional, the effect is the same.

From this melting pot of experience, personality, and social context, a group identity forms. It might do more recent would-be underground movements some good to remember that if you do everything else right, and have a cohesive community of vital people who have the means to produce their work, this happens almost all on its own. You needn't brand before you have an identity.

A movement is an ideal which holds the lure of total freedom, a sweet taste that often quickly sours on the tongue, which is nevertheless integral, and indispensable to the creative spirit. Like any good myth, or art itself, there's cultural value in it, and there is a kind of truth in it, even if it is also a lie in a literal sense—as Pablo Picasso said, "Art is a lie that makes us realize truth at least the truth that is given us to understand. The artist must know the manner whereby to convince others of the truthfulness of his lies." A movement is, at best, just such a lie.

So many bookshelves are littered with books—mostly unread—which were purchased because of the allure of the author's persona. The personal myths of a movement's personalities, of its members, help to solidify the identity of movement; for example, the anecdotes about Burroughs, Kerouac, Ginsberg, and so on, which also helps perpetuate the myth of the movement as a whole. This isn't to say that "William Tell routine"—the stories around the death of Burroughs' wife that underwrites the movie biographization of *Naked Lunch*—did or didn't happen, but as it moves into the realm of myth, it ceases to matter. The greater your success as an artist, the less your actual life, even your work, matters. A movement is a game of whisper down the lane.

It's been observed in numerous places that Hunter S. Thompson drew a similar inference, from the Faulknerian "fiction is the best fact." If we look at Gonzo, Hunter S. Thompson was also well aware of the myth-building necessary to have any kind of success as a writer, even if the caricature or double that he created in many ways became a cage. Personality often brands a movement, and defines what the movement comes to mean in the public imagination.

> I'm never sure which one people expect me to be. Very often, they conflict—most often, as a matter of fact. ...I'm leading a normal life and right along side me there is this myth, and it is growing and mushrooming and getting more and more warped. When I get invited to, say, speak at universities, I'm not sure if they are inviting Duke or Thompson. I'm not sure who to be.—Hunter S. Thompson, 1978 BBC documentary

Finally, there is the individual works themselves—books, paintings, movies, comics, sculptures—unique for each artist or group of collaborators, but which would in no way exist without the myth and untold reality that lurks behind it, people living, growing, arguing, fucking, and ultimately dissipating and dying as they did. But you'll notice that in the context of movements, the actual art is mentioned last. This isn't incidental.

APPROPRIATION AND ASYMMETRICAL POWER

Lack of originality is often a challenge lobbed at the Beats, from critics and eventually the general public, once it was no longer protected by the aura of cool. But that criticism misses the point. The Beats openly appropriated inspiration from bebop, from Buddhism—which was seeing a new, if still very muted, popularity in the West—and from other cultures and political ideas at that time. None of it was "original" in that sense, but the melange was, for better or worse, unique. Even the ways Buddhism and bebop were both decontextualized and re-interpreted as free-wheeling riffing rather than structured disciplines created new versions of them in the public imagination.[67]

The vitality of a message, its ability to strike the heart or the mind and wring things out of us we didn't even know we had in us, often speaks louder than being the first to play that rhythm. The employed techniques, the medium—even the components themselves could have been used a thousand times before. So what? The atoms that make up a tsetse fly or an orangutan aren't after all so different.

This is equally true in business, where the innovators take something that's being done, and figure out how to amplify, to do it better, or more efficiently. Attempts at complete originality usually result in useless and often downright bizarre gizmos that at the end of the day do several incompatible things poorly and nothing well. "No one thought of it before" doesn't necessarily mean it's a good idea.

The art of the collage, montage, bricolage, DJing, "mashups", and the like demonstrate what we all do as thinkers, as painters, as poets, or even as scientists. The message of the collage approach is clear enough: do not be afraid to show and honor your influences, and at the same time, don't be afraid to break those idols or re-use them in unforeseen ways. Once all norms or exemplars are cast off, innovation ceases, and we are left with sheer monotony, a kind of aperionic echo-chamber of vacant and meaningless variety. One of the keys to Bowie's enduring success was that he recognized this implicitly, and his ruminations and early ventures into the Internet in the 1990s remain a touchstone for anyone who seeks to use the medium for creative purpose.

This has conflicting implications for the intersection of media and copyright law, as people increasingly think of the Internet as the new Commons. Though this narrative arc has moved increasingly in corporate interest, as we see the progression from Napster to Torrents to the gradual erosion of Net neutrality. Information wants to be free, on one hand, and free informa-

---

[67] There's a certain dishonesty in portraying Western ontology with an Eastern aesthetic as representative of Eastern spirituality. But as a syncretic creation, it's not a far cry from the English propensity for linguistic theft.

tion doesn't butter any parsnips on the other. This falls in that category of unexpected consequences. Whether it's good, bad, or more likely both, the dichotomies of the virtual/irl are the sandbox that future creative movements are going to be playing in.

Artists appropriate. Nearly every artist we know of has acquired and adapted and remixed other sources. Austin Kleon's book *Steal Like An Artist* deals with this in a practical manner. Kleon states throughout the book that, "nothing is original... all creative work builds on what came before." Art is always a morally ambiguous process. Ethics in this regard is a different question than utility, let alone aesthetic value, and may not, matter all that much in the final summation from the perspective of an artist, aside from the court of public opinion. This was the root of Kierkegaard's anxiety in *Either/Or*. The aesthetic sin is not to steal, but to steal poorly. In the process, hopefully that material is filtered through one mind, one history, one style, so that the result is something new. Although for some artists, like John Cage, removal of authorial intention became the goal. Yet even then, we remember the myth of the artist. The intentional erasure of the author defines them in those empty spaces. There's no escaping style. No one can tell your story the way you can. Our stories are also never truly our own.

The street art habit of "tagging", painting a signature in public spaces is in a sense the quintessential artistic act—it all amounts to staking your momentary claim on eternity with hand prints on the cave wall, or dicks scribbled atop the Mona Lisa. Duchamp's "Fountain"—which was inarguably a urinal—is arguably art because it was placed in a gallery with his name beside it. It's an attack on the centralized power of the art world to sanctify art as product, more than comment on artistic merit. But nevertheless it has come to be seen as the stock example of the hubris of modern art, of "anything can be art," or "I'm an artist because I stole this urinal." As Hunter S. Thompson said in an interview with the Atlantic Online in 1997,

> Yeah, it's a validation process. Faulkner said that American troops wrote "Kilroy was here" on the walls of Europe in World War II in order to prove that somebody had been there—"I was here"—and that the whole history of man is just an effort by people, writers, to just write your name on the great wall.

We can go a step further. Misunderstanding and appropriation can be a great method for cultural creation. Think misunderstood Chinese philosophy and German Idealism, American Transcendentalism or The Beats. Schopenhauer's misinterpretation of Buddhism, or Nietzsche's, or Bowie's appropriation of Kabuki or queer culture, all change what they are by inventing a new double.[68] They make a unique creature—constructed par-

---

[68] Though it's worth mentioning that there are thousands if not millions of diverse "Buddhisms" within even any traditional cultural source, and in these cases two, appropriation, misunderstanding, and power dynamics are factors in what those distinctions are.

tially by way of misunderstanding and category mismatch. The creative process is never *ex nihilo*, and it would do us well to actually recognize that.

Though there is a continuum of authenticity, at best it approaches the limit without ever reaching it, for no one truly owns a culture. Where we criticize for appropriation and lack of originality, we should instead scrutinize hierarchies of power. Appropriation doesn't cause asymmetrical power structures to exist, though it can mirror it, since social power gives some greater means to plunder than others. That may sound like an abstract distinction but its repercussions are dead literal.

The same power structures exist in countercultural societies as anywhere else, they just map differently. Many criticisms have been lodged over the years—Kerouac's misogyny and alcoholism, Ginsberg's expressed fondness for young boys, Burroughs' romance with guns and heroin (and young boys). Maybe some of the disappointment is in the expectations that counterculture is somehow supposed to transcend the norm.

To the extent that these criticisms are valid, they point toward a larger fact. As clear as it is that new art and culture can be created through appropriation, we do not make ourselves anew in this transformation. Sexism, racism, and so on don't disappear within a countercultural setting. They are just carved in relief, through embracing "deviant" aesthetics, as homosexuality was at the time. But the underlying power structures remain. This is the problem, not de facto appropriation, and it is a key reasons we selected the Beats as an example of movement—not because it bears emulation, but because it offers itself up so readily to this critique.

Power structures in America have long lent themselves to the benefit of white men, a fictional group identity who have allowed elites of that class to the upper hand in what labor and property they can borrow, adapt, or outright "discover." (Media industry speak for "plunder.") That bears scrutiny, though it won't be fixed by refusing to explore outside the milieu of our upbringing. These separate issues have grown over and atop one another in the public dialog. Critique of power is always needed—but we should make a distinction here between method, history and intent. Pluralism and multiculturalism is anathema to the separatism of monocultures vying for hegemony, and mainstream liberal rhetoric about appropriation as a form of moralizing, especially bare of an emphasis on power rather than ownership of ideas, is completely off the rails.

Yet it is true that the histories that we write of Beats or famous thinkers disproportionately emphasizes those that social power centralizes. This is a call for ever expanding "niche markets", which will invariably still benefit those with the power to leverage it.

Structures of power don't change with a new paint job. Doubling down on antiquated concepts of intellectual property, or blanket ideas of cultural ownership, won't ultimately help anyone except corporations.

What can be done? It almost seems that such things can only happen blindly, naturally, like bees pollinating flowers. We can build systems that re-enforce some instincts more than others, and we can do it without being defined by the labels that people want to define us with. This is the manner of myth—the explicit story is false, yet the implicit assumptions it's based on tells a truth about the speaker that they aren't even aware of. The ways we narrativize movements is telling. The Beat and Hippie movements hoped that primal territorial and ideological conflicts, wanton greed and corruption, were some sort of prolonged hold-back rather than the results of an underlying structural reality. The Beats were cynical where the Hippies were optimistic, but both movements were founded on a kind of naive romanticism, that dropping out might lead to redemption.

We may be better off erecting our tent cities of the mind rather than all clustering about the same crumbling museum.

INTERLOPERS

So long as these movements have fuel, they'll have the attention of the powers that be, business and government both. People will come in and out, and others might wonder at interlopers or heaven forbid, moles. Any glance at FBI and CIA history with fringe groups explains the context of this paranoia. They had a file on Jefferson Airplane of all things. And just because you're paranoid doesn't mean they're not out to get you.

The role dictatorships have played in silencing creative voices is well known—the first revolutionary act in such cases can merely be speaking your mind. But the role of expression in pluralist societies is far more complex than simple ideals of free speech might have us believe. What about the state covertly using the arts to broadcast messages to its enemies abroad?

> ... no one would think to add Abstract Expressionist painting to a list that includes fast food and Walt Disney products. Nevertheless, the work of such artists as Jackson Pollock, Mark Rothko, and Willem de Kooning wound up as part of a secret CIA program during the height of the Cold War, aimed at promoting American ideals abroad. The artists themselves were completely unaware that their work was being used as propaganda. On what agents called a "long leash," they participated in several exhibitions secretly organized by the CIA ...

It may be of little surprise that the FBI has paid attention to Burning Man and similar events. Yet again, one may be better off asking, why would they not? Anything that is popular enough to work may one day become the foundation for subversive corporate or state propaganda.

Life as an artist is certainly easier being funded than not, all things being equal. If a federal agency secretly pays to do what you were already doing to show up the Ruskies, and that thing happens to be getting shitfaced and splattering paint, well. Get the turpentine and paint. All those involved in movements that aren't yet international marketing campaigns can merely say: bring it on.

Hunter would be proud.

> It's a rare goddamn trip for a locked-in, rent-paying writer to get into a gig that, even in retrospect, was a kinghell, highlife fuck-all from start to finish... and then to actually get paid for writing this kind of manic gibberish seems genuinely weird; like getting paid for kicking Agnew in the balls. So maybe there's hope. Or maybe I'm going mad...—Comments on Fear and Loathing in Las Vegas in The Great Shark Hunt: Strange Tales from a Strange Time

SAY YOU WANT A REVOLUTION

The magazine will foster consciousness among each of the group's members of the ties that bind him to the others, and of the nature of these ties. It will open an era of real friendship and will ask that ideas not be placed above people. It will also give to the group the meaning of an elective and not gregarious [community]. Individuals meet—a true meeting, leading to an act of love, to a creative spasm—and something may be born of their individual conjugal act. The magazine will pronounce itself against all militant action or spectacular activism, to which it will oppose magic action—love being the key to all magic. —Letter from Jindrich Heisler to Kiesler, Dec 13, 1947

Anarchosocialism has a dubious future in mainstream America, but it may be the only way genuine creative movements can gestate within larger cultures that uphold very different ideals. These disparate collectives need to navigate the balance between individual and collective good, and these can be deceptively turbulent waters. For a movement to have integrity, everyone must be true to themselves, yet for that to come about, it needs solidarity of purpose. This is a dilemma. We need one another for critique, for diversity, for sustainability. We need each other to build the myth of a movement. Even by not engaging in PR you are engaging in PR.

Without an alignment of collective and mutual best interest, a movement cannot survive. It will collapse in on itself before it attains any sort of critical mass. This seeming paradox is part of what keeps many creative individuals disenfranchised, biting at each others ankles. They're arguing about the wrong things, and focusing their energy and attention in the wrong place. Movements only occur when people learn to work together towards common goals, to hell with the labels.

Living movements require no closed manifestos, no party lines, no armbands, tattoos or uniforms. (Save them for the PR events.) They need to share agreed upon goals that represent mutually agreed upon objectives, not prescribed identities. What is needed is space to meet up and share ideas and collaborate, a means of making the relevancy of our work evident outside the insular and seemingly elitist circles that form around such groups and the ability to eat and pay rent without completely shilling the underlying premise; resources, an understanding of mutual benefit, safety, and aid, and a determination that goes far beyond any benefit that aesthetic posturing could possibly provide. As Frederick Douglass said,"I would unite with anybody to do right; and with nobody to do wrong." Invisible structures and histories condition our behavior, and we ought to be mindful of that.

Last but not least, movements require time, and colossal dedication. The question worth asking is not what we can imagine, but what we can realize. As in many times in the past, there is a strong and demonstrable need for creative movements and cultural revolutions that the mainstream culture may neither recognize, understand, nor support. All these facts do not mean that you should not, or can not, bring it about. Supposing this is a course that speaks to you, barring bad luck and the "acts of God," the only real barrier is in ourselves, in the forms of egotism, laziness, isolation, a lack of vision, planning, lack of collective resources, or making the wrong compromise at the wrong time.

We have no need for a movement so long as it is for the sake of fashion, so long as we hobble ourselves or one another or use elitism or ideological disagreements as excuses that keep us from getting something done. Nor do we have any use for these things if they are anything but a means to an end which realize the common goals of its members and manifest that purpose. It doesn't matter if today you consider yourself a Pagan, a Christian, or a Muslim, a plumber, an artist, or an information architect. Religion, gender, all symbolic presentation is mutable and ever-changing. So long as we can mutually find the fulcrum point of a common ground, and a common good, to lift us all up with. If, on the other hand, we signal our identities the same but can find no such leverage, we'd probably be better off going our own ways. We can have our ideological arguments over tea; there is no ideology which trumps someone being a genuine, open-minded, passionate person, and no party line agreement can provide reparations if they're not. It is not liberalism that needs to opposite traditionalism, it is pluralism, derived from the philosophy of the distributed ad hoc network. And very likely, the fear over a complete leveling of group identity at the hands of liberal pluralism —which is a key nationalist talking point—is something of a bogeyman, since human society isn't a product of forethought in the sense of conscious design. Pluralism after all isn't everyone becoming the same but rather everyone accepting difference that isn't a mortal threat.

This is also a question of consistency. If the society we want is innately pluralistic, multi-cultural, and based on tolerance, then there has to be a certain concession to the rigidity of symbolic cultural boundaries, (which is a big part of the illusion of a static identity). Many people want a pluralist society, but they also want to say this group owns this idea or practice and that one owns that one, or that identity can't cross multiple boundaries or change over time (heaven forbid a lesbian sleep with men, or a man should transition to a woman). It's like running in two directions at once. We adhere, then, to a standard of identity as a palimpsest, and as forever in flux.

Anxiety about identity is one of the mass psychological forces that was leveraged into a win for Trump, Brexit, and who knows what next, the force of animus behind most modern nationalist movements. The goal there is to increase the granularity of distinction between social groups. Their end game is literally black and white, human or not.

We're socially atomized. "We" have numbers but they're useless without common causes that don't collapse into battles over who has the right to X and who doesn't. This grounds all discussion in identifying which identities are oppressed versus which are privileged, with the binaristic idea that the only political question is whether one "sides with" the oppressed or the privileged. This rejects all other considerations—tactical or strategic effectiveness, universal rights, conceptual consistency, et cetera—as not merely secondary, but as nothing other than illegitimate apologetics for privilege. Intersectionality asserts that all forms of oppression must be recognized and all oppressed groups' needs addressed together. But in order to secure claims in the diffuse consensus process—both to occupying an oppressed position in general and in marking an identity in a particular context—articulating the details of one's oppression with vigor and detail is rewarded, and thus implicitly encouraged. The question of who is oppressed in what context is central; there is no other road to legitimacy. But there is no explicit principles by which to adjudicate competing claims to the oppressed position. The result is that oppressed classes are identified by an unarticulated process of consensus among members of a community. Membership in that circle is ratified by ever-escalating performance of ever-more-inaccessible community shibboleths. This is unsteady ground to build any movement upon.

Cultural revolution isn't going to be found in a common manner of dress, speech, or ideology. If it is found at all, it will come in the chance meeting of equals in the Wasteland, and the work they do to water the desert until it flowers.

SELECTED BIBLIOGRAPHY

Adorno, T. W., & Horkheimer, M. (2016). Dialectic of enlightenment. London: Verso.

Bataille, G., & Richardson, M. (2006). The absence of myth: writings on surrealism. London: Verso.

Bataille, G., & Dalwood, M. (1986). Erotism: death & sensuality. San Francisco: City Lights Books.

Baudrillard, J., & Glaser, S. F. (2014). Simulacra and simulation. Ann Arbor: The University of Michigan Press.

Campbell, J. (1962). The masks of God. London: Secker & Warburg.

Debord, G. (2014). The society of the spectacle. Berkeley, CA: Bureau of Public Secrets.

DeLanda, M. (2013). A new philosophy of society: assemblage theory and social complexity. London: Bloomsbury.

DeLanda, M. (2014). A thousand years of nonlinear history. New York: Swerve Editions.

Dundes, A. (1980). Interpreting folklore. Bloomington: Indiana University Press.

Eliade, M., (1987) The Sacred and The Profane: The Nature of Religion. Harcourt Brace Jovanovich.

Gray, J. (2014). The silence of animals on progress and other modern myths. London: Penguin Books.

Gray, J. (2016). The soul of the marionette: a short enquiry into human freedom. London: Penguin Books.

Harari, Y. N. (2016). Sapiens: a brief history of humankind. Toronto, Ontario: Signal, McClelland & Stewart.

Harris, M. (1991). Cannibals and kings: the origins of cultures. New York: Vintage Books.

Jung, C. G., Henderson, J. L., Franz, M. V., Jaffé, A., & Jacobi, J. (2013). Man and his symbols. Bowdon, Cheshire, England: Stellar Classics.

Mannheim, K. (1955). Ideology and Utopia: An Introduction to the Sociology of. Harvest Books.

Monroe, A. (2005). Interrogation machine: Laibach and NSK. Cambridge. Mass.: MIT Press.

Pieper, J. (1999). The end of time: a meditation on the philosophy of history. San Francisco: Ignatius Press.

Reich, W. (2015). Mass psychology of fascism. Place of publication not identified: Aakar Books.

Snyder, T. (2016). Black earth: the holocaust as history and warning. Tim Duggan Books.

Toulman, S. Janik, A. (1996). Wittgenstein's Vienna. Ivan R. Dee; New edition edition.

Vattimo, G. (2003). The end of modernity: Nihilisme dan hermeneutika dalam budaya pos modern. Yogyakarta: Sadasiva.

Woodley, D. (2010). Fascism and political theory: critical perspectives on fascist ideology. London: Routledge.

The Work of Art in the Age of Ontological Speculation : Walter Benjamin Revisited. (n.d.). Walter Benjamin and Art. doi:10.5040/9781472547811.ch-006

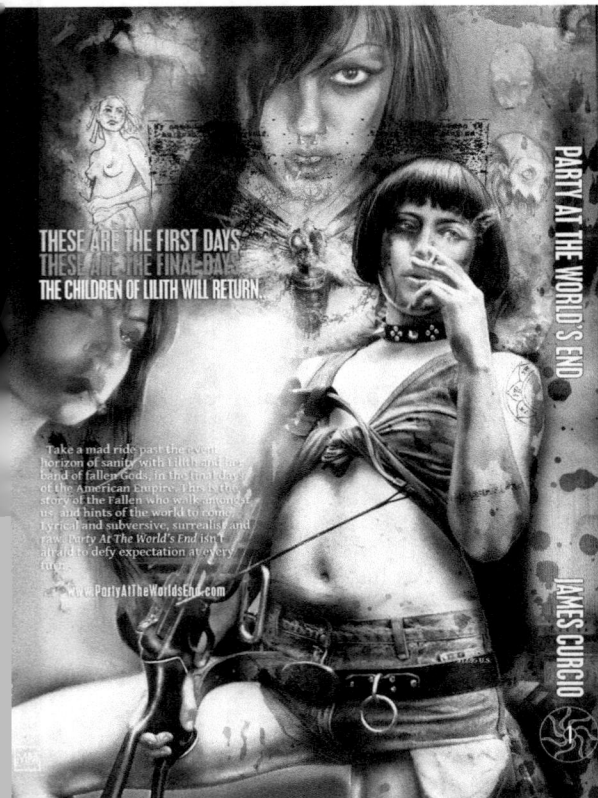

PARTY AT THE WORLD'S END

AVAILABLE NOW ON AMAZON

Take a mad ride past the event horizon of sanity with Lilith, Dionysus, and their band of Fallen Gods, in the final days of the American Empire.

After the fiasco at Rushmore, they knew there would be more bodies. But they joined the cause anyway. They stood up to the US Government and said "you've got to kill me in the sunlight." But Lilith said, "Do it under cover of moonlight." She wanted everyone to watch the bloodbath on Facetime, shaky footage of government-hired mercenaries lobbing mortar fire into the fallen nation's sons and daughters. Hundreds of teens strewn about like discarded dixie cups after a rave in a field, between two bluffs in the Black Hills. Curiously close to the death toll at Wounded Knee. I was wrong. They weren't just blind fools, they were the bloody sacrifice, offered up by Lilith in her mad ploy for immortality. But the time to fight and win was over, now was the time to die a hero's death that would be heard round the world. Even as the one candle goes out, another, darker one comes to light. — Dionysus

Party At The World's End is a lyrical and subversive retelling of Euripides' *The Bacchae* in the age of anonymity and alternate identities.

Book 1 of the Fallen Cycle: this is the story of those Fallen who walk amongst us, and hints of the world that is to come.

WWW.FALLENCYCLE.COM

TALES FROM WHEN I HAD A FACE
IN PRODUCTION

2018

A battle between the light of remembrance and dark of forgetting; the burden of tradition, and the cost of progress.

Young Ayta was descended from legends, but she was also an only child born to immigrants in a big city. A city where she didn't belong and never would.

She was named after her Gran, the sole surviving shaman of a lost tribe said to wander still, somewhere out there in the Siberian Taiga. "Old Bark," they also called her. "Night's shroud," the wild witch of the woods. Then, on her 7th birthday, there came a knock on the door. Stern, like wood rapping against wood. And Gran was there, a thing of myth, now just a stooped old woman with a broken face and hair like tree roots.

From that day forward, she was Ayta's only confidant. Through her tales, Gran carries her granddaughter out of the isolation of that youth to Alterran—a land of the distant future where tribes ruled by symbol and portent face their own struggle between the unifying force of a budding Empire and the apocalyptic ravages of the Children of Lilith.

But Gran would not live forever, and Ayta must come to terms with her legacy, bearing ancestral myth in a modern world that has no need for what it sees as childish things. What she does not realize is the incredible cost, no matter the choice we make, or path we take.

An existential fairytale, told for those of us that may have grown up, but still remember the uncertainty of a world steeped in the occult logic of dreams.

WWW.FALLENCYCLE.COM

ABOUT THE AUTHOR:

James Curcio's career as polymath or dilettante (depending who you ask) began around 2001 when he graduated Bard college with the world's most lucrative degree (Philosophy), and co-founded a media collective. Partially inspired by The Factory, they cranked out media by day for clients ranging from local business to Glaxo Smith Kline and Roche, and avant-garde art weirdness by night.

He left that partnership in NY to focus on a music project in LA, based on Jack Parson's Babalon Working, which worked out for them about as well as it did for Jack. Following that was ten years half lived on couches, futons, festivals, and conventions across America. During this time he worked on numerous transmedia projects. Some of these included *Join My Cult!*, a postmodern occult novel satirizing postmodern occultism published by New Falcon, (also of Aleister Crowley and Robert Anton Wilson), Disinfo's anthology *Generation Hex*, which was launched at Alex and Allyson Grey's Chapel of Sacred Mirrors, and collaboration with Joseph Matheny and Dave Szulborski, two pioneers of Alternate Reality Games, on various popular ARG related comics, podcasts and websites. He co-starred in a bi-weekly "Gonzomentary" web series. This LSD-soaked, mangled gibberish inexplicably won the Outstanding Lead Actor Award and Outstanding Writing by the 2013 LA Web Series Festival, while receiving an Honorable Mention for Best Documentary at the 6th Philadelphia Independent Film Festival. He ceased musical live performance in 2005 with an opening act for Front242, only since releasing studio collaborations on obscure labels you've never heard of.

He was editor-in-chief of Rebel News, an independent news outlet he founded with "House of Cards" consultant Gregg Housh. He keeps the dilettante tradition of corrupting the youth alive; his previous non-fiction anthologies, *Apocalyptic Imaginary* and *The Immanence of Myth* were both curriculum materials for several lit and philosophy courses at SUNY Binghamton, 2010-12.

Present projects include *Tales From When I Had A Face*, an illustrated novel in the transmedia Fallen Cycle, *Narrative Machines: Modern Myth, Revolution, and Propaganda*, and endless research for the forthcoming anthology, *Masks: Bowie and Artists of Artifice*.